Grammar for Reading German

Form C Revised Edition

A Second Year Workbook with Recognition Exercises

By K. Roald Bergethon
and Ellis Finger, Lafayette College

Houghton Mifflin Company • Boston
Dallas • Geneva, Illinois   Hopewell, New Jersey • Palo Alto • London

Under the editorship of
William G. Moulton,
Princeton University

Printed in the U.S.A.
ISBN: 0-395-26085-X

PREFACE

Grammar for Reading German is written for intermediate college courses in reading German. It is designed to supplement whatever reading texts — literary, general, scientific — may be used in a particular course. Graduate students have found it an economical means to prepare for the use of German in research.

The *primary intent* of the book is to order and intensify the experience which the student gains in reading. The ultimate objective is to increase the skill in reading mature German to a degree that could otherwise be attained only by reading more pages of German than is possible in normal class circumstances.

Grammar for Reading German contains sixteen grammar units with exercises, four optional review exercises, vocabularies for the exercises, a grammatical appendix, and answer sheets for the exercises. The sixteen main units review and present important facts of German grammar. The appendix contains a summary of basic facts (declension, conjugation, etc.) which the students should have learned in their basic courses but may need to review.

The *approach to the grammar* is strictly from the viewpoint of the English-speaking reader. The student is not told how to form the future or passive; instead he is told what possibilities must be kept in mind when a form of *werden* occurs. German constructions which cause little or no difficulty in reading are in general not discussed. While the book treats particular difficulties such as the extended adjective construction, it is the fundamentals of case and word order, demanding major adjustments on the part of the English-speaking reader, which are emphasized directly and indirectly throughout the book.

The *exercises* practice recognition and test interpretation of the phenomena which are described in each grammar section. So that the practice situation will be as realistic as possible, the sentences used in the exercises have been culled from cultural histories or literary documents written for a German public. They are not easier from the standpoint of vocabulary or content than advanced reading texts, for the students must learn to use their grammatical knowledge under the conditions which normally obtain when they are reading mature material. It was possible now and then to bring together sentences from various sources and get a group of sentences with some unity of content. But the primary objective throughout was to have a testing point in every sentence so as to provide concentrated practice. For that reason, and to avoid disagreeable artificiality, most of the exercises consist of disconnected sentences. These do, however, generally state a fact, an idea or opinion which may elicit interest and at least give the student the impression that the sentence says something.

The *four optional review exercises* may be used at the discretion of the teacher. They contain additional practice material of the kind used in the exercises for the sixteen main units. They also include Reviews of Strong Verbs which emphasize the most frequent patterns of vowel change in this group of words.

The element of *time* — the student's and the teacher's — was a great consideration in constructing the book. It is a major premise that the book be used with the least possible cost in class time. The grammar presentation is full and amply illustrated so that it should not be necessary to take class time to set forth the material.

It is intended that the exercises be completed at home by the student. Though some straightforward translation is necessary and desirable, the exercises in large part utilize multiple choice questions, completion and fill-in translation and similar devices in order to provide the maximum practice with the least expenditure of time. The answer sheets also help save the student's time.

The nature of the questions, the answer sheets and an Instructor's Answer Key ease the burden of correction. The Instructor's Key can save the teacher's own time in correction; because the Key is full and often provides alternate answers, correction of exercises may be delegated to advanced undergraduate or graduate assistants.

Working vocabularies omit words marked with an asterisk in Wadepuhl and Morgan, *Minimum Standard German Vocabulary* (Crofts, N.Y., 1945), except where a knowledge of gender of nouns or principal parts of verbs is demanded by the exercises, or when the English equivalent of a familiar word in a particular context might not be easily apparent to the student. Some high frequency words which students seem to forget easily are, however, included in the working vocabularies.

The sixteen lessons of the grammar should easily be covered in a semester in addition to reading. Teachers will, of course, vary the pace at which *assignments* are made. Some units are long and difficult enough to make a full day's assignment alone. Others may well be assigned along with other work. The author suggests scheduling the grammar study in the first two-thirds of the semester, alternating grammar practice with reading.

If the exercises are corrected outside the classroom, the class hours for which grammar assignments are made can be effectively utilized for practice in sight reading. This workshop method of reading enables the class to cover almost as much reading material as would ordinarily be assigned for homework. Perhaps even more important than coverage is the practice in intelligent guessing which the student obtains while working through new material with the rest of the class and the instructor.

The author hopes that use of the grammar will do more than increase the student's skill in reading German. All too often reading selections of intrinsic literary value or stimulating content become almost solely material for translation practice, grammatical analysis, vocabulary study and, finally, test questions. If the burden of rigorous study is put on the grammar and relegated in part at any rate to homework time, then class meetings can be devoted more freely to the enjoyment and discussion of the values and content of the reading material. In this way the grammar should not only help the student to attain greater proficiency in reading, but should also provide the means for increasing the direct pleasure and benefit from the reading.

K. Roald Bergethon

ACKNOWLEDGEMENTS

The present form of *Grammar for Reading German* owes much to early testing of its approach in classes at Brown University and to helpful comments during its inception from colleagues Alan Holske, Detlev Schumann and W. Freeman Twaddell, as well as from friends Rolf and Margot Polack. It has been improved through contributions of Frank X. Braun, formerly of the University of Michigan, who provided exercises for Form B, and of Ellis Finger, Lafayette College, who in the execution of the present revised form helped amplify the grammar presentation in addition to supplying the material for the exercises. Rado Pribic of Lafayette College graciously reviewed and helped better the new exercises. I am grateful also for advice and comments provided by W. G. Moulton, under whose general editorship the book appears.

K. R. B.
Lafayette College
Easton, Pennsylvania

TO THE STUDENT

This book can help you in reading advanced German.

The grammar analysis in the sixteen main units approaches German from the viewpoint of understanding and translation. In these sections it is assumed that you know the basic material which is summarized for review and reference in the Appendix.

The exercises give you practice in recognizing and interpreting the phenomena discussed in the grammar analyses in as realistic a fashion as seemed practicable. Sentences used in the exercises have been collected from books written for a German public. The vocabulary is mature; you will have to look up many words. But after all, you must learn to use your grammatical knowledge in reading which contains unfamiliar words. You will find after a while that understanding the grammatical habits of German will help you in making intelligent guesses at the meanings of words which are new to you.

The working vocabularies contain mainly words which you are not expected to know. However, words which are familiar to you are included when the exercises call for information about gender, declension, or principal parts of verbs. Should you fail to recognize a word which is omitted from the vocabularies, you can probably find it in the vocabulary of almost any reader you may be using.

Before you begin to work on the exercises, read in the Appendix §61 and §103, on *Nouns* and *Verbs in the dictionary or vocabulary*. You would also do well to familiarize yourself with §85 on the *Meanings of the prepositions and postpositions*. All of these sections will help you with vocabulary problems.

CONTENTS

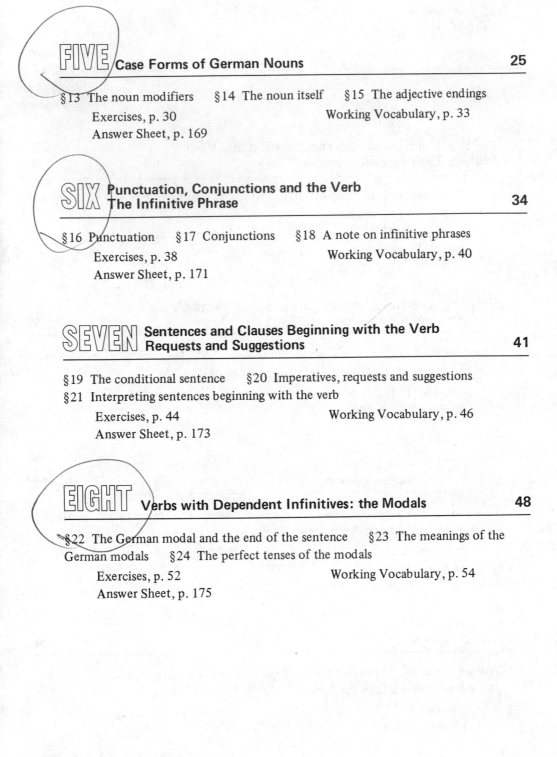

GRAMMATICAL APPENDIX

Grammar for Reading German

Form C   Revised Edition

ONE

The German Sentence: Subject and Verb
The Pronoun *man*

The subject, the verb, and the object of the verb or the predicate nominative are the backbone of the sentence. Find these, and the other parts of the sentence usually fall into place.

Because you speak English, you have the habit of expecting the subject of a statement to precede the verb. Compare the widely different meanings of the following sentences where the only structural difference is the order of the words:

The world needs the artist.—Subject precedes verb.
The artist needs the world.—Subject precedes verb.

1 / Subject and verb in German

In the main clause of a German statement the subject may precede, but will as often follow the verb. Only the verb has its specific place in the German sentence. The inflected verb of the German main clause or simple sentence is normally the second element of the sentence; any one element or logical unit may precede the verb. The subject may be the first element; but if an object, adverb, phrase or clause is the first element in the statement, the subject follows the verb.

Die Welt braucht den Künstler.   *The world* needs the artist.
Den Künstler braucht *die Welt.*

Der Buchdruck hat schon im 16. Jahr-   *The art of printing* obtained great cul-
hundert große kulturelle Bedeutung   tural importance even in the 16th
erlangt.   century.
Schon im 16. Jahrhundert hat *der
Buchdruck* große kulturelle Bedeutung erlangt.
Große kulturelle Bedeutung hat *der
Buchdruck* schon im 16. Jahrhundert erlangt.

If you approach the German sentence expecting the subject to precede the verb, you will make mistakes and lose time. When you read German, use case forms, agreement between verb and subject, and context to help you find the subject.

2 / Identifying the subject of the German sentence

a / Case forms

Some case forms are in themselves enough to identify the subject. The form *der Mensch* can only be the nominative singular, since *Mensch* is a masculine noun which takes a plural ending. It must be either the subject of a sentence or a predicate nominative.

However, often we can determine definitely which noun in a sentence is the subject only through a process of elimination. Compare the sentences:

> *Das Tier* sieht aber *den Jäger* nicht.   But *the animal* does not see the hunter.

> *Das Tier* sieht aber *der Jäger* nicht.   But *the hunter* does not see the animal.

Both sentences contain the neuter form *das Tier* which is both nominative case (subject form) and accusative case (object form). In the first sentence we know that *das Tier* is the subject only because we also know that *den Jäger* is in the accusative case and cannot be the subject. In the second sentence the form *der Jäger*, being the nominative case, can only be the subject; therefore, *das Tier* must be the object.

Not only neuter nominative and accusative are similar. Actually, if we look at a table of case forms, we find that only the masculine noun singular has a nominative form distinct from the accusative. Compare:

	MASCULINE	NEUTER	FEMININE	PLURAL
NOM.	*der* Tag	das Herz	die Frau	die Tage, Herzen, Frauen
ACC.	*den* Tag	das Herz	die Frau	die Tage, Herzen, Frauen

Moreover, there are forms like *der Arbeiter, der Wagen, der Flügel* which are both nominative singular and genitive plural.

> *Der Arbeiter* will mehr Geld.   *The workingman* wants more money.
> Die Häuser *der Arbeiter* waren klein.   The homes *of the laborers* were small.

The nominative singular and the genitive plural are identical for all masculine nouns which add neither umlaut nor ending in the plural. For example,

NOM. SINGULAR	NOM. PLURAL	GEN. PLURAL
der Lehrer	die Lehrer	*der Lehrer*
der Wagen	die Wagen	*der Wagen*
der Flügel	die Flügel	*der Flügel*

Thus only in a minority of instances can we find the subject of a German sentence simply through direct recognition of a nominative form. Most of the time we must do two things: recognize possible subject forms, and eliminate non-subject forms.

b / Agreement between subject and verb

An important aid in finding the subject of the German sentence is the agreement in number and person between subject and verb. In the sentence, *Diese Schriften machte Lessing bekannt* (Lessing made known these writings), we recognize that *Lessing* must be the subject because the verb form is that of the third person singular. *Die Schriften* is plural and could not be the subject.

Note   You can see from the above that it is exceedingly important to know well the case forms of nouns and pronouns, tense forms and endings of verbs. If you are not sure about this basic information, turn to the Appendix §59-66 and refresh your memory.

3 / The pronoun *man*

The indefinite pronoun *man* is singular and is accompanied by a singular verb. You can avoid confusion if you remember that *man* is always the subject of the sentence or clause in which it occurs.

Man can often be translated as *one, people, we, they, you*, etc.

Man schließt, daß dies der Fall ist.	*One concludes* that this is the case. *We conclude*, etc.
Man wollte seine Lehre nicht annehmen.	*People refused* to accept his teachings. *They refused*, etc.

However, just as often it is better to translate a sentence with *man* by substituting an English passive construction for German *man* plus an active verb.

Man bewundert Beethoven als einen der größten Musiker aller Zeiten.	*Beethoven is admired* as one of the greatest musicians of all time. Cf. People admire Beethoven, etc.
Man hält ihn für einen großen Wissenschaftler.	*He is considered* (to be) a great scientist. Cf. People consider him, etc.

Note   The pronoun *man* can never be translated with the English word "man."

The accusative form for *man* is *einen*, the dative *einem*. The possessive adjective used in referring to *man*, or one of its forms, is *sein*.

Das erinnert *einen* an Zeiten, wo *man* glücklicher war.	That reminds *one* of times when *one* was happier.
Für *die seinen* sorgt *man* zuerst.	*One* takes care of *one's own* (family) first. *People* take care of *their own* (families) first.

Exercises

Note Answer sheets for all exercises are provided on pp. 161-200.
The symbol ☆ indicates examples.

I In the spaces on the answer sheet indicate the case(s) and number for each noun below. If any form serves for two cases, you must give both. Use the following abbreviations:

Nom.	for nominative	*sg.*	for singular
Acc.	for accusative	*pl.*	for plural
Dat.	for dative		
Gen.	for genitive		

☆ QUESTION   ANSWER
   a jeden Versuch   a *Acc. sg.*
   b der Zeit   b *Dat. sg., Gen. sg.*
   c der Lehrer   c *Nom. sg., Gen. pl.*

1 diese Gefühle		11 der Dynamik
2 den Politiker		12 des Stückes
3 dem Volk		13 keine Revolutionen
4 einer Form		14 der Stoffe
5 unsere Fragen		15 dem Ende
6 der Unruhen		16 der Techniker
7 den Werken		17 welches Mittel
8 das Publikum		18 die Komponisten
9 den Forschungen		19 den Lehren
10 diese Kenntnis		20 viele Produkte

II Enter on the answer sheet the letter identifying the subject form for the verb at the left.

1 macht   (a) der Werke   (b) alle Politiker
             (c) dieses Philosophen   (d) das Publikum
2 bringt   (a) diese Lehre   (b) dem Techniker
             (c) der Zeit   (d) Produkte
3 finden   (a) die Gleichheit   (b) dieses Ende
             (c) andere Mittel   (d) die Analyse
4 hat   (a) neuer Stoffe   (b) ihre Frage
             (c) der Unruhen   (d) dem Politiker
5 glaubte   (a) der Philosophen   (b) mancher Wissenschaftler
             (c) viele Politiker   (d) den Techniker
6 kannten   (a) alle Gelehrten   (b) des Publikums
             (c) der Dirigent   (d) jeder Komponist
7 kamen   (a) keine Lehre   (b) die Frage
             (c) die Techniker   (d) welche Unruhe

8	spielte	(a) der Gefühle	(b) unsere Formeln
		(c) die Dynamik	(d) diese Jahrhunderte
9	sind	(a) jede Revolution	(b) unser Wissenschaftler
		(c) keine Form	(d) wichtige Forschungen
10	suchten	(a) solche Werke	(b) der Völker
		(c) andere Musik	(d) unsere Kenntnis

III   Copy on the answer sheet the complete subject of each sentence.

1 Die Gleichheit hat die Französische Revolution *nicht* gebracht; sie hat nur zu einer anderen Form der Ungleichheit geführt.

2 Das Ende der Unruhen sahen die Franzosen nicht.

3 Die ersten Aktiengesellschaften entstanden gegen Ende des 19. Jahrhunderts.

4 Die alte Lehre der Dynamik stellte Einstein in Frage.

5 Um die Jahrhundertwende wandelte sich durch die Forschungen Plancks und Einsteins das physikalische Weltbild.

6 Gerade zur Auffindung neuer elementarer Stoffe war die Spektralanalyse gut geeignet.

7 Leider haben die Staatspräsidenten ein besseres Mittel zur Rüstungskontrolle nicht gefunden.

8 Nicht allen schönredenden Politikern soll ein Volk glauben, auch wenn es einen Führer suchen muß.

9 Der Wissenschaftler liefert dem Techniker die nötigen Formeln; (10) diese Formeln verwandelt der Techniker in neue Produkte für die Industrie.

IV   Copy on the answer sheet the subject of each sentence. Consider as part of the subject all words and phrases which modify the subject directly.

☆   QUESTION: Das Mittelalter und die Jahrhunderte des Überganges zur Neuzeit glaubten die ganze Welt von geistigen Mächten erfüllt und belebt.

ANSWER: *Das Mittelalter und die Jahrhunderte des Überganges zur Neuzeit*

1 Die Meisterwerke von J. S. Bach brachte der Komponist/Dirigent Felix Mendelssohn-Bartholdy etwa um 1840 wieder zur Kenntnis seines Berliner Publikums.

2 Dem späten 18. Jahrhundert und dem frühen 19. Jahrhundert waren sie so gut wie unbekannt.

3 Damals spielte man fast ausschließlich die Musik von Mozart, Haydn und Beethoven.

4 Die früheren Leistungen der deutschen Tonkunst kannten nur wenige Gelehrte und Musikwissenschaftler.

5 Dank dieser "Neuentdeckung" kamen die *Johannes-Passion,* die *Matthäus-Passion* und vor allem die *Messe in h-moll* wieder auf die Liste der beliebtesten Konzertstücke unserer Zeit.

V   On the answer sheet write translations of the following sentences.

1 Man bewunderte Michelangelo, (2) aber man fürchtete ihn auch.

3 Man weiß nicht immer, was recht ist.

4 Man kann sich nicht vorsichtiger ausdrücken.

5 Man brachte uns etwas zu essen.

Working Vocabulary

die Aktiengesellschaft, -en   stock company
die Analyse, -n   analysis
die Auffindung, -en   discovery, location
sich aus·drücken   express oneself
     ausschließlich   exclusive(ly)
     beleben   animate
     beliebt   popular, favorite
     betrachten   study, view, regard
     bewundern   admire
     damals   then, at that time
     dank   thanks to
der Dirigent (-en), -en   conductor (music)
die Dynamik   dynamics, study or theory of dynamics
     elementar   elementary, basic
das Ende, -n   end, goal, result
     entstehen, entstand, entstanden   arise, begin
     erfüllen   fill, fulfill
     etwa   about, approximately
     fast   almost
die Form, -en   form, shape
die Formel, -n   formula
die Forschung, -en   research, work of research
die Frage, -n   question; in Frage stellen call into question, challenge
     fürchten   fear
     geeignet   suited, appropriate
das Gefühl, -e   feeling, sentiment
     geistig   mental, intellectual, spiritual
der Gelehrte   scholar, man of knowledge (for declension see Appendix §73)
     glauben   believe, think, be convinced
die Gleichheit, -en   equality, similarity
das Jahrhundert, -e   century
die Jahrhundertwende, -n   turn of the century
die Kenntnis, -se   knowledge, familiarity; zur Kenntnis bringen   bring to (someone's) notice or attention
der Komponist (-en), -en   composer
das Konzertstück, -e   concert piece, selection
die Lehre, -n   doctrine, theory, teaching
     leider   unfortunately

die Leistung, -en   achievement, product
     liefern   furnish, provide with
die Liste, -n   list
die Macht, ٜe   force, power
das Meisterwerk, -e   masterpiece
die Messe, -n   mass; die Messe in h-moll the "Mass in B Minor"
das Mittel, –   means, way
das Mittelalter   Middle Ages
die Musik   music
der Musikwissenschaftler, –   musicologist
die Neuentdeckung, -en   new discovery
die Neuzeit   modern times
     nötig   necessary
die Passion   passion (play); die Johannes-Passion   the "St. John Passion"; die Matthäus-Passion   the "St. Matthew Passion"
der Philosoph (-en), -en   philosopher
der Politiker, –   politician
das Produkt, -e   product
das Publikum   audience, public
die Revolution, -en   revolution
die Rüstungskontrolle, -n   arms control, supervision of arms agreements
     schönredend   fine-spoken, flattering
die Spektralanalyse, -n   spectrum analysis
der Staatspräsident (-en), -en   head of state, national president
der Stoff, -e   element, material
das Stück, -e   piece
der Techniker, –   technician, technical engineer
die Tonkunst   music
der Übergang, ٜe   transition
     unbekannt   unknown
die Ungleichheit, -en   inequality
die Unruhe, -n   unrest, disturbance
     verwandeln   convert, change (into)
das Volk, ٜer   people
     vorsichtig   cautious, careful
sich wandeln   change, become altered
das Weltbild, -er   view of life, theory of life
das Werk, -e   work, composition
der Wissenschaftler, –   scientist
die Zeit, -en   time

TWO

The Hinge of the German Sentence: the Verb
Verbs with Modifiers

In English we use the same word order in both main and subordinate clauses. If we have a compound verb, one verb follows close upon the other. For example,

> The scientists *(1) tried (2) to keep* secret the success of their experiments because they *(1) could* not *(2) foresee* the consequences of their work.

4 / Position of the verb in German statements

a / The inflected verb
• *Main clause.* As stated in Unit One, the inflected verb of the main clause in a German statement is normally the second element of the sentence. The first element may be the subject, the object, an adverb, a phrase, a whole clause, or some other logical unit. But there will be only one such logical unit and then the inflected verb.[1]

Schiller, Deutschlands größter Dramatiker, *lebte* im 18. Jahrhundert.	Schiller, Germany's greatest dramatist, lived in the 18th century.
Im Jahre 1805 *starb* Schiller.	In the year 1805 Schiller died.
Obgleich er krank war, *arbeitete* Schiller sehr schwer.	Although he was sick, Schiller worked very hard.

• *Subordinate clause.* In a subordinate clause the inflected verb comes at or near the end of the clause.

Obgleich er krank *war*, arbeitete Schiller sehr schwer.	Although he was sick, Schiller worked very hard.

b / The infinitive and past participle
The infinitive and past participle come at or near the end of any clause.

In a main clause the infinitive or past participle is, therefore, separated from its inflected auxiliary verb.

---

[1] There are exceptions to the generalization stated. The coordinate conjunctions (*und, oder, denn, aber, allein, sondern*) and responses like *Ja, Nein, Oh, Ach,* are not considered as "first elements" in determining the position of the inflected verb. The sentence "Er kommt nicht." retains the same word order after any of these words: "Nein, er kommt nicht." "Denn er kommt nicht." Certain other expressions do not affect the position of the inflected verb in a main clause; see the illustrations in Unit Sixteen, §50. Also, the position of the inflected verb in the result clause of a conditional sentence is not affected by the frequently used introductory words *so* and *dann*; see illustrations in Unit Seven, §19.

Die Leihbibliothek *(1) hat* das 18. Jahrhundert *(2) erfunden.*	The 18th century *(1-2) invented* the lending library.
Wir *(1) werden* keine tiefgreifende Veränderung der Lage *(3) erwarten (2) können.*	We *(1) shall* not *(2) be able (3) to expect* any radical change in the situation.

In a subordinate clause the infinitive and/or participle are close to the inflected verb at the end of the clause—but the verbs appear in the reverse of the English order.

Der Einfluß, den Nietzsche um 1900 auf die Literatur *(2) ausgeübt (1) hat,* war sehr groß.	The influence which Nietzsche *(1-2) exerted* upon literature around 1900 was very great.
Wer *sich* mit einer Wissenschaft *(3) bekannt (2) machen (1) will,* muß sich auch mit deren Geschichte beschäftigen.	Whoever *(1) wishes (2-3) to acquaint himself* with a science must also concern himself with its history.

Note   The verb in translating. Never make up your mind about the meaning of any verb form in a German sentence before you have read the whole clause or sentence. Be sure you have all the elements of the verb before you begin translating.

When you translate, remember the peculiarities of English. Begin your translation with the subject unless there is good reason to do otherwise; let the complete verb follow immediately after the subject.

5 / The separable verb or verb phrase[1]

In German the separable modifier of a verb[2] tends toward the end of the main clause or simple sentence and is thus separated from its verb.

Das moderne Bankwesen *blühte* im Jahrzehnt 1850-60 in Deutschland *auf.*	The modern banking system *began to flourish* in Germany in the decade 1850-60.
Nach den Revolutionen von 1848 *setzte* die Reaktion *ein.*	After the revolutions of 1848 the reaction *set in.*

In the subordinate clause, both modifier and verb come near the end of the clause and the two are written together as one word, the modifier preceding the verb. This occurs also in the case of the infinitive or past participle forms; for here again both modifier and verb are found at the end of the clause or sentence.

Es läßt sich behaupten, daß das Mittelalter in zahlreichen Überresten noch bis heute *fortlebt.*	It can be maintained that the Middle Ages *live on* even today in numerous survivals.
Sie wollte mit unserer Familie *zurückfahren.*	She wanted *to return* with our family.

---

[1]See also Appendix §96.

[2]Sometimes called "the stressed or accented adverb with a verb" or "the separable prefix of a verb."

If *zu* must be expressed with the infinitive, it is inserted between the separable modifier and the verb, and all three are written together as one word. Similarly, the participial prefix *ge-,* where required, comes between the separable modifier and the verb.

Es gelang nach schwerer Arbeit *fest-zustellen,* daß dies der Fall war.	After (much) hard work it was possible *to establish* that this was the case.
Goethe *ist* in Wohlstand *aufgewachsen.*	Goethe *grew up* in comfortable circumstances.

Note   Almost any verb in German may be used with a separable modifier. A reader can rarely be sure he has the complete verb until he has seen the end of the sentence.

Remember that separable verbs are listed in vocabularies according to the first letter of the modifier. The verbs of the German examples above would be listed as *aufblühen, einsetzen, fortleben, zurückfahren, feststellen, aufwachsen.*

6 / Other modifying elements at the end of the German clause

a / Verb complexes
German also has looser word complexes which act in some ways like the separable verb compounds but which remain separate words at all times. The modifying element is sometimes just a word, sometimes a phrase. Like the modifier of the separable verb compound, these modifying elements are usually near the end of the sentence or clause.

Die Arbeit *nimmt* nur sehr langsam *ihren Fortgang.*	The work *proceeds* but slowly.
Heute noch *zieht* man die Zurückführung der Elemente auf einen einzigen Urstoff *in Betracht.*	Today we still *take into consideration* (the possibility of) tracing the elements back to a single original substance.

b / Adverbs and predicate adjectives
Nicht and other German adverbs also appear near the end of a sentence or clause.

Allein Long *veröffentlichte* seine Entdeckung *nicht.*	But Long *did not publish* his discovery.
Hier werden wir die Geschichte dieser Entwicklung nur *kurz umreißen.*	Here we will just *briefly outline* the history of this development.

Grammatically important adjectives often appear at or near the end of the clause or sentence.

Außerdem *ist* in Heines Werken der Einfluß des Volksliedes deutlich *erkennbar.*	Moreover, the influence of the folk song *is* clearly *recognizable* in Heine's works.

Observe that in most of the illustrations the English version brings together the verb and the modifying element, adjective, or adverb.

Exercises

I   On the answer sheet write the infinitive form of the separable verb in each of the following sentences or clauses. For reflexive verbs include *sich*.

☆   QUESTION   ANSWER
  a Diese Behauptung ist nicht   a *annehmen*
     ohne Weiteres anzunehmen.
  b Solche Verhältnisse liegen   b *vorliegen*
     besonders bei Cholera vor.
  c Unsere Zeit droht an ihren   c *zugrunde gehen*
     Errungenschaften zugrunde
     zu gehen.

1 Goethe hat die Welt immer als Künstler angesehen.
2 Die deutsche "Geniezeit" geht in wesentlichen Zügen auf Rousseau zurück.
3 Für Napoleon blieb aber der Erfolg selten aus.
4 Die Völkerwanderung riß die östlichen Stämme vom germanischen Leib los (5) und
   streute sie über das römische Reich aus.
6 Als der erste Weltkrieg ausbrach, (7) setzte sich die deutsche Jugend sehr wirksam
   ein.
8 Viele Völker und Nationen haben an dem zweiten Weltkrieg teilgenommen.
9 Amerika und Rußland gingen als die beherrschenden Weltmächte aus dem zweiten
   Weltkrieg hervor.
10 Im unmittelbaren Anschluß an die Pariser Konferenz von 1926 fand die jährliche
   Völkerbundtagung in Genf statt.
11 Nach der Wirtschaftskrise von 1929 breiteten sich Arbeitslosigkeit und soziales
   Elend aus.
12 Vico hatte die Kühnheit, der Geschichte den Vorrang vor allen Wissenschaften
   zuzubilligen.
13 Als Kulturkritiker hat Nietzsche eine mächtige Wirkung auf seine Zeit ausgeübt.
14 Dann gab Adenauer nach (15) und schloß sich dem Vorschlag des Finanzministers
   an.

II   For each of the following sentences there is a word-for-word translation which omits the verb complex. Rewrite these sentences in correct English word order, completing the translation as you do so.
1 Im 18. Jahrhundert stellten neue Strömungen der Philosophie die Grundlagen des
   christlichen Glaubens in Frage.
   In the eighteenth century _____ new trends in philosophy the foundation of
   the Christian faith _____ .
2 Philosophen wie Russell und Whitehead nahmen auf die religiösen Gefühle keine
   Rücksicht.
   Philosophers like Russell and Whitehead _____ religious emotions _____ .

3 Als wichtiges Mitglied der Dessauer "Bauhaus" Schule (1925 ff.) brachte Walter Gropius die maßgebenden Muster der modernen Architektur zustande.
As an important member of the Dessau Bauhaus School (1925 ff.) _____Walter Gropius the normative models of modern architecture _____ .

4 Willy Brandt brachte hierauf das deutsche Wirtschaftsproblem zur Sprache.
Willy Brandt _____ then the German economic problem _____ .

5 DeGaulle versuchte immer, sein Volk gegen ungerechte Angriffe in Schutz zu nehmen.
DeGaulle tried always his people against unjust attacks _____ .

III Translate the entire sentence.
1 Die Ergebnisse eines chemischen Versuchs sind von vielen Faktoren abhängig.
2 Galilei war von der Richtigkeit seiner Entdeckungen völlig überzeugt.
3 Den schwachen Dramen der Restoration-Zeit waren Shakespeares Werke weit überlegen.
4 Der Dichter gehört nicht der Vergangenheit an, er reicht in die Zukunft hinüber.
5 Mit dem Ausgang der Potsdamer Konferenz waren viele Amerikaner gar nicht zufrieden.

Working Vocabulary

abhängig dependent
an·gehören belong to
an·nehmen (·nimmt), ·nahm, ·genommen accept, assume
sich *an·schließen, o, o* join with, agree with
der *Anschluß, ─sse* connection
an·sehen (ie), a, e view, regard
die *Arbeitslosigkeit* unemployment
aus·bleiben, ie, ie be lacking, fail to appear
aus·brechen (i), a, o break out, erupt
sich *aus·breiten* spread (itself) out, expand
der *Ausgang, ─e* conclusion, outcome, closing, exit
aus·streuen scatter, disperse
aus·üben exert, exercise, practice
die *Behauptung, -en* assertion, claim
beherrschend ruling, dominant
besonders especially
der *Dichter, ─* poet, writer
drohen threaten, be in danger of
das *Elend* misery, suffering
sich *ein·setzen* commit oneself, become engaged (in)
die *Entdeckung, -en* discovery
der *Erfolg, -e* success

das *Ergebnis, -se* result
die *Errungenschaft, -en* accomplishment
der *Finanzminister, ─* minister of finance
die *Frage, -n* question; *in Frage stellen* raise doubts about, call into question, challenge
das *Genie, -s* genius; *die Geniezeit* the period idealizing the genius (a label for the pre-Romantic period of German literature)
die *Geschichte, -n* history, story
hervor· gehen, ·ging, ·gegangen proceed, go forth, come out of
hinüber·reichen extend, reach over
jährlich annual
die *Jugend* youth, young people
die *Kühnheit, -en* audacity, boldness
der *Kulturkritiker, ─* critic of culture
der *Künstler, ─* artist
der *Leib, -er* body
los·reißen, i, i tear loose
mächtig powerful
nach·geben (i), a, e give in, yield
östlich eastern
das *Reich, -e* empire, kingdom
die *Restoration-Zeit* Restoration period

die *Richtigkeit, -en* accuracy, correctness
     römisch Roman
die *Rücksicht, -en* consideration; *Rück-
     sicht nehmen* give consideration (to),
     take into consideration, pay attention
     (to)
der *Schutz* protection, shelter; *in Schutz
     nehmen* defend
     selten rare(ly), unusual(ly)
die *Sprache, -n* speech, language; *zur
     Sprache bringen* broach a theme, raise
     (a topic) for discussion
der *Stamm, ⁻e* tribe, trunk
     statt·finden, a, u take place
     überlegen superior
     überzeugen convince
die *Vergangenheit* past
das *Verhältnis, -se* condition, relationship
der *Versuch, -e* experiment
das *Volk, ⁻er* people, race
die *Völkerbundtagung, -en* meeting of the
     "Völkerbund" (League of Nations)
die *Völkerwanderung, -en* migration of a
     people, nation or tribe
     völlig fully, completely
     vor·liegen, a, e be (present), exist

der *Vorrang* pre-eminence, superiority
der *Vorschlag, ⁻e* proposal, suggestion
     weit wide, far, remote; *weiter* far-
     ther, further, additional; *ohne Weiteres*
     without further ado
der *Weltkrieg, -e* world war
die *Weltmacht, ⁻e* world power
     wesentlich essential, basic
     wirksam effective(ly)
die *Wirkung, -en* effect
die *Wirtschaftskrise, -n* economic crisis
die *Wissenschaft, -en* field of study,
     science
     zu·billigen grant, concede
     zufrieden content, pleased, happy,
     satisfied
der *Zug, ⁻e* traits, characteristics; train
     zugrunde gehen, ging, gegangen be
     ruined
die *Zukunft* future
     zurück·gehen, ·ging, ·gegangen go back,
     return, be based on
     zustande·bringen, ·brachte, ·gebracht
     accomplish, bring about (into being)
     establish

haben and sein

The function and meaning of *haben* or *sein* can be clear only when you have seen the entire clause or sentence. To put it another way, any form of *sein* or *haben* should direct your attention toward the end of the clause or sentence.

7 / *haben* and *sein* as independent verbs

Haben (to have, own) and *sein* (to be, exist) are independent verbs and may occur alone.

Wer *hat,* dem wird gegeben.	To everyone who *has* shall be given.
Hunger *ist* der beste Koch.	Hunger *is* the best cook.

8 / *haben* and *sein* with past participles

a / The perfect tenses[2]

Haben and *sein* may be used in combination with past participles to form the perfect tenses (English *have tried, had tried*). As indicated in §4, b, the past participle comes at or close to the end of the clause or sentence.

When used as perfect auxiliaries both *sein* and *haben* are translated with forms of English *have*.

Belagerungen und Erstürmungen *(1) haben* ganze Städte *(2) zerstört.*	Sieges and assaults *(1) have (2) destroyed* whole cities.
Einsteins Arbeit *(1) ist* für die Entwicklung der Atombombe wichtig *(2) gewesen.*	Einstein's work *(1) has (2) been* important for the development of the atomic bomb.

[1]For conjugations of *haben* and *sein* see Appendix §98.
[2]See also Appendix § 88.

Schon im 18. Jahrhundert *(1) waren*   Similar views *(1) had (2) arisen* as
ähnliche Anschauungen *(2) ent-*   early as the 18th century.
standen.

It is often possible, sometimes necessary to translate the perfect tense in German
with a simple past verb or with a past verb-phrase (*did* + verb).

Goethe *ist* im Jahre 1832 *gestorben.*   Goethe *died* in the year 1832.

Hat Brahms wirklich nur drei Sonaten   *Did* Brahms really *compose* only three
für Klavier *komponiert?*   sonatas for piano?

b / *sein* with a past participle

As we have seen, *sein* with a past participle is often translated with English *have.*
Sein has this meaning when it is used as a perfect auxiliary with *intransitive* verbs indicating change of place or condition and with the participles *gewesen* and *geblieben* (*ist
gewesen* has been; *ist geblieben* has stayed).

Er *ist* nach Berlin *gereist.*   He *has gone* to Berlin.

Er *war* schon *gestorben.*   He *had* already *died.*

Sie *sind* nicht lange hier *geblieben.*   They *did* not *stay* here very long.

Forms of *sein* may also occur with the past participles of transitive verbs. In
such cases the past participle functions as an adjective and *sein* will be translated with
English *to be.*

Die Tür *ist geschlossen.*   The door *is closed.*

Mit dieser Reaktion *ist* ein Verbrauch   There *is* a consumption of heat *con-*
von Wärme *verbunden.*   *nected* with this reaction.

Compare with the above:

Die *geschlossene* Tür . . .   The *closed* door . . .

Der mit dieser Reaktion *verbundene*   The consumption of heat *connected*
Verbrauch von Wärme . . .   *(in connection)* with this reac-
                                                tion . . .

See also Unit Thirteen, *The Verb as Adjective.*

9 / *sein* and *haben* plus an infinitive with *zu*

Sein and *haben* may have dependent infinitives with *zu.* The dependent
infinitive is found at or near the end of the clause or sentence.

Usually the construction *sein* or *haben* plus an infinitive with *zu* expresses the fact
that an action is possible, necessary, or obligatory.

Haben with a dependent infinitive introduced by *zu* seldom causes difficulty for the
English speaking reader. The usages in German and English appear recognizably similar.

Er *hat* heute schwer *zu arbeiten.*   He *has to work* hard today.

Er wird schon mit mir *zu tun haben.*   He is certainly going *to have to do*
                                                (*deal*) with me.

Man *hat* Vorsicht *auszuüben.*

It *is necessary to* (one *must*) *practice* caution.

An infinitive with *zu* which depends on *sein* has passive force. There are a few expressions in English that are comparable.

No one *is to blame.*

i.e., No one *is to be blamed.*

There *is* a great task *to perform.*

i.e., There *is* a great task *to be performed.*

This food *is* not fit *to eat.*

i.e., This food *is* not fit *to be eaten.*

An infinitive with *zu* dependent on *sein* will usually be translated with the English passive. Because the effect of the construction is to state possibility, necessity or obligation, appropriate modal auxiliaries or their equivalents may have to be employed in the English renderings.

Die Zwillinge *waren* nicht von einander *zu unterscheiden.*

The twins *could* not *be told apart.*
It *was* not *possible to tell* the twins *apart.*

Hier *sind* Vorsichtsmaßregeln *zu treffen.*

Here precautionary measures *are to be taken.*
Here precautionary measures *ought to be taken.*

In erster Linie *sind* die Gebrüder Grimm *zu nennen.*

The Grimm brothers *must be mentioned* first of all.

Note   An infinitive may appear in the same sentence with a form of *sein* or *haben* and be dependent not on *haben* or *sein* but on some other word in the sentence. In such cases the infinitive with *zu* can usually be translated with an active infinitive in English.

Auf diesem Gebiete *ist* noch *viel zu tun.*

In this field there *is* still *much to do* (or *to be done*).

Hier *hat* der Soziologe und Staatswissenschaftler noch *viel zu leisten.*

Here the sociologist and political scientist still *have much to accomplish.*

Das *war* sehr *schwer zu verstehen.*

That *was* very *hard to understand.*

Er *hatte* offenbar *die Absicht,* einen Wortstreit *einzuleiten.*

He obviously *had the intention* (*intended*) *to begin* a quarrel.

Exercises

I   Write on the answer sheet the letter which identifies the subject of the following verb forms.

1	sind	(a) der Gedanke	(b) den Zusammenbruch	
		(c) die Waffen	(d) die Bedeutung	
2	hat	(a) die Dichter	(b) sein Glaube	
		(c) den Gedanken	(d) dieses Ausbruchs	
3	habe	(a) Sie	(b) wir	
		(c) ihr	(d) ich	
4	waren	(a) seines Lebens	(b) der Vorstoß	
		(c) diese Reden	(d) die Gegenwart	
5	hatte	(a) der Ablauf	(b) die Gefühle	
		(c) seines Studiums	(d) der Gedanken	
6	ist	(a) die Antike	(b) lange Kriege	
		(c) der Anzahl	(d) Liebesgedichte	
7	haben	(a) der Arbeiter	(b) die Natur	
		(c) diese Gefühle	(d) keine Börse	
8	habt	(a) er	(b) wir	
		(c) sie	(d) ihr	
9	war	(a) Erfahrungen	(b) seine Leistung	
		(c) alte Reden	(d) der Waffen	
10	hatten	(a) der Sprachen	(b) das Bürgertum	
		(c) die Reformation	(d) die Künstler	

II   In the following sentences translate the word or phrase in italics.
A Toynbee (1→) *hat* den Plan seiner Weltgeschichte (←1) *abgerundet*, indem er aus den Erfahrungen seines Lebens neue Erkenntnisse (2) *gewonnen hat* und auch seine Anschauungen (3) *weitergebildet hat*.
B Ein langes Studium vergangener Kulturen (4→) *hat* Toynbee auf die eigene Gegenwart aufmerksam (←4) *gemacht*.
C Nach Toynbee (5) *hat* die Geschichte einen zyklischen Ablauf.
D Die Kultur der Azteken (6→) *haben wir uns* ungefähr auf einer Entwicklungsstufe wie die der römischen Kaiserzeit (←6) *vorzustellen*.
E Schon am Ende des 15. Jahrhunderts (7→) *hatte* Columbus den ersten Vorstoß nach Westen (←7) *gemacht*.
F Richard Wagner (8) *hatte nicht* das geringste Interesse für französische Malerei.
G Bei Spengler (9) *hat* jede Kultur ihre eigene Moral.
H Spengler (10→) *hat* bis zu seinem Tod an einem Werk der Metaphysik (←10) *gearbeitet*.

III   On the answer sheet write the letter which identifies the best translation of *sein* as it is used in each sentence.
1 In Österreich *war* der Faschismus vor 1940 noch nicht voll und offen zum Ausbruch gekommen.
(a) was   (b) could (be)   (c) had   (d) has

III   On the answer sheet write the letter which identifies the best translation of *sein* as it is used in each sentence.
1   In Österreich *war* der Faschismus vor 1940 noch nicht voll und offen zum Aus-
    bruch gekommen.
    (a) was   (b) could (be)   (c) had   (d) has
2   Deutschland wußte, daß England militärisch nicht zu besiegen *war*.
    (a) could (be)   (b) had (to)   (c) had (been)   (d) must
3   Bis zum Zusammenbruch der New Yorker Börse in 1929 *war* Amerikas wirtschaft-
    liche Entwicklung glänzend *gewesen*.
    (a) had been   (b) was   (c) could have been   (d) was to be
4   Napoleons Popularität *ist* zum Teil auf seine Persönlichkeit zurückzuführen.
    (a) is being   (b) has   (c) will   (d) can (be)
5   Die große Waffe der Arbeiter *ist* der Streik.
    (a) has   (b) is   (c) was   (d) can (be)
6   Seit dem Erlöschen der Hansa *ist* die deutsche Flagge von den Meeren fast ver-
    schwunden.
    (a) was   (b) has   (c) had   (d) could (have been)
7   Die Sprechweise Lenins *war* nicht volksmäßig, sondern Kunstsprache des Theoreti-
    kers.
    (a) was   (b) has   (c) had   (d) is
8   Das Jahr 1517 *ist* jedermann bekannt als das Geburtsjahr der Reformation.
    (a) was   (b) has   (c) can (be)   (d) is
9   Auf den ersten Weltkrieg wie auf den zweiten *war* ein kalter Krieg der Verdächti-
    gungen gefolgt.
    (a) could (be)   (b) had   (c) was   (d) did
10 Die historische Bedeutung Trotzkis *ist* immer noch nicht richtig einzuschätzen.
    (a) will   (b) has   (c) can (be)   (d) was

IV   On the answer sheet write translations of the subject and of the complete verb or verb complex in each sentence or clause.
     (1) Petrarcha war der erste große Propagandist der Antike. (2) Er ist unermüdlich im Sammeln alter Manuskripte gewesen: (3) ihm ist die Wiederentdeckung einer gan-zen Anzahl von Briefen und Reden Ciceros zu verdanken. (4) Dieser große Gelehrte ist aber durch andere Leistungen epochemachend geworden. (5) Die ersten großen Lie-besgedichte in italienischer Sprache hat er geschrieben, (6) und dieser Dichter hat die Form des Sonetts geschaffen, (7) das seither die Lieblingsgattung der europäischen Dichter geworden ist. (8) Er ist vor allem als der erste empfindsame Mensch anzusehen. (9) Auch war er dem Altertum gegenüber völlig christlich orientiert. (10) Als Mensch und Künstler war dieser Sohn des 14. Jahrhunderts eine ganz moderne, komplexe Natur.

Working Vocabulary

der Ablauf, "-e flow, movement
   ab·runden round out, complete
   all all, entire; *vor allem* above all
das Altertum, "-er antiquity
die Antike classical antiquity

die Anschauung, -en view, observation
   an·sehen (ie), a, e view, regard, look at
die Anzahl, -en number, quantity; *eine
   ganze Anzahl* a goodly number, quite a
   number

der *Arbeiter, –*   worker, laborer
aufmerksam   attentive, conscious; *einen*
auf etwas aufmerksam machen   call
one's attention to something
der *Ausbruch, ¨e*   eruption; *zum Ausbruch*
kommen   break out, erupt
der *Azteke (-n), -n*   the Aztec
die *Bedeutung, -en*   significance, meaning
bekannt   (well-)known, familiar
besiegen   conquer, defeat
die *Börse, -n*   stock market, purse
das *Bürgertum*   bourgeoisie, citizenry,
middle class
christlich   Christian
der *Dichter, –*   poet
eigen   own
ein·schätzen   assess, judge
empfindsam   sentimental, sensitive
die *Entwicklung, -en*   development
die *Entwicklungsstufe, -n*   stage or phase of
development
epochemachend   epoch-making
die *Erfahrung, -en*   experience
die *Erkenntnis, -se*   insight, knowledge
das *Erlöschen*   extinction, disappearance
die *Flagge, -n*   flag, banner
folgen   follow
das *Geburtsjahr, -e*   birth year
der *Gedanke (-ns), -n*   thought, idea
das *Gefühl, -e*   feeling, sentiment
gegenüber   in relation to, facing,
opposite
die *Gegenwart*   the present (time)
der *Gelehrte*   scholar, man of learning (for
declension see Appendix §73)
gering   slight, small
die *Geschichte, -n*   history, story, tale
gewinnen, a, o   gain, acquire
glänzend   brilliant, splendid
der *Glaube (-ns)*   faith, belief
die *Hansa*   Hanseatic League
indem   while, as, in that, by (doing)
das *Jahrhundert, -e*   century
die *Kaiserzeit*   era of emperors
der *Krieg, -e*   war
der *Künstler, –*   artist
die *Kunstsprache, -n*   literary (sophisti-
cated, technical) language
die *Leistung, -en*   achievement, accomplishment
das *Liebesgedicht, -e*   love poem
die *Lieblingsgattung, -en*   favorite genre

die *Malerei, -en*   painting
das *Meer, -e*   sea, ocean
die *Metaphysik*   metaphysics
die *Moral*   morality, ethical code
die *Natur, -en*   personality, character type;
nature
orientieren   locate, give direction to;
christlich orientiert   with (having) a
Christian perspective
das *Österreich*   Austria
die *Persönlichkeit, -en*   personality
die *Rede, -n*   speech, address
richtig   correct
römisch   Roman
das *Sammeln*   collecting
schaffen, schuf, a   create, produce
seit   since
seither   since then
die *Sprache, -n*   language, speech
die *Sprechweise, -n*   manner of speaking
der *Streik, -e*   strike
das *Studium, -ien*   study
der *Teil, -e*   part; *zum Teil*   in part, partially
der *Theoretiker, –*   theoretician
unermüdlich   tireless
ungefähr   about, approximately
die *Verdächtigung, -en*   suspicion, insinua-
tion
verdanken   owe, be indebted to, be
owing (due) to
vergangen   past
verschwinden, a, u   disappear, vanish
volksmäßig   popular, down-to-earth
völlig   fully, completely
vor allem   above all
sich *vor·stellen*   imagine, think of
der *Vorstoß, ¨e*   (forward) movement,
advance, thrust
die *Waffe, -n*   weapon
weiter·bilden   continue to develop,
advance
die *Weltgeschichte*   world history
der *Weltkrieg, -e*   world war
das *Werk, -e*   work, book
die *Wiederentdeckung, -en*   rediscovery
wirtschaftlich   economic
zurück·führen   trace back (to), attribute (to)
der *Zusammenbruch, ¨e*   collapse
zyklisch   cyclical

FOUR

werden

Werden[1], like the verbs *haben* and *sein,* should direct your attention to the end of the clause or sentence. Besides being an important independent verb, *werden* serves as the auxiliary of both the future tense and the passive voice.

10 / werden as an independent verb

Werden as an independent verb means *to become, to grow, to get (to be).*

Der Krieg *wird* für alle, für den Bürger wie den Soldaten, immer gefähr- licher.	War *is becoming (is growing, is getting to be)* more and more dangerous for everyone, for the civilian as well as for the soldier.
Schopenhauer *wurde* der Modephilo- soph der zweiten Hälfte des 19. Jahr- hunderts.	Schopenhauer *became* the fashionable philosopher of the second half of the 19th century.
Daltons Atomtheorie *ist* als Arbeits- grundlage bald sehr wichtig *gewor- den.*	Dalton's atomic theory soon *became* very important as a basis for work.

11 / werden as the future auxiliary

a / The future[2]
Werden when used with a dependent infinitive functions as the future auxiliary. It must then be translated with the English future auxiliaries *shall* or *will* or *be going to.*

Auch mit ethischen Problemen *werden* wir uns *beschäftigen müssen.*	We *shall* also *have to concern* ourselves with ethical problems.
Man weiß gar nicht, was in der Zukunft *geschehen wird.*	One knows nothing at all about what *is going to happen* in the future.

---

[1] For the complete conjugation of *werden* see Appendix §98.
[2] See also Unit Sixteen, §53.

b / The future perfect[1]

The future perfect is formed from the present tense of *werden* and the perfect infinitive of the main verb. Compare the position of the verbs in German and English.

Vor dem Jahr 2000 *(1) werden* wir über das Atom als neue Quelle der Energie viel *(3) gelernt (2) haben.

Before the year 2000 we *(1) will (2) have (3) learned* much about the atom as a new source of energy.

Viele glauben, daß der Begriff der „Freiheit" sich vor dem Ende dieses Jahrhunderts sehr *(3) geändert (2) haben (1) wird.*

Many people believe that the concept of "freedom" *(1) will (2) have (3) changed* a great deal by the end of this century.

12 / *werden* as the passive auxiliary

a / Basic passive pattern

Werden when used with a past participle functions as the passive auxiliary and must be translated with the English passive auxiliary *to be.*

Man *wird* heute nicht mehr so rasch *befördert.*

Today one *is* no longer *promoted* so rapidly.

Today people *are* no longer *being promoted* so rapidly.

Staat und Kirche *wurden getrennt.*

The state and the church *were separated.*

Es *(1) werden* wohl später einige von unseren Vorstellungen als Aberglaube *(3) bezeichnet (2) werden.*

Some of our ideas *(1) will* probably *(2) be (3) considered* as superstition at a later time.

In the perfect tenses of the passive the past participle *geworden* loses its *ge*-prefix.

„Figaros Hochzeit" (Mozart) *(1) ist* zuerst gleichgültig *(3) aufgenommen (2) worden.*

"The Marriage of Figaro" (Mozart) *(1-2) was (3) received* with indifference at first.

Ganze Völker *(1) waren* mit absurden Rassentheorien *(3) vergiftet (2) worden.*

Whole peoples *(1) had (2) been (3) poisoned* with absurd theories about race.

b / Expansion to identify agent

The basic form of the passive sentence illustrated above may be expanded to identify the agent or instrument of the action. The agent or instrument is then introduced by either *von* (by) or *durch* (by, by means of).

Heute *werden von* den Forschern täglich neue Entdeckungen *gemacht.*

Today new discoveries *are being made* every day *by* the researchers.

[1]See also Unit Sixteen, §53.

Im Jahre 1066 *wurde* England *von* den Normannen *erobert.*	In 1066 England *was conquered by* the Normans.
Oft *werden durch* einen genialen Gedanken neue Arbeitsfelder *erschlossen.*	Often new fields of endeavor *are opened up by* an idea which bears the stamp of genius.

c / Contraction to express action only

On the other hand, the passive construction may eliminate all mention of either recipient (subject) or agent of the action. The sentence will then express only the fact that an action is taking place, has taken place, or will take place. In translating such a sentence into English we must usually provide a logical subject, often the action itself or an implied agent of the action.

Es wird hier gearbeitet.	There is work going on here.
(*Literally:* There is being worked here.)	Work is going on here.
Es wurde gestern abend getanzt.	There was dancing last night.
(*Literally:* There was danced last night.)	Last night we went dancing.
Es ist schon zu viel geredet worden.	There has been too much talk already.
(*Literally:* There has been talked too much already.)	

Es in such sentences really serves only as a grammatical filler or "dummy." It may, therefore, be omitted if another word is to be given first position for reasons of emphasis, style or rhythm.

Hier wurde eifrig gearbeitet.	Here the work went on with great enthusiasm.
(*Literally:* Here was zealously worked.)	*Or if the reference is known:*
	Here he (they) worked with zeal.
Nach dem Arzt ist schon geschickt worden.	Someone has already sent for the doctor.
(*Literally:* For the doctor has been sent already.)	The doctor has already been sent for.
Ihm wird sicher geholfen werden.	He will surely be helped.
(*Literally:* Him will surely be helped.)	Someone will surely help him.

Exercises

I   Enter on the answer sheet the letter which identifies the correct translation of the form of *werden* in italics in each sentence or clause.

A   Der Rhein und die Wartburg *wurden* heilige Stätte für die Romantiker.

   1   (a) became   (b) were   (c) had become   (d) were growing

B   Unter vielen afrikanischen Völkern *werden* die alten Sitten ungeändert bleiben.

   2   (a) are being   (b) will   (c) become   (d) are

C   Am Ende des 19. Jahrhunderts *wurde* die englische Außenpolitik scharf kritisiert.

   3   (a) was growing (b) became   (c) would   (d) was

D   Der Friede unter den Völkern (4) *wird* gesichert sein, wenn das Menschenrecht auf die Muttersprache, Kultur und Religion geachtet und geschützt (5) *wird*.

   4   (a) is   (b) will   (c) becomes   (d) is turning

   5   (a) is   (b) grows   (c) will   (d) becomes

E   Für Deutschland *ist* die Ostpolitik während des ersten Weltkriegs zur Katastrophe *geworden*.

   6   (a) is becoming (b) has been   (c) became   (d) had grown

F   Die Existenzphilosophie *wurde* von Martin Heidegger und Karl Jaspers entwickelt und von Jean-Paul Sartre effektvoll verwertet.

   7   (a) will   (b) was   (c) was becoming (d) grew

G   Hoffnung ist eine Kraft, die in den Völkern niemals aussterben *wird*.

   8   (a) becomes   (b) is   (c) grows   (d) will

H   Hindenburg beharrte auf seiner alten Forderung, Reichskanzler zu *werden*.

   9   (a) become   (b) being   (c) grow   (d) will

I   Der Besuch zwischen Brandt und Pompidou *war* durch Privatgespräche vorbereitet *worden*.

   10   (a) had become (b) had been   (c) became   (d) was

J   Im 15. Jahrhundert *wurde* Italien zum Schauplatz regionaler Machtkämpfe.

   11   (a) was   (b) got   (c) has been   (d) became

K   Wichtig an dieser Unterhaltung ist nicht so sehr, was gesagt wurde, denn es (12→) *ist* schon oftmals gesagt (←12) *worden* und (13→) *wird* auch noch oftmals gesagt (←13) *werden*.

   12   (a) has become (b) was   (c) will have been (d) has been

   13   (a) will be   (b) will become   (c) will have been (d) will grow

L   Die Musikkritik spielt eine bedeutsame Rolle, da die Fähigkeit und der Mut zu selbständigem Urteil immer seltener *werden*.

   14   (a) are   (b) will   (c) are becoming (d) are going to

M   Auf allen Gebieten der Technik *werden* neue Erfolge und Ergebnisse erzielt.

   15   (a) grow   (b) are being   (c) will   (d) are becoming

II   For each sentence you are given a translation which omits only the verb. On the answer sheet write the English verb phrase that would best complete the sentence.

☆   QUESTION: William Gilbert wurde zum Begründer der Lehre von der Elektrizität und dem Magnetismus.

William Gilbert _____ the founder of the science of electricity and magnetism.

ANSWER: *became*

1 Gerade in diesen Wochen wurde die Stellung der Brandt Regierung durch schwere innerpolitische Kämpfe gefährdet.
It was in these very weeks that the position of the Brandt government _____ by serious internal struggles.

2 Die Pariser *Figaro* Zeitung ist zu einer Institution geworden, einem Blatt, (3) das überall in der Welt gelesen und geachtet wird.
The Parisian newspaper *Figaro* (2) _____ an institution, a journal which (3) _____ and _____ all over the world.

4 Als praktischer Politiker und als politischer Theoretiker ist Meinecke durch den Gang der Ereignisse gerechtfertigt worden.
As a practical politician and as a political theoretician Meinecke _____ by the course of events.

5 „Der Friede, den wir erkämpfen werden," sagte Friedrich Meinecke (6) „wird ein Erzieher zu wahrer und vernünftiger Staatskunst für uns werden."
The peace which we (5) _____ (6) _____ a guide to true and rational statesmanship for us.

7 Was Napoleon auf dem Schlachtfeld verloren hatte, wurde von dem geistvollsten aller Kongreßteilnehmer, Talleyrand, wiedergewonnen.
What Napoleon had lost on the battlefield _____ by Talleyrand, the most ingenious of all participants in the Congress.

8 Durch den Bastillensturm am 14. Juli 1789 wurde das *ancien régime* gesturzt.
The *ancien régime* _____ through the storming of the Bastille on July 14, 1789.

9 Über die Berliner Krisenjahre 1961 und 1962 ist viel geschrieben worden.
Much _____ about the Berlin crisis years 1961 and 1962.

10 Der jüngste Roman von Solschenizyn wird nicht in Rußland erscheinen.
Solzhenitsyn's most recent novel _____ in Russia.

III   Translate.
1 Bei uns wird viel musiziert.
2 Im Laboratorium wird nicht geraucht.
3 Auf seine erste Frage wurde nicht sofort geantwortet.
4 Gegen Intoleranz soll überall gekämpft werden.
5 Dem Kranken konnte nicht geholfen werden.

Working Vocabulary

achten   respect, honor

antworten   answer

die *Außenpolitik*   foreign policy

aus·sterben (i), a, o   die out, disappear

bedeutsam   significant, important

beharren   persist in, remain firm

der *Besuch, -e*   visit

effektvoll   effective(ly), to good effect

entwickeln   develop, evolve

der *Erfolg, -e*   success

das *Ergebnis, -se*   result, product

erkämpfen   gain through struggle (by fighting), fight to get

erscheinen, ie, ie   appear, (of a book) be published

erzielen   attain, achieve

die *Existenzphilosophie, -n*   existentialist philosophy

die *Fähigkeit, -en*   ability

die *Forderung, -en*   demand

der *Friede (-ns)*   peace

das *Gebiet, -e*   area, territory

gefährden   endanger, threaten

heilig   holy, sacred

die *Hoffnung, -en*   hope, optimism

die *Intoleranz*   intolerance

kämpfen   fight, combat

die *Kraft, ¨e*   power, force

das *Laboratorium, -ien*   laboratory

der *Machtkampf, ¨e*   power struggle

das *Menschenrecht, -e*   human right(s)

die *Musikkritik, -en*   music criticism, critique

musizieren   make music

der *Mut*   courage

die *Muttersprache, -n*   native language, mother tongue

niemals   never

oftmals   often

die *Ostpolitik*   (foreign) policy toward Eastern Europe

das *Privatgespräch, -e*   private talk, conversation

rauchen   smoke

rechtfertigen   vindicate, justify

der *Reichskanzler, –*   chancellor (of the Reich)

der *Rhein*   Rhine river

die *Rolle, -n*   role

der *Romantiker, –*   romanticist, author or poet of the Romantic period

scharf   sharp

der *Schauplatz, ¨e*   scene, arena

schützen   protect, defend

selbständig   independent

selten   rare, unusual; *immer seltener* more and more rare

sichern   secure, assure

die *Sitte, -n*   custom, practice

sofort   immediately, right away

die *Statt, ¨e*   place, location

stürzen   overthrow

die *Technik, -en*   technology, technique

überall   all over, everywhere

ungeändert   unchanged

die *Unterhaltung, -en*   conversation, amusement

das *Urteil, -e*   judgment

verwerten   make use of, apply

vor·bereiten   prepare, make ready

die *Wartburg*   Wartburg, 13th century castle of Landgrave Herman I of Thuringia

der *Weltkrieg, -e*   world war

wichtig   important

wieder·gewinnen, a, o   win back, regain

FIVE

Case Forms of German Nouns

Unit One pointed out that the subject, the verb and the object or predicate nominative are the backbone of the sentence. It was also stressed that in reading German we must not expect the subject to precede the verb as it normally does in English. We must instead look for the subject (almost anywhere in the sentence or clause), assemble the complete verb, and identify the object or predicate nominative, if there is any.

The same unit also pointed out that to identify subjects (or objects and predicate nominatives) in German we must do several things simultaneously:

1 recognize subject and object forms,
2 eliminate words which are not subject or object forms,
3 check for agreement of the verb with possible subject forms,
4 use the context.

This unit discusses more specifically the forms of nouns and their modifiers in regard to recognizing the function of a noun in a sentence.[1]

13 / The noun modifiers[2]

You are probably familiar with tables which show the declension of the noun modifiers in somewhat the following manner.

		MASCULINE	NEUTER	FEMININE	PLURAL
Definite	NOM.	*der*	*das*	*die*	*die*
Article	ACC.	*den*	*das*	*die*	*die*
	DAT.	*dem*	*dem*	*der*	*den*
	GEN.	*des*	*des*	*der*	*der*
dieser-	NOM.	dies *er*	dies *es*	dies *e*	dies *e*
words	ACC.	dies *en*	dies *es*	dies *e*	dies *e*
	DAT.	dies *em*	dies *em*	dies *er*	dies *en*
	GEN.	dies *es*	dies *es*	dies *er*	dies *er*
ein-	NOM.	kein	kein	kein *e*	kein *e*
words	ACC.	kein *en*	kein	kein *e*	kein *e*
	DAT.	kein *em*	kein *em*	kein *er*	kein *en*
	GEN.	kein *es*	kein *es*	kein *er*	kein *er*

[1]For a summary of the functions of cases see Appendix §55-58.
[2]See also Appendix §59.

Such tables, however, do not bring out clearly a fact which is important in reading German. If we count the number of case-gender-number places in the above tables, we find a total of sixteen case-gender-number places (four gender or plural series, each with four cases). But if we look at the forms themselves, we find that there are only six forms of the definite article, only six forms of the *ein*-words, and only five forms of the *dieser*-words.

Clearly, then, any given form of a noun modifier (say *der*) appears in more than one place in the table, and in any given sentence *der* has one of several possible functions.

It is, therefore, important to know the forms of the noun modifiers so well that you can easily recognize all the possible functions of each. Study the summaries below which show the possible case, gender and number indications for each form in the tables.

CASE, NUMBER, AND GENDER INDICATIONS OF THE NOUN MODIFIERS

Definite Article

das	das Kind	Nom. or Acc. singular (Neuter)
dem	dem Mann, Kind	Dat. singular (Masculine or Neuter)
den	den Mann	Acc. singular (Masculine)
	den Leuten	Dat. plural
der	der Mann	Nom. singular (Masculine)
	der Frau	Dat. or Gen. singular (Feminine)
	der Leute	Gen. plural
des	des Mannes, Kindes	Gen. singular (Masculine or Neuter)
die	die Frau	Nom. or Acc. singular (Feminine)
	die Leute	Nom. or Acc. plural

dieser-words: *dieser, jeder, jener, mancher, solcher, welcher*

dies *e*	diese Frau	Nom. or Acc. singular (Feminine)
	diese Leute	Nom. or Acc. plural
dies *em*	diesem Mann, Kind	Dat. singular (Masculine or Neuter)
dies *en*	diesen Mann	Acc. singular (Masculine)
	diesen Leuten	Dat. plural
dies *er*	dieser Mann	Nom. singular (Masculine)
	dieser Frau	Dat. or Gen. singular (Feminine)
	dieser Leute	Gen. plural
dies *es*	dieses Kind	Nom. or Acc. singular (Neuter)
	dieses Mannes, Kindes	Gen. singular (Masculine or Neuter)

ein-words: *ein, kein, mein, dein, sein, ihr, unser, euer*

kein	kein Mann	Nom. singular (Masculine)
	kein Kind	Nom. or Acc. singular (Neuter)
kein *e*	keine Frau	Nom. or Acc. singular (Feminine)
	keine Leute	Nom. or Acc. plural
kein *em*	keinem Mann, Kind	Dat. singular (Masculine or Neuter)
kein *en*	keinen Mann	Acc. singular (Masculine)
	keinen Leuten	Dat. plural
kein *er*	keiner Frau	Dat. or Gen. singular (Feminine)
	keiner Leute	Gen. plural
kein *es*	keines Mannes, Kindes	Gen. singular (Masculine or Neuter)

14 / The noun itself[1]

The essence of the lesson to be drawn from the above summaries is that we can practically never determine the case of a noun solely on the basis of its modifier. The only reliable ending is *-em,* which is always dative singular. In almost all other instances, one must keep an open mind until additional information about the noun is obtained.

a / The gender and the singular and plural forms of nouns

The forms *der Affe* and *der Grenze* are similar in appearance. But the information we draw from the form *der* with these two words is not the same when we know that *Affe* is a masculine noun and that *Grenze* is a feminine noun. We realize then that *der Affe* is nominative singular and that *der Grenze* is either dative or genitive singular. The form *den Teilchen* may look like a masculine accusative singular; but anyone who knows that *Teilchen* is a neuter noun realizes immediately that *den Teilchen* must be dative plural.

As far as the article and the general appearance of the noun are concerned, the form *den Gärten* might be either the accusative singular (masculine) or dative plural. But if we know that *Gärten* is the plural form of *der Garten,* then it is apparent that *den Gärten* can only be the dative plural. How many cases might one not have to consider for the form *der Krämpfe,* if one knew nothing about the noun! But once we know that *Krämpfe* is the plural of *der Krampf,* then we can easily identify the form *der Krämpfe* as genitive plural.

When a German sentence seems difficult and confusing, the reason is often that the reader does not recognize the functions of the nouns in it. Make it a habit to note the gender and plural form for every noun that you look up in a vocabulary or dictionary. (See Appendix §61.)

b / The case endings of nouns

• *The genitive ending of masculine and neuter nouns.* The *-s* or *-es* genitive ending of most masculine and all neuter nouns is always helpful. But when neuter nouns are accompanied by *dieser*-words the noun ending in the genitive case is crucial. Thus, for example, the *-(e)s* genitive ending is the decisive difference between *dieses Buch* (nominative or accusative) and *dieses Buches* (genitive), between *manches Kloster* (nominative or accusative) and *manches Klosters* (genitive).

• *The dative plural ending.* All plural nouns except those which end in *-n* or *-s* must add *-n* in the dative plural. When you see a modifier ending in *-en* and a noun ending in *-n,* you should, therefore, be hesitant to assume that the noun is in the accusative case (masculine). There are a few masculine nouns whose accusative singular ends in *-n,* e.g., *den Wagen, den Herrn.* But most of the time a modifier ending in *-en* with a noun which ends in *-n* (e.g., *den Lehrern, den Messern, den Frauen*) will mean that you are dealing with a dative plural.

Get in the habit of looking at the ending of a noun before you decide it is in a certain case.

---

[1]For a complete summary of the noun declension, see Appendix §60.

Note   In some instances only the context can help you determine the case of a particular form.

The most obvious instances are the neuter singular nominative and accusative (*das Kind*), the feminine singular nominative and accusative (*die Frau*), the feminine singular dative and genitive (*der Frau*), the plural nominative and accusative (*die Männer, Kinder, Frauen*). See Unit One, 2, a.

There are two other less frequent instances of this kind:

• Masculine nouns with the same form in both singular and plural have identical nominative singulars and genitive plurals.

NOM. SINGULAR	NOM. PLURAL	GEN. PLURAL
der Lehrer	die Lehrer	*der Lehrer*
der Enkel	die Enkel	*der Enkel*
der Spaten	die Spaten	*der Spaten*

But see §15, *b* on p. 29.

• Two types of masculine nouns have identical accusative singulars and dative plurals:

1   Masculine nouns which end in *-en* and have the same form in both singular and plural:

NOM. SINGULAR	ACC. SINGULAR	NOM. PLURAL	DAT. PLURAL
der Wagen	*den Wagen*	die Wagen	*den Wagen*
der Spaten	*den Spaten*	die Spaten	*den Spaten*

2   Masculine nouns which end in *-n* or *-en* in all cases except the nominative singular (see Appendix §60, C, 2):

NOM. SINGULAR	ACC. SINGULAR	NOM. PLURAL	DAT. PLURAL
der Mensch	*den Menschen*	die Menschen	*den Menschen*
der Knabe	*den Knaben*	die Knaben	*den Knaben*

15 / The adjective endings[1]

a / Strong adjective endings

So-called strong adjective endings give information about the case, number, and gender of a noun. They are used when adjectives come before nouns which have no preceding article, *dieser-*, or *ein-*word, and when adjectives follow *ein-*word forms without case or gender endings.

Since the strong adjective endings are in the main the same as the endings of the *dieser-*words, they can be of considerable help. But, as with the *dieser-*words themselves, you must remember that any strong adjective ending may serve several cases.

[1]For the complete summary of the adjective declension, see Appendix §67-73.

A table showing typical strong adjective endings is given here for your convenience. See also Appendix §69.

	MASCULINE	NEUTER	FEMININE	PLURAL
NOM.	gut *er* Wein	kalt *es* Wasser	heiß *e* Suppe	klein *e* Kinder
ACC.	gut *en* Wein	kalt *es* Wasser	heiß *e* Suppe	klein *e* Kinder
DAT.	gut *em* Wein	kalt *em* Wasser	heiß *er* Suppe	klein *en* Kindern
GEN.	gut *en* Weines	kalt *en* Wassers	heiß *er* Suppe	klein *er* Kinder

NOM.	ein gut *er* Wein	ein klein *es* Kind
ACC.		ein klein *es* Kind

b / Weak adjective endings

The weak adjective endings are essentially neutral. They are used when there is a preceding definite article, *dieser*-word, or *ein*-word with a characteristic case ending. (See tables Appendix §70.) But even these endings may be of help in a few instances.

The weak adjective endings are -*e* (in all nominative singulars and in the accusative of the feminine and neuter singulars) and -*en* (in all other cases). Hence:

● If the noun modifier is *die, diese, keine,* etc., and you are not sure about the gender and the forms of the noun, the adjective endings -*e* and -*en* will indicate whether a noun is singular or plural.

die *(diese, keine)* gut *e* Lampe	-*e* → singular
die *(diese, keine)* groß *en* Kräfte	-*en* → plural

● If the noun modifier is *der, dieser, jener,* etc., and the noun is a masculine with the same form in singular and plural, the adjective ending -*e* will indicate a nominative singular and the ending -*en* will tell you the noun is a genitive plural.

der *(dieser)* alt *e* Wagen	-*e* → nominative singular
der *(dieser)* alt *en* Wagen	-*en* → genitive plural

● If the noun modifier is *der, dieser, jener,* etc., and you do not know the gender and the singular and plural forms of the noun, the endings -*e* and -*en* will tell you whether you can eliminate any possibilities.

der *(dies er)* froh *e* Optimismus	Nominative singular (masculine)
der *(dies er)* neu *en* Religion	Not nominative singular (masculine) (It is dative or genitive of a singular feminine.)
der *(dies er)* neu *en* Formen	Not nominative singular (masculine) (It is genitive plural.)

c / Adjectival nouns: a note

Adjectives with weak or strong endings may be used to form nouns. See Appendix §73.

Exercises

I   On the answer sheet identify the case and number of each noun. If the noun can be either of two cases, identify both. Use the usual abbreviations.

☆   QUESTION   ANSWER
   a   dem Vater   a   *Dat. sg.*
   b   die Farben   b   *Nom. pl., Acc. pl.*
   c   der Arbeiter   c   *Nom. sg., Gen. pl.*

1 der Richtung	16 unserer Regierung
2 den Stämmen	17 diese Plätze
3 den Staat	18 eine Chance
4 dieses sinnlose Streben	19 den Eintritt
5 jedes Bundes	20 hohen Grades
6 unsere Pflege	21 dem Fundament
7 allen Wissenschaften	22 höchste Zeit
8 großen Nutzen	23 der Würde
9 wichtige Erfindungen	24 starke Gefühle
10 jedes Vorbild	25 dieses Glied
11 der neuen Technik	26 den Gesetzen
12 dem Menschen	27 des Deutschen
13 keine Möglichkeit	28 der Umbruch
14 des Lebens	29 schönen Künsten
15 viele Bürger	30 aller Kulturen

II   For each noun with a number before it there is a grammatical description giving its case and function[1] in the sentence. Enter on the answer sheet the letter identifying the correct description of each noun. In addition to the usual abbreviations for case and number, the following are used:

dir.	direct	*poss.*	possession, relation of source, etc.
ind.	indirect	*pred.*	predicate
indef.	indefinite	*prep.*	preposition(al)
obj.	object	*subj.*	subject

☆   QUESTION: (1) Der *Bürger* soll sich als Glied des Ganzen fühlen und aus (2) dem *Gefühl* (3) seiner *Würde* auch (4) einen hohen *Grad* von Patriotismus bekommen.

1 (a) Nom. sing., subj.
   (b) Nom. sing., pred. nom.
   (c) Acc. sing., dir. obj.
   (d) Gen. pl., poss.

2 (a) Dat. pl., ind. obj.
   (b) Dat. sing., prep. obj.
   (c) Gen. pl., prep. obj.
   (d) Acc. sing., dir. obj.

---

[1]For a summary of the functions of cases see Appendix §55-58.

3 (a) Gen. sing., poss.
  (b) Gen. pl., poss.
  (c) Nom. sing., subj.
  (d) Dat. sing., ind. obj.

4 (a) Nom. sing., pred. nom.
  (b) Dat. pl., prep. obj.
  (c) Acc. sing., dir. obj.
  (d) Gen. sing., indef. time

ANSWER: 1 *a* 2 *b* 3 *a* 4 *c*

A (1) Der *Pietismus* schuf (2) den *Deutschen,* wie Goethe sagte, (3) das *Fundament* (4) einer sittlichen *Kultur.*

1 (a) Nom. sing., subj.
  (b) Nom. sing., pred. nom.
  (c) Gen. sing., indef. time
  (d) Dat. sing., ind. obj.

2 (a) Acc. sing., dir. obj.
  (b) Acc. sing., prep. obj.
  (c) Dat. pl., prep. obj.
  (d) Dat. pl., ind. obj.

3 (a) Nom. sing., subj.
  (b) Nom. sing., pred. nom.
  (c) Acc. sing., dir. obj.
  (d) Gen. sing., poss.

4 (a) Gen. sing., poss.
  (b) Gen. pl., prep. obj.
  (c) Dat. sing., ind. obj.
  (d) Dat. pl., prep. obj.

B (5) Der Deutsche *Bund* (1834) hat gerade durch seine Mangelhaftigkeit (6) dem *Streben* (7) der *Deutschen* aller Schichten und (8) aller *Stämme* (9) die *Richtung* auf (10) den nationalen *Staat* gegeben.

5 (a) Gen. pl., poss.
  (b) Gen. sing., poss.
  (c) Nom. sing., subj.
  (d) Dat. sing., dat. of reference

6 (a) Dat. pl., ind. obj.
  (b) Dat. sing., ind. obj.
  (c) Acc. sing., dir. obj.
  (d) Gen. sing., poss.

7 (a) Nom. sing., subj.
  (b) Gen. pl., poss.
  (c) Dat. sing., ind. obj.
  (d) Acc. pl., dir. obj.

8 (a) Dat. sing., ind. obj.
  (b) Nom. sing., pred. nom.
  (c) Gen. sing., prep. obj.
  (d) Gen. pl., poss.

9 (a) Acc. sing., dir. obj.
  (b) Acc. pl., dir. obj.
  (c) Nom. sing., pred. nom.
  (d) Nom. pl., subj.

10 (a) Acc. sing., dir. obj.
  (b) Dat. pl., prep. obj.
  (c) Acc. sing., prep. obj.
  (d) Dat. sing., prep. obj.

C Robert Bunsen war (11) ein *Vorbild* (12) der *Pflege* (13) der *Wissenschaft*; aus (14) seinen *Erfindungen* (15) *Nutzen* für sich zu ziehen, lag ihm fern.

11 (a) Nom. sing., pred. nom.
  (b) Nom. sing., subj.
  (c) Acc. sing., dir. obj.
  (d) Dat. sing., dat. of reference

12 (a) Nom. sing., pred. nom.
  (b) Dat. sing., ind. obj.
  (c) Gen. pl., prep. obj.
  (d) Gen. sing., poss.

13 (a) Gen. pl., poss.
  (b) Gen. sing., poss.
  (c) Nom. sing., pred. nom.
  (d) Dat. sing., ind. obj.

14 (a) Nom. pl., subj.
  (b) Acc. pl., dir. obj.
  (c) Dat. pl., prep. obj.
  (d) Dat. pl., ind. obj.

15 (a) Nom. sing., subj.
  (b) Acc. sing., dir. obj.
  (c) Acc. pl., prep. obj.
  (d) Dat. pl., prep. obj.

D   (16) Die *Sozialdemokraten* wollen mit ihrem Eintritt in (17) die *Regierung*
(18) nächstes *Jahr* (19) die *Chance* etwas vergrößern, daß Arbeitsplätze (20) den
kleinen *Lohnempfängern* erhalten bleiben.

16 (a) Acc. pl., dir. obj.
   (b) Acc. pl., prep. obj.
   (c) Nom. sing., subj.
   (d) Nom. pl., subj.
18 (a) Acc. sing., def. time
   (b) Gen. sing., indef. time
   (c) Nom. sing., pred. nom.
   (d) Acc. sing., dir. obj.
20 (a) Acc. sing., dir. obj.
   (b) Acc. pl., prep. obj.
   (c) Dat. pl., dat. of reference
   (d) Gen. pl., poss.

17 (a) Dat. sing., ind. obj.
   (b) Nom. sing., pred. nom.
   (c) Acc. pl., prep. obj.
   (d) Acc. sing., prep. obj.
19 (a) Nom. sing., subj.
   (b) Nom. sing., pred. nom.
   (c) Acc. sing., dir. obj.
   (d) Acc. sing., prep. obj.

E   Auf keinem Gebiet (21) der *Kunst* scheint (22) der *Umbruch* (23) der modernen
Zeit (24) die *Gesetze* (25) der klassischen *Ästhetik* so umstürzlerisch beiseitegeschoben
zu haben wie in der Dramatik.

21 (a) Gen. pl., prep. obj.
   (b) Gen. sing., poss.
   (c) Dat. sing., dat. of reference
   (d) Nom. sing., subj.
23 (a) Dat. sing., ind. obj.
   (b) Gen. pl., prep. obj.
   (c) Nom. sing., pred. nom.
   (d) Gen. sing., poss.
25 (a) Nom. sing., subj.
   (b) Dat. sing., dat. of reference
   (c) Gen. sing., poss.
   (d) Acc. sing., dir. obj.

22 (a) Dat. sing., ind. obj.
   (b) Nom. sing., subj.
   (c) Gen. sing., indef. time
   (d) Gen. pl., poss.
24 (a) Acc. pl., dir. obj.
   (b) Acc. sing., dir. obj.
   (c) Nom. pl., subj.
   (d) Dat. pl., ind. obj.

F   Die Technik wird uns (26) eines *Tages* (27) die *Möglichkeit* geben, (28) den
Menschen (29) ein besseres, schöneres und würdigeres *Leben* zu schaffen, als es sich
(30) unsere *Vorfahren* jemals vorstellen konnten.

26 (a) Acc. pl., dir. obj.
   (b) Gen. sing., indef. time
   (c) Dat. sing., ind. obj.
   (d) Nom. pl., pred. nom.
28 (a) Acc. sing., dir. obj.
   (b) Acc. pl., dir. obj.
   (c) Nom. pl., pred. nom.
   (d) Dat. pl., ind. obj.
30 (a) Gen. pl., indef. time.
   (b) Dat. pl., ind. obj.
   (c) Nom. pl., subj.
   (d) Acc. pl., dir. obj.

27 (a) Acc. sing., dir. obj.
   (b) Nom. sing., pred. nom.
   (c) Acc. pl., prep. obj.
   (d) Gen. pl., poss.
29 (a) Nom. sing., subj.
   (b) Gen. sing., prep. obj.
   (c) Acc. sing., dir. obj.
   (d) Acc. pl., dir. obj.

Working Vocabulary

der *Arbeiter, –* worker
der *Arbeitsplatz, ¨e* job, place of employment
die *Ästhetik* aesthetics
beiseite·schieben, o, o push aside, dismiss
bekommen, bekam, o receive, gain, get
der *Bund, ¨e* union, confederation, band, tie
der *Bürger, –* citizen
die *Chance, -n* opportunity, chance
der *Deutsche* the German (for declension see Appendix §73)
die *Dramatik* drama, the theater
der *Eintritt, -e* entrance, entry, admission
die *Erfindung, -en* invention
erhalten (ä), ie, a save, keep; *erhalten bleiben* be kept, be preserved, be maintained
fern far, distant (see *liegen*)
sich *fühlen* feel
das *Fundament, -e* basis, foundation
das *Ganze* the whole (For declension see Appendix §73.)
das *Gebiet, -e* area, domain
das *Gefühl, -e* feeling
gerade just, exactly, precisely
das *Gesetz, e* law
das *Glied, -er* member, part
der *Grad, -e* degree, level
jemals ever
die *Kultur, -en* culture
die *Kunst, ¨e* art
das *Leben, –* life
liegen, a, e lie, be situated; *einem fern liegen* be far from someone's thoughts
der *Lohnempfänger, –* wage earner, worker
die *Mangelhaftigkeit* inadequacy, defectiveness, imperfection

der *Mensch (-en), -en* human being, man
die *Möglichkeit, -en* possibility
nächst next
der *Nutzen, –* use, profit, gain, advantage
der *Patriotismus* patriotism
die *Pflege, -n* care, cultivation
der *Pietismus* pietism
der *Platz, ¨e* place, location
die *Regierung, -en* government
die *Richtung, -en* direction, course
schaffen, schuf, a create, make, provide
scheinen, ie, ie seem, shine
die *Schicht, -en* layer, class (in society)
sinnlos senseless, meaningless
sittlich moral, ethical
der *Sozialdemokrat (-en), -en* Social(istic) Democrat
der *Stamm, ¨e* tribe, race
der *Staat, -en* nation, state
das *Streben* aspiration, striving
der *Tag, -e* day; *eines Tages* one day, some day
die *Technik, -en* technology, technique
der *Umbruch, ¨e* (radical) change, transformation
umstürzlerisch revolutionary
der *Vater, ¨* father
vergrößern increase, augment
das *Vorbild, -er* model, example, ideal
der *Vorfahr (-en), -en* ancestor, forefather
sich *vor·stellen* imagine, dream of
wichtig important
die *Wissenschaft, -en* science, knowledge
die *Würde, -n* worthiness, dignity
würdig worthy, dignified
die *Zeit, -en* time, era, period
ziehen, zog, gezogen pull, draw; *Nutzen ziehen* derive use, make gains

Punctuation, Conjunctions and the Verb
The Infinitive Phrase

One of the ways of finding the verb in a German sentence is simply to recognize a verb form which you know, or to recognize that a word, because of its form, can be nothing but a verb. But in a complicated sentence, or in a sentence with complex verb forms, it is often helpful to know where you can expect to find the verbs.

16 / Punctuation

a / In general

Marks of punctuation can be helpful in locating verbs. Infinitives, past participles, verb modifiers, and inflected verbs in subordinate clauses are usually at or near the end of the sentence or clause. They are, therefore, generally found before some mark of punctuation.

Racine hat sein größtes Werk, „Phèdre", *geschrieben,* um seinen alten Lehrern *zu beweisen,* daß eine Tragödie christlich und moralisch sein *könne.*	Racine wrote his greatest work, "Phèdre," to prove to his old teachers that a tragedy could be Christian and moral.

Periods, colons, question and exclamation marks are used in about the same way in both German and English.

Freud war nur ungern Arzt *geworden.*	Freud had only reluctantly become a doctor.
Ist mit dieser Reaktion ein Verbrauch von Wärme *verbunden?*	Is consumption of heat connected with this reaction?
Halten Sie sich bereit, sofort *fortzu-fahren!*	Be ready to leave immediately!

b / The comma

English and German are similar in using the comma to separate words in a series, nouns in apposition, and interjections. But there are some important differences in usage.

In English the comma serves to separate from each other main clauses introduced by conjunctions and to set off certain subordinate clauses.

In German, on the other hand, the comma separates any meaning unit which contains a verb from other like units of the sentence. Thus every clause in the German sentence, be it main or subordinate clause, is set off from every other clause by commas. The infinitive phrase,[1] too, is most often separated by a comma from the clause to which it belongs.

Man sagte ihm, daß es schwer sein würde, geldliche Unterstützung zu bekommen.	They told him that it would be hard to get financial support.

Moreover, the comma in German frequently serves to separate two main clauses which in English would normally be separated by a semicolon.

Diese Vermutung steht zwar mit den Tatsachen im Einklang, sie ist jedoch immer noch eine Vermutung.	This conjecture is, to be sure, in harmony with the facts; nevertheless, it is still only a conjecture.

c / Use of the comma to help establish meaning

When the sense of a sentence is not readily apparent, it is a good idea to work within commas which enclose a unit of meaning containing a verb. You must remember, of course, that any clause may contain within it another clause. Remember, too, that an infinitive phrase set off by commas may be needed to complete the sense of the unit within which you are working.

Here is an example of how the use of commas may help:

Nicht die Wahrheit, in deren Besitz irgend ein Mensch ist, oder zu sein vermeinet, sondern die aufrichtige Mühe, die er angewandt hat, hinter die Wahrheit zu kommen, macht den Wert des Menschen. (Lessing)

Using the commas to separate clauses and find verbs is one way to identify the meaningful sections of the sentence:

Nicht die Wahrheit / in deren Besitz irgend ein Mensch *ist* / oder *zu sein vermeinet* / sondern die aufrichtige Mühe / die er *angewandt hat* / hinter die Wahrheit *zu kommen* / *macht* den Wert des Menschen.

When each section is understood, this complex-looking sentence resolves into a main clause and two subordinate clauses (each one with a supplement).

Main clause:

Nicht die Wahrheit sondern die aufrichtige Mühe macht den Wert des Menschen.	Not the truth but sincere effort determines the worth of the person.

Subordinate clause 1 with two verbs:

in deren Besitz irgend ein Mensch ist, oder zu sein vermeinet,	in the possession of which a person is or thinks he is,

Subordinate clause 2 with infinitive phrase:

die er angewandt hat, hinter die Wahrheit zu kommen,	which he has made to search for the truth,

[1]See §18.

Now the sentence can easily be put together:

> Not the truth, in the possession of which a person is or thinks he is, but the sincere effort which he has made to search for the truth, determines the worth of the person.

17 / Conjunctions

Another aid in finding the verb is a knowledge of the conjunctions. If you know, for example, that the conjunction *daß* always introduces a subordinate clause, then you will also expect the verb to be at the end of that clause. On the other hand, if you see the conjunction *denn* you can expect to find the inflected verb the second element of that clause, i.e., following upon either the subject, or the object, or an adverb, etc. In short, it is helpful to know which conjunctions introduce main clauses and which introduce subordinate clauses.

a / Coordinating conjunctions
The conjunctions which introduce coordinate or main clauses are:

aber	but	*denn*	for
allein	but	*oder*	or
sondern	but (on the contrary)	*und*	and

Remember: After these conjunctions there is one element and only one (subject, or object, or adverb, etc.), then the inflected verb.

b / Subordinating conjunctions
Conjunctions which introduce subordinate or dependent clauses are:

als	as, when	*da*	since (causal)
wie	as, when	*weil*	because
wenn	when, if	*damit*	in order that
bis	until	*daß*	that, so that
bevor	before	*ohne daß***	without ... ing**
ehe	before	*ob*	whether, if
*indem**	while, by, in that, as*	*wenn*	if, when
		als ob	as if
während	while	*als wenn*	as if
nachdem	after	*auch wenn*	even if
je nachdem	according to the way that; depending on (how)	*wenn ... auch*	even if
		obgleich	although
		obwohl	although
		wenngleich	although, even though
seitdem	since (of time)	*wenn ... gleich*	although, even though
sobald	as soon as		

*Indem man den Stoff heizt ...   While one heats the substance ...
                                         In hea*ting* the substance ...
                                         By hea*ting* the substance ...

**Ohne daß er es wußte ...   *Without* his kno*wing* it ...

The following question words are also used as subordinating conjunctions:

wann	when	*wo*	where
warum	why	*woher*	where . . . from, whence
wie	how	*wohin*	where . . . to, whither

Remember: These conjunctions should direct your attention toward the end of the clause where the verb will ordinarily be.

c / Other common connectives

The relative pronouns *der, die, das; welcher; wer; was; da(r)-* and *wo(r)-* also introduce subordinate clauses and should cause you to expect that the verb will normally be found at the end of the clause. For illustrations see Unit Ten, §30, §31, §32 a and c.

d / The conjunction *da*

The conjunction *da* (since) is often confused with the adverb *da* (there, then) especially when the word *da* comes at the beginning of a sentence or clause. The position of the verb is the key. Compare:

Da auf diesem Gebiete noch viel *zu tun ist,* ist die Unterstützung durch den Staat dringend notwendig.

Since much remains to be done in this field, the support of the state is urgently necessary.

Da ist aber noch sehr viel zu tun, und die Unterstützung durch den Staat ist dringend notwendig.

There much remains to be done, and the support of the state is urgently necessary.

After the conjunction *da* (since) the inflected verb comes at the end of the clause. If the sentence or clause begins with the adverb *da* (there, then), the inflected verb (which must be the second element of a main clause) follows immediately upon *da*.

18 / A note on infinitive phrases[1]

Both English and German have so-called "infinitive phrases" consisting of an infinitive with objects(s), or modifiers(s), or both. In German these phrases are normally separated from the rest of the sentence by commas.

Er hofft, *einen neuen Wagen zu bekommen.*

He hopes *to get a new car.*

Es wäre besser, *heute abend zu Hause zu bleiben.*

It would be better *to stay home tonight.*

In the English infinitive phrase the infinitive usually comes first, whereas in German the infinitive is the last element of the phrase. In translating German infinitive phrases you must begin usually at the end, i.e., with the infinitive. Then let object(s) or modifiers(s) follow. See illustrations above.

But if an infinitive phrase is introduced by a preposition, you must begin with the preposition. Let the infinitive follow immediately, and then pick up the other elements of the phrase.

[1]See also Appendix §84.

Um Wasserstoff *zu gewinnen,* zersetzt man Wasser durch Elektrolyse.

In order to obtain hydrogen we decompose water by means of electrolysis.

Ohne mit der Homerischen Götterwelt einigermaßen bekannt *zu sein,* kann man viele Dichtungen aus der Neuzeit nicht verstehen.

Without being acquainted to some extent with the Homeric gods one cannot understand many poetic works of the modern era.

Anstatt (Statt) neue poetische Formen *zu schaffen,* bleiben viele Dichter bei den geläufigen Gattungen der klassichen Tradition.

Instead of creating new poetic forms, many poets stay with (keep on using) the customary types of the classical tradition.

Notice that the infinitives in the second and third illustrations above are rendered by gerunds (being, creating). The English gerund is frequently the equivalent of a German infinitive.

Exercises

I   Conjunctions and other connectives used in the sentences below are listed on the answer sheet. In the space next to each conjunction which introduces a (coordinate) main clause enter the symbol *Co*; enter the inflected verb of the clause if the conjunction introduces a subordinate clause.

☆   QUESTION

Da seine Theorie zunächst kein Gehör fand, setzte Harvey seine Versuche und Beobachtungen fort, denn er war seiner Sache ziemlich sicher.

Since his theory was at first not well received, Harvey continued his experiments and observations, for he was fairly sure of his case.

ANSWER

Da   *fand*

denn   *Co*

1   Die bedeutendste Persönlichkeit, die während der gemäßigten Phase der Französischen Revolution hervortrat, war Graf Mirabeau.

The most important personality that came forward during the moderate phase of the French Revolution was Count Mirabeau.

2   Es ist immer ein Zeichen von schöpferischer Begabung, wenn ein Mensch die Fähigkeit besitzt, Gegebenheiten zu sehen und mit ihnen zu operieren. Ein solcher Mensch war Mirabeau.

It is always a sign of creative talent when a person has the ability to see actualities and to deal with them. Mirabeau was such a person.

3 Er war für die Jakobiner, als sie keinen Krieg wollten, weil er sah, daß dieser nur den Sieg der Anarchie bedeuten würde.	He was on the side of the Jacobins when they did not want war because he saw that war would only mean the triumph of anarchy,
4 Aber er war gegen die Jakobiner, als sie radikale Demokratie forderten, denn er sah, daß diese ebenfalls zur Anarchie führen müsse.	But he was against the Jacobins when they demanded radical democracy, for he saw that this policy also would necessarily lead to anarchy.
5 Als der König daran dachte, nach Paris zu gehen, äußerte Mirabeau Mißfallen, da er wußte, daß dieser Schritt höchst gefährlich war.	When the king thought he ought perhaps go to Paris, Mirabeau expressed his displeasure, since he knew that this step was highly dangerous.
6 Er scheute sich nicht, vom Hof große Geldsummen anzunehmen, und doch kann man ihn nicht bestochen nennen, denn er wußte, daß sie ihn nicht von seiner klar gezogenen Richtlinie abbringen würden.	He was not reluctant to accept large sums of money from the members of Court, and yet one cannot speak of his being bribed, for he knew that these sums would not divert him from his clearly-drawn course.

II   Using again the sentences in Exercise I, write on the answer sheet the first and last words of the main clauses and infinitive phrases. The answer sheet indicates how many main clauses (abbreviation MC) and infinitive phrases (abbreviation IP) there are in each sentence.

☆   QUESTION

Um Wasserstoff zu gewinnen, zersetzt man Wasser durch Elektrolyse.	To obtain hydrogen we decompose water through electrolysis.

ANSWER   IP *um   gewinnen*   MC *zersetzt   Elektrolyse*

III   In the following sentences translate the phrases or clauses printed in italics.
1 Die Nationalsozialisten setzten den Reichstag in Brand, *um einen äußerlichen Anlaß* für die politische Verfolgung der Kommunisten *zu schaffen.*
2 Goethe hat Kants Schriften gelesen, *ohne davon beeinflußt zu werden.*
3 *Längst bevor die Französische Revolution* nach Deutschland *kam*, waren alle Blicke nach Paris gerichtet.
4 *Da das deutsche Volk jetzt geteilt ist*, kann man nicht von **einer** deutschen Nation sprechen.
5 Galilei schickte seine Schriften zu einem holländischen Verleger, *damit sie* ohne Zensur *erscheinen konnten.*
6 Brandt versuchte, seine Ostpolitik weiterzuführen, *ohne daß seine Regierung* dadurch *geschwächt wurde.*
7 Man wußte nicht, *ob das Bild von Rembrandt selbst war* oder von einem seiner Schüler.
8 Es muß eine Aufgabe der Außenpolitik sein, *bei allen Konflikten im Spiel zu bleiben*, (9) *ohne aber das Odium auf sich zu laden*, (10) *sie bewußt vertieft zu haben.*

Working Vocabulary

der **Anlaß, -"(ss)e** cause, motive, occasion, reason

die **Aufgabe, -n** task, job, assignment

äußerlich outward, external, evident, apparent

die **Außenpolitik, -en** foreign policy

beeinflussen influence

bewußt consciously, deliberately

das **Bild, -er** picture, painting

bleiben, ie, ie remain, continue (see *das Spiel*)

der **Blick, -e** gaze; *alle Blicke richten* turn everyone's eyes

der **Brand, -"e** fire, flames(s); *in Brand setzen* set on fire

damit so that

erscheinen, ie, ie appear (of a book), be published

französisch French

holländisch Dutch

laden (ä), u, a load, charge; *auf sich laden* incur, bring upon oneself

längst long (ago)

der **Nationalsozialist(-en), -en** National Socialist

das **Odium** stigma, odious charge, hateful onus

die **Ostpolitik, -en** (foreign) policy toward Eastern Europe

die **Regierung, -en** government

der **Reichstag** German Parliament from 1871 until 1933, also the building in which the German Parliament met

richten direct, aim (see *der Blick*)

schaffen, schuf, a create, make, produce, provide

schicken send

die **Schrift, -en** writing(s)

der **Schüler, –** student, apprentice

schwächen weaken

setzen put, set (see *der Brand*)

das **Spiel, -e** play, game; *im Spiel bleiben* remain involved, stay in the game, continue to play a role or have a hand (in things)

teilen divide

die **Verfolgung, -en** persecution, prosecution

der **Verleger, –** publisher

versuchen try, attempt

vertiefen deepen, intensify

das **Volk, -"er** people, nation

weiter· führen continue, develop further, expand

wissen (weiß), wußte, gewußt know

die **Zensur, -en** censorship

Sentences and Clauses Beginning with the Verb Requests and Suggestions

In the preceding units it has been stressed that: (a) in a statement the finite verb of the main clause is normally the second element of the sentence; and (b) in most subordinate clauses the finite verb is the final element.

Sometimes the finite verb comes at the beginning of the sentence, or is the first word in a main clause following a coordinating conjunction.[1] This initial position of the finite verb should put you on your guard, for this position may mean one of several things. To understand the intent of the writer in putting the finite verb first, it is necessary to take the rest of the sentence into consideration.

The three[2] most frequent types of sentences in which the finite verb comes first are: the question, the condition, and the imperative or suggestion. The finite verb may begin a question in English (Have you . . . ? Do you have . . . ?) as well as in German *(Haben Sie . . . ?)*, and so this kind of sentence in German occasions the English speaking reader very little difficulty. The condition and the imperative or suggestion require discussion in some detail before we turn to a comparison of the three types.

19 / The conditional sentence

In stating a condition contrary to fact in English, we occasionally omit the conjunction *if.* When this is done the verb must come first in the clause.

> *If I had seen* him, I would have told him about it.
>
> *Had I seen* him, I would have told him about it.

The same procedure is permissible in German in stating any condition. The verb is then the first element in the clause. The result clause or conclusion usually begins with *so* or *dann.*[3]

Wenn man ein Gas in einem geschlossenen Behälter *erwärmt,* (so) steigt der Druck darin.	*If* gas is heated in a closed container, (then) the pressure rises in the container.
Erwärmt man ein Gas in einem geschlossenen Behälter, *so* (or *dann*) steigt der Druck darin.	

---

[1] The inflected verb of the main clause normally comes first after a subordinate clause, the subordinate clause being the first element of the sentence: (1) *Ob diese Behauptung wahr ist,* (2) *können wir hier nicht entscheiden.*

[2] A fourth type of sentence beginning with the inflected verb is discussed in Unit Sixteen, §49.

[3] *So* and *dann* in a result clause do not affect the word order. See footnote on p. 7.

20 / Imperatives, requests and suggestions

An imperative is a verb form used in direct address to give commands or exhortations.

Sei (Seid, Seien Sie) ruhig!	*Be* quiet!
Habe (Habt, Haben Sie) Geduld!	*Have* patience!
Gib (Gebt, Geben Sie) acht!	*Pay* attention!

See Appendix §95 for the formation of the imperatives.

Note   The infinitive or past participle is sometimes used in German to give commands or advice.

Bitte, *achtgeben!*	*Pay attention,* please.
Nur nicht *aufregen!*	Above all, don't *get excited.*
Aufgemerkt!	*Pay attention!*

a / The first-person plural request or suggestion

In addition to the imperative associated with the pronoun "you" there is another very common request or suggestion form. This is a request which includes listener and speaker, or reader and author in a companionship where the pronouns "we" and "us" become appropriate. Typical English examples of this type of request begin with "Let us . . . ."

The "Let us . . ." type of request in German is similar in form to the polite imperative, but it substitutes the pronoun *wir* for the pronoun *Sie.*

Versuchen wir, das zu erklären!	*Let's try* to explain that.
Nehmen wir als Beispiel . . .	*Let us take* as an example . . .
Nehmen wir an, daß . . .	*Let us assume* that . . .

b / The third-person singular request or suggestion

A further type of request or suggestion is addressed to someone as a third person. In English such a sentence would begin with "Let the reader . . . ."

In German this type of request is a third person singular form consisting of the stem of the infinitive and the ending *-e.* The only exceptional form is that for *sein,* where the third person request form is *sei.*

The subject of this form is the person to whom the request or suggestion is made. Whereas the pronoun *wir* must always follow the verb in the "Let us" type of request, the subject of the third person singular form may either precede or follow the verb.

Man stelle sich vor . . .	*Let the reader imagine* . . .; or simply:
Or: Nun *stelle man sich vor* . . .	*Imagine* . . .
Man denke nur an Flaubert.	*Let the reader* but *think* of Flaubert.
Or: *Denke man* nur an Flaubert.	Or: *Just think* of Flaubert.
Der Laie nehme sich in acht . . .	*Let the layman exercise care* . . .

c / Other uses of the suggestion forms

Suggestion broadly interpreted may also include a wish, a proposition, a concession, a statement of intent. Hence one often finds the forms described above in the following types of sentences.

Mö*ge* es ihm gelingen.	May he succeed. I hope he will succeed.
Ge*be* Gott . . .	May God grant . . .
Die Figur a *sei* . . .	Let the figure a be (represent) . . .
Man fixier*e* irgendeinen Punkt o . . .	Let any point o be fixed . . .
Es *sei* noch einmal betont . . .	Let it be emphasized once more . . .

The third person plural may also occur in sentences stating intent, propositions, etc. Especially frequent in such sentences are the verb forms *seien* and *mögen*.

Zum Schluß *seien* die Ergebnisse angegeben.	In conclusion let the results be given. In conclusion I give the results.
Einige Beispiele *mögen* dies veranschaulichen.	Perhaps some examples will make this clear. I shall try to make this clear with some examples.

21 / Interpreting sentences beginning with the verb

It is possible to find at the beginning of a sentence or main clause a verb form which can be interpreted in three ways.

Nehmen wir an . . .	Do we assume . . . ? Let us assume . . . If we assume . . .

Whenever you see a verb at the beginning of a German sentence or main clause, or following immediately upon a coordinating conjunction connecting two main clauses, look at the rest of the sentence for a key to the interpretation of the verb's unusual position.

Two types of sentences beginning with the verb have fairly definite "sign-posts."

—A question is always punctuated with a question mark.

—When *wenn* is omitted from the conditional clause, the following result clause almost always begins with either the word *so* or *dann*.

If neither of these "sign-posts" is present or if the sentence is punctuated with an exclamation mark, the sentence is probably a suggestion or request.

Ist diese Tatsache aber so aufzufassen?	But *is* this fact to be interpreted in this way?
Ist diese Tatsache aber so aufzufassen, *so (dann)* kann unsere Annahme nicht bestehen.	*If*, however, this fact is to be interpreted in this way, then our assumption cannot stand.

Fassen wir jetzt alle Ergebnisse *zu-*   *If we summarize* all the results, (then)
     sammen, so (dann) gelangen wir   we arrive at the concept . . .
     zum Begriff . . .

Fassen wir jetzt alle Ergebnisse *zusam-*   *Let us* now *summarize* all the results.
     men. (!)

Exercises

I On the answer sheet enter the letter identifying the imperative, request or suggestion form in each of the groups.

1 (a) Wir bleiben	(b) Bleiben wir	(c) Bleibe ich
2 (a) Ist	(b) Sind	(c) Sei
3 (a) Er hat	(b) Er habe	(c) Er hatte
4 (a) Stellt	(b) Stellst	(c) Stellte
5 (a) Man sitze	(b) Man sitzt	(c) Sitzt man
6 (a) Seien wir	(b) Sind wir	(c) Wir sind
7 (a) Der Student versucht	(b) Der Student versuche	(c) Der Student versuchte
8 (a) Man glaubt	(b) Glaubt man	(c) Glaube man
9 (a) Ich denke	(b) Der Leser denke	(c) Denke ich
10 (a) Wir vergessen nicht	(b) Vergessen wir nicht	(c) Haben wir vergessen
11 (a) Werde ich	(b) Ich werde	(c) Werde man
12 (a) Er möge	(b) Mag er	(c) Er mag
13 (a) Hofften wir	(b) Wir hoffen	(c) Hoffen wir
14 (a) Kam	(b) Kommt	(c) Kommst
15 (a) Sie bringen	(b) Sie bringt	(c) Bringen Sie

II On the answer sheet enter the letter which identifies the best English translation of
the verb phrase in italics in each sentence.

1 *Kann man* Mahlers Symphonien mit denen Beethovens *vergleichen?*
    (a) Let one compare   (b) They compare   (c) If people compare
    (d) Can we compare

2 *Denken wir* an den Übergang vom Mittelalter zur Neuzeit oder an die Zeit der
    Französischen Revolution.
    (a) If we consider   (b) Let us consider   (c) Do we consider
    (d) We consider

3 "*Wollen wir* mächtig im Frieden bleiben, so müssen wir auch die Freiheit der
    anderen Völker achten." (Friedrich Meinecke)
    (a) May we wish   (b) Do we want   (c) If we want   (d) We want

4 *Hüten wir uns* davor, Philosophie mit einem neuen Kunststil gleichzusetzen.
    (a) Let us guard   (b) We guard   (c) If we guard   (d) Do we guard

5 *Möge* uns *die Zukunft* einen dauernden Frieden *bringen!*
    (a) If the future brings   (b) May the future bring   (c) Will the future bring
    (d) The future brings

6 *Unterstreichen wir* diese wichtige Tatsache: Das Ende der Weimarer Republik
   kam, bevor der Nationalsozialismus zur Macht gelangt war.
   (a) Let us emphasize   (b) We are emphasizing   (c) If we emphasize
   (d) Do we emphasize

7 *Gliedert sich die Musikwissenschaft auch* in viele Teilgebiete, so sind doch alle eng
   miteinander verbunden.
   (a) Musicology is divided also   (b) Is musicology even divided   (c) May musicology also be divided   (d) Even if musicology is divided

8 *Dürfen wir* Pasteur zu den größten Naturforschern *rechnen?*
   (a) If we include   (b) Let us include   (c) We may include   (d) Can we
   include

9 *Möge die Arbeit* der Vereinten Nationen *sich* auf der Grundlage der großen Begriffe Freiheit, Friede, und Einigkeit *vollziehen.*
   (a) If the work may be accomplished   (b) Will the work be accomplished
   (c) May the work be accomplished   (d) The work may be accomplished

10 *Vergleicht man* Preußen mit Frankreich, so erkennt man die unterschiedlichen
   Ziele der Politik.
   (a) Does one compare   (b) If we compare   (c) Let us compare
   (d) People compare

11 *Seien Sie versichert,* daß wir Ihren Entschluß durchaus billigen.
   (a) Are you assured   (b) If you are assured   (c) Can I assure you
   (d) Be assured

12 *War* Wagners **Tristan und Isolde** von großer Bedeutung, so ist doch **Der Ring der
   Nibelungen** von noch weit höherem Rang.
   (a) Though **Tristan und Isolde** was   (b) Was **Tristan und Isolde**   (c) May
   Tristan und Isolde be   (d) **Tristan und Isolde** was

13 *Vergessen wir nicht,* daß im 18. Jahrhundert auch Fahrenheit und Réaumur lebten.
   (a) Let us not forget   (b) If we do not forget   (c) Do we forget   (d) We
   do not forget

14 *Nehmen wir* Spenglers Diagnosen nur als Beobachtungen eines phantasiereichen
   Sehers, so ergeben sich doch Perspektiven, die den Blick auf neue Landschaften
   eröffnen.
   (a) Let us regard   (b) We regard   (c) Do we regard   (d) Even if we
   regard

15 "*Hat* **Tonio Kröger** den Vorzug der größeren Frische, der jugendlichen Empfindung, so ist **Der Tod in Venedig** ohne Zweifel das reifere Kunstwerk und die gelung-
   enere Komposition." (Thomas Mann judges two of his best-known works.)
   (a) If **Tonio Kröger** has   (b) Does **Tonio Kröger** have   (c) **Tonio Kröger** has
   (d) May **Tonio Kröger** have

III On the answer sheet write translations of the phrases in italics in the following
sentences.

1 *Man erinnere sich* an die großen Romane von Balzac.
2 *Möge Ihre Reise* schön und genußreich *sein!*
3 *Fangen wir* zunächst mit dem Gedicht von Yeats *an.*
4 *Versuche* vor Augen zu halten, wie tief Einsteins frühe Theorien reichten.

5 *Beeilen wir uns nicht* bei diesem höchst wichtigen Argument.
6 *Sei nicht voreilig* und (7) *wende nicht ein,* daß der Versuch nicht ganz gelungen ist.
8 *Glaube niemand,* daß unser Kanzler nicht ehrlich handelt!
9 In diesem Zusammenhang sei auf die grundlegende Arbeit von Heisenberg *hinge-wiesen.*
10 *Denkt* an die peinlichen Opfer unserer Vorfahren!
11 *Gibt es nicht sehr große Individuen,* die besonderes Unglück gehabt haben?
12 *Frage sich* doch *jeder,* wie er in seine Zeit einwirken kann.
13 *Beschäftigen wir uns* zunächst mit dem Aufbau des Wassers.
14 *Man denke sich* einen Punkt, der sich auf einer geraden Linie bewegt; (15) im Augenblicke t *befinde sich der Punkt* etwa an der Stelle q.

Working Vocabulary

achten respect, have regard for
der *Aufbau* ([e]s), -ten building, erection, structure, (re)construction, synthesis
das *Auge, -n* eye (see *halten*)
der *Augenblick, -e* moment
die *Bedeutung, -en* meaning, significance
sich *beeilen* hurry, make haste
sich *befinden, a, u* be, feel, find oneself (in a particular location)
der *Begriff, -e* concept, idea
die *Beobachtung, -en* observation
sich *beschäftigen* occupy oneself, concern oneself
besonder particular, special, exceptional, singular
sich *bewegen* move
billigen approve (of), agree (with)
der *Blick, -e* eye, view (see *eröffnen*)
dauern last, continue, endure
denken, dachte, gedacht (an) think (of), consider; *sich denken* conceive, imagine
durchaus thoroughly, completely
dürfen (darf), durfte, gedurft may, be in a position to, be permitted
ehrlich honest
die *Einigkeit* unity, concord, harmony
ein·wenden object, take exception (to), enter objection (to, that)
ein·wirken have influence, have an effect (on)
die *Empfindung, -en* sentiment, perception
eng tight, close
der *Entschluß, ⁻(ss)e* decision
sich *ergeben (i), a, e* result, follow, be produced

sich *erinnern* remember, be reminded
eröffnen open, start; *den Blick auf neue Landschaften eröffnen* bring new vistas to view
etwa nearly, about; perhaps (for example)
die *Frische* freshness
geben (i), a, e give; *es gibt* there is (are)
das *Gedicht, -e* poem
gelangen reach, arrive (at); *zur Macht gelangen* come to power
gelingen, a, u succeed; *gelungen* successful, well done
genußreich pleasant, enjoyable
gerade straight, direct
gleich·setzen equate
sich *gliedern* be divided into, be composed of, form
die *Grundlage, -n* foundation, base
grundlegend fundamental, basic
halten (ä), ie, a hold, keep; *vor Augen halten* keep in mind (in view)
handeln act, behave
hin·weisen, ie, ie refer to, point to
hoch, höher, höchst high, great;
höchst highly
hoffen hope
sich *hüten* guard, be on guard; *sich hüten vor* guard against, be careful in regard to
das *Individuum (-s), -duen* individual
jugendlich youthful
der *Kanzler, –* chancellor
der *Kunststil, -e* style (of art)

die *Landschaft, -en* landscape (see
eröffnen)
die *Macht, ̈e* power, strength
miteinander with each other, together
das *Mittelalter* Middle Ages
der *Naturforscher, –* natural scientist
die *Neuzeit* modern time(s)
der *Nibelung (-en), -en* In German mythology, a race of dwarfs
das *Opfer, –* sacrifice
peinlich painful, agonizing, embarrassing
phantasiereich imaginative, ingenious, fanciful
das *Preußen* Prussia
der *Punkt (es), -e* point
der *Rang, ̈e* class, order, rank
rechnen count, reckon, include, consider; *rechnen zu* consider, count among
reichen reach, extend
reif mature
die *Reise, -n* trip, journey
der *Roman, -e* novel
der *Seher, –* prophet, seer
die *Stelle, -n* place, position
die *Tatsache, -n* fact
das *Teilgebiet, -e* branch, department

der *Übergang, ̈e* transition
das *Unglück* misfortune, bad luck, affliction
unterschiedlich different, diverse, distinct
unterstreichen, i, i emphasize, underscore
verbinden, a, u connect, relate
die *Vereinten Nationen* the United Nations
vergessen (i), a, e forget
vergleichen, i, i compare
versichern assure, insure, make sure (of)
der *Versuch, -e* trial, experiment, attempt
versuchen try, attempt
sich *vollziehen, -zog, -zogen* be accomplished, be effected
voreilig hasty, premature, precipitate
der *Vorfahr (-en), -en* ancestor
der *Vorzug, ̈e* superiority, the form or feature of excellence, advantage
weit vast, much, wide
das *Ziel, -e* goal, aim, objective
zunächst (at) first, to begin with
der *Zusammenhang, ̈e* connection, context
der *Zweifel, –* doubt; *ohne Zweifel* without a doubt

Verbs with Dependent Infinitives: the Modals

The so-called modal auxiliaries might also be called "incomplete verbs." If someone says to you suddenly: "You must" or "You ought" your immediate response is: "I must (ought to) do what? " The modal auxiliary generally states a relationship (ability, necessity, obligation, permission, possibility, etc.) between the subject and action and therefore needs a "completion verb" to make sense. Sometimes this "completion verb" is expressed, sometimes it is understood from the context.

22 / The German modal and the end of the sentence

The German modal auxiliary, like the English, needs a "completion verb" except in a limited number of idiomatic uses. This "completion verb" is an infinitive and comes toward the end of the clause or sentence. Any form of *dürfen, können, mögen, müssen, sollen, wollen* should, therefore, direct your attention toward the end of the clause.

As in the case of *haben, sein* and *werden,* you cannot know how to translate the modal auxiliaries until you have seen the whole clause or sentence. Most modal auxiliaries have more than one meaning, and this meaning does not become clear until the whole context is known.

23 / The meanings of the German modals[1]

Below is a summary of the meanings of the modals in some common uses. You should study this summary well, observing especially the English equivalents of the modals in the various tenses. English lacks complete conjugations of the modals and must, particularly in the past tenses, use circumlocutions.

A use common to the modals is to express subjective states of mind, conjectures or personal viewpoints. In addition to the primary meanings of the modals there are idiomatic uses to be noted.

- *dürfen, (darf), durfte, gedurft*—to have permission or authority to

    Man *darf* gehen.   One *is permitted to* go.
                                         One *may* go.

[1]For tables showing the conjugation of the modals, see Appendix §99.

Wir *dürfen* heute sagen, daß . . .	Today we *may* say that . . .
	Today we *are in a position to* say that . . .
Er *durfte* also bleiben?	Then he *was allowed to* remain?

Idiomatic and subjective uses of *dürfen* include:

Man *darf* sich kaum denken . . .	One *hardly dares* imagine . . .
Es *dürfte* jetzt zu spät sein.	It *is probably (seems)* too late now.

See also the note on page 51 about *dürfen* in the negative.

- *können (kann), konnte, gekonnt*—can, to be able to, to be in a position to

Er *kann* es tun.	He *can* do it.
	He *is able to* do it.
Sie *konnte* schon lesen.	She *was* already *able to* read.
	She already *knew how to* read.

Idiomatic and subjective uses of *können* include:

Er *kann* Deutsch.	He *knows* German.
Das *kann* sein.	That *may* be.
Er *kann* uns *gesehen haben.*	He *may have seen* us.
	He *probably saw* us.
	It *is possible (probable)* that he saw us.

- *mögen (mag), mochte, gemocht*—may (possibility); to like, to have a mind to, to be inclined to

Er *mag* krank sein.	He *is perhaps* sick.
	He *may be* sick.
Er *mochte* krank sein.	He *was probably* sick.
	Maybe he *was* sick.
Er *mag* nur kommen.	*Let* him come.
Man *mag* das nicht glauben.	One does not *like (want) to* believe that.
Das Publikum *hat* aber die Farbe des Präparats nicht *gemocht.*	But the public *did* not *like* the color of the preparation.

See also below and illustrations in §20c of Unit Seven for the use of *mögen* to express intent.

Möge dieses Werk einen Fortschritt bedeuten.	*May* this work constitute a step forward.
	I hope that this work *will* constitute a step forward.

• *müssen (muß), mußte, gemußt*—must, to have to

    Man *muß* schwer arbeiten.   One *must* work a great deal.
                                    One *has to* work a great deal.

    Man wird schwer arbeiten *müssen.*   One will *have to* work hard.

Idiomatic and subjective uses of *müssen* include:

    Sie *muß* doch jetzt hier sein.   *Surely* she *is* here by now.
                                      It is very likely that she *is* here now.

    Er *muß* das Buch gelesen haben.   He *must have read* the book.
                                      He *has surely read* the book.

See also the note on page 51 about *müssen* in the negative.

• *sollen (soll), sollte, gesollt*—to be obliged to, to be supposed to, to be said to. See also §38.

    Soll ich morgen kommen?   *Shall* I come tomorrow?
    Er *soll* morgen anfangen.   He *is supposed to* begin tomorrow.
                                      He *is to* begin tomorrow.

    Er *sollte* in zehn Tagen fertig sein.   He *was to (was supposed to)* be ready
                                      in ten days.

    Er soll sofort kommen.   *Let him (Tell him to)* come right away.

    Es *soll* sehr teuer sein.   It *is supposed to* be very expensive.
                                      It *is said to* be very expensive.

    Er *sollte* zu der Zeit schwer krank   He *was said (supposed, thought) to* be
      sein.   very sick at that time.

• *wollen (will), wollte, gewollt*—will, to want to, to intend to

    Er *will* morgen anfangen.   He *wants to* begin tomorrow.
                                      He *intends to* begin tomorrow.

    Er *will* es aber.   But he *will (is determined to)* do it.

    Er *wollte* nicht dabei sein.   He *did* not *want to* be present.
                                    He *did* not *intend to* be there.
                                    He *was determined* not *to* be there.

    Dies *wollen* wir an einem Beispiel   *Let us* make this clear with an ex-
      klar machen.   ample.

Idiomatic and subjective uses of *wollen* include:

    Er *will* eine großartige Entdeckung   He *claims to* have made a tremendous
      gemacht haben.   discovery.

    Blumen *wollen* gepflegt sein.   Flowers *must* be tended.
                                      Flowers *ought to* be tended.

Die Tatsachen *wollten* aber mit der Theorie *nicht* übereinstimmen.	The facts *refused to* conform to the theory.
	The facts, however, *simply did not* conform to the theory.

- *dürfen* and *müssen* with a negative

When *dürfen* is used with *nicht* the force of the basic meaning *not to be allowed* is generally best translated with *must not.*

Ich *darf* es *nicht.*	I *am not allowed to* (do it).
	I *must not* (do it).
Man *darf* es sich aber *nicht* so vorstellen.	But one *must not* conceive of it in this way.

On the other hand, *müssen* with *nicht* states that the subject is not compelled to do something.

Man *muß* zwar *nicht.*	To be sure, one *does not have to.*
Was man *nicht* tun *muß,* tut man nicht.	What one *does not have to* do, one does not do.
	What a person *is not required to* do, he won't do.

24 / The perfect tenses of the modals

In the perfect tenses the modal auxiliaries have two past participle forms. Sometimes they use a regular past participle (*ge . . . t*). Sometimes the infinitive form functions as a past participle.

a / Perfect tenses of modals without dependent infinitives

When used without an expressed dependent infinitive the modals have a regular past participle form in the perfect and pluperfect tenses.

Er *hat* es *gemußt.*	He has had to. (He has had to do it.)
Er *hatte* es *gemußt.*	He had had to. (He had had to do it.)

Note   If the "completion verb" with a modal is understood (here, for example, study), German often uses *es* as a sort of reference to this understood verb. In English this *es* is sometimes omitted in translating, sometimes replaced by the indefinite *do it.*

b / Perfect tenses of modals with dependent infinitives

If the modal in the perfect or pluperfect tense has an expressed dependent infinitive, then the modal's infinitive functions as a past participle. We then get what is called the double-infinitive construction.

Er *hat* schwer *arbeiten müssen.*	He *has had to work* hard.
Er *hatte* schwer *arbeiten müssen.*	He *had had to work* hard.

c / Position of the double infinitive construction

The double infinitive must always be the last element of its clause. Even the inflected verb in the subordinate clause must precede the double infinitive.

Obgleich er manches Hindernis *(1) hat (3) überwinden (2) müssen,* ist es ihm gelungen.

Although he *(1) has (2) had (3) to surmount* many an obstacle, he has succeeded.

cf. Obgleich er manches Hindernis *(2) überwinden (1) mußte,* gelang es ihm.

Although he *(1) had (2) to surmount* many an obstacle, he succeeded.

Note   Like the modal auxiliaries, the following verbs form double infinitive constructions with their dependent infinitives when used in a compound tense: *hören, lassen, sehen;* rarely also: *helfen, lernen.*

Exercises

I   On the answer sheet one form of each modal verb is entered under one of the headings listed in the example below. In the spaces provided, enter the other four forms of the verb.

☆   ANSWER

Infinitive	*Present*	*Past*	*Participle*	
	3rd Person Singular		Without Dependent Infinitive	With Dependent Infinitive
lassen	*läßt*	ließ	*gelassen*	*lassen*

II   On the answer sheet enter the letter that identifies the best translation of the word or phrase in italics in each sentence, clause or phrase.

A Der Historiker (1) *muß* Einsicht in den Gang der praktischen Politik haben, um sie richtig beurteilen zu (2) *können.*

   1   (a) had to   (b) have to   (c) has to   (d) should

   2   (a) can   (b) be able to   (c) could   (d) has been able to

B „Die amerikanisch-sowjetische Entspannung *darf* nicht stillstehen," meinte Breschnew.

   3   (a) must (not)   (b) is (not) allowed to   (c) may (not)

      (d) might (not)

C Seit dem Ende des zweiten Weltkriegs ist es unklar geblieben, wie die Europäer der Zukunft entgegentreten *sollen.*

   4   (a) are said to   (b) intend to   (c) should have   (d) are to

D Nach Luther *soll* die Gemeinde ihren Pfarrer selbst wählen *dürfen.*

   5   (a) is said to be allowed to   (b) must not allowed to   (c) would be allowed to   (d) is to be allowed to

E Dichter wie Mallarmé und Verlaine *wollten* keine bestimmten Gedanken verkünden.
   6 (a) do (not) want to   (b) had (not) wanted to   (c) did (not) intend to
      (d) should (not) claim to
F Einige Kritiker *wollen* in Warhol einen bedeutenden Künstler erkennen.
   7 (a) claim to   (b) had wanted to   (c) will   (d) were able to
G Bei den Ägyptern *muß* der Bauwille gewaltig *gewesen sein.*
   8 (a) had been necessary   (b) has been   (c) must have been
      (d) must be
H Daß ein Gleichgewicht geschaffen *werden mußte,* folgte aus der Natur der
europäischen Verhältnisse.
   9 (a) is to be   (b) had to be   (c) will have to be   (d) will have had
      to be
I Die Entwicklung der Musik *mag* auch bei den einzelnen Völkern unterschiedlich
verlaufen sein.
   10 (a) may have occurred   (b) is said to be occurring   (c) has been
      allowed to occur   (d) would have occurred

III Translate the word or phrase in italics. Be sure that your translation suits the idiomatic sense of the whole sentence.
   1 Es *mag* eine Enttäuschung *gewesen sein,* (2) daß die Dresdener Konferenz *hat
ausfallen müssen.*
   3 *Man* wird doch *sagen dürfen:* (4) einer *darf niemals* Opportunist *sein.*
   5 Wilson *soll sich* als Bannerträger eines neuen Menschheitsideals *empfunden haben.*
   6 Der Krieg *darf* kein Mittel der Politik *sein.*
   7 Die Theoretiker der Aufklärung *wollten* den Gesetzen der Vernunft und der
Moral *folgen.*
   8 Der mathematische Sinn der Azteken *muß* sehr entwickelt *gewesen sein,* denn
ihr arithmetisches System war auf dem schweren Prinzip der Potenzierung
aufgebaut.
   9 Galilei *soll* auf seine Theorie des freien Falls im Pisa-Turm *gekommen sein.*
   10 Daß die alte Musik dem heutigen Hörer bisweilen fremd *klingen mag,* macht sie
nicht weniger interessant und mindert nicht ihre historische Bedeutung.

IV Translate.
   1 Wenn man überhaupt von „balance of power" sprechen kann, (2) dann muß
man auch an Rußland denken.
   3 Der Staatsman muß die Kraft haben, (4) taktische Rückschläge hinnehmen zu
können.
   5 Beethoven muß als Abseitiger angesehen werden.
   6 Ein einzelnes Werk kann nicht eine ganze Bibliothek ersetzen wollen.
   7 Wir dürfen die Zähigkeit der Tradition nicht unterschätzen.
   8 Die Sozialisten konnten das bürgerliche Leben nicht verändern.
   9 Picasso soll viele Motive aus der afrikanischen Volkskunst übernommen haben.
   10 Nicht alle Menschen mögen klassische Musik.

Working Vocabulary

abseitig   set apart, eccentric; *der Absei-*
tige   eccentric, one who stands apart,
aloof   (for declension see Appendix
§73)
der Ägypter, –   Egyptian
auf·bauen   construct, build (up)
die Aufklärung, -en   clarification, explanation; the Enlightenment
aus-fallen (ä), -fiel, a   be cancelled
der Azteke (-n) -n   the Aztec
der Bannerträger, –   standard bearer
der Bauwille (-ns), -n   urge to build
bedeutend   important, significant
die Bedeutung, -en   meaning, importance
bestimmt   definite, specific
beurteilen   judge
die Bibliothek, -en   library
bisweilen   occasionally, sometimes
bleiben, ie, ie   remain, stay
bürgerlich   middle-class, bourgeois
denken, dachte, gedacht   think; *an*
etwas denken   think of, consider
der Dichter, –   poet, writer
einige   several, a few
einmal   once, at one time
die Einsicht, -en   insight, understanding
einzeln   single, individual
sich empfinden, a, u   view oneself,
feel
entgegen·treten (· tritt), · trat, · getreten
approach, move toward
die Entspannung, -en   relaxing of tension,
détente
die Enttäuschung, -en   disappointment
entwickeln   develop
die Entwicklung, -en   development
erkennen, erkannte, erkannt   recognize,
see
ersetzen   replace
der Fall, ̈-e   fall; case, instance
folgen   follow
der Gang, ̈-e   course, process
der Gedanke (-ns), -n   thought, idea
die Gemeinde, -n   (church) congregation,
community, parish
das Gesetz, -e   law
gewaltig   strong, intense
das Gleichgewicht   equilibrium, balance
die Grundzahl, -en   base number
heutig   contemporary, of today

hin·nehmen (· nimmt), · nahm, · genom-
men   accept, bear, put up with
der Historiker, –   historian
klassisch   classical
die Kraft, ̈-e   power, strength
meinen   be of (express) the opinion,
say, mean
das Menschheitsideal, -e   humanitarian ideal
mindern   lessen, reduce
das Mittel, –   means, way
die Moral, -en   morals, ethics
das Motiv, -e   motif, theme
niemals   never
der Pfarrer, –   minister, clergyman
die Potenzierung, -en   exponential math-
ematics, positional notation
richtig   correct, accurate
der Rückschlag, ̈-e   set-back, reversal,
defeat
schaffen, schuf, a   create, bring about
der Sinn, -e   sense, faculty, intelligence,
understanding, meaning
der Sozialist (-en), -en   socialist
der Staatsmann, ̈-er   statesman
still·stehen, · stand, · gestanden   stand
still, stop
taktisch   tactical
der Theoretiker, –   theoretician
der Turm, ̈-e   tower
überhaupt   generally, on the whole,
at all
übernehmen (-nimmt), -nahm, übernom-
men   take over, adopt (stylistic elements)
unterschätzen   underrate, under-
estimate
unterschiedlich   different, distinct,
diverse
verändern   change, alter
das Verhältnis, -se   relation, relationship,
circumstance
verkünden   proclaim, announce
verlaufen (-äu), ie, au   occur, run
die Vernunft   reason, intellect
das Volk, ̈-er   people, nation
die Volkskunst   folk art
wählen   choose, elect
weniger   less
das Werk, -e   work, publication, book
die Zähigkeit   tenacity, toughness, viscosity
die Zukunft   future

The Reflexive Construction
The Verb *lassen*

Both German and English use a number of so-called reflexive constructions where the object of the verb refers back to the subject. But German has a greater number of these constructions, and the reflexive construction in German has a wider field of use than in English. Consequently, the two languages often use different constructions to express the same thing.

25 / The reflexive object[1]

a / Form

In the first and second person singular and plural the reflexive object has the same form as the personal pronouns: *mich, mir; uns; dich, dir; euch.* For the third person of both singular and plural there is the special form *sich* (himself, herself, itself; themselves, each other; yourself, yourselves). The form *sich* is both dative and accusative.

b / Position

The reflexive pronoun generally has a position well forward in the clause or phrase in which it occurs. Very often, therefore, it is separated from the verb of which it is the object.

Man *freut sich* über diese Entdeckung.	One rejoices over this discovery.
Viele deutsche Schrifsteller haben *sich* für die Ideen der französischen Revolution *begeistert*.	Many German authors were enthusiastic about the ideas of the French Revolution.
Bunsen wollte *sich* diesem Streit *entziehen.*	Bunsen wanted to withdraw from this dispute.
Ohne *sich* um die anderen zu *kümmern*, setzte er seine Arbeit fort.	Without paying any heed to the others, he continued his work.

[1]For tables showing the conjugation of the reflexive construction, see Appendix §97.

26 / Translating the reflexive construction

a / German reflexive, English reflexive

Some German reflexive constructions may be translated with English reflexives.

Gegen diesen Angriff hat er *sich* nicht *verteidigen* können.	He was not able to *defend himself* against this attack.
Galen *beobachtete sich* selbst sehr genau.	Galen *observed himself* very carefully.

b / German reflexive, English verb, idiom or passive construction

For other German reflexives there are, however, no corresponding English constructions of the same meaning.

• Most of these reflexive verbs in German may be translated with an English verb or idiom without a reflexive object.

Viele deutsche Schriftsteller *begeisterten sich* für die Ideen der französischen Revolution.	Many German authors *were enthusiastic* about the ideas of the French Revolution.
Ein Mythos beginnt *sich* um die Gestalt Schweitzers *zu bilden.*	A myth is beginning *to form* around the figure of Schweitzer.
Es *entspann sich* eine lange und unerfreuliche Polemik.	There *ensued* a long and disagreeable controversy.

• A number of German reflexive constructions are translatable only with a passive construction in English.

Die Lösung dieses Problems wird *sich* noch *finden.*	The solution of this problem will still *be found.*
Diese Abweichungen *erklären sich* daraus, daß . . .	These deviations *are to be explained* by the fact that . . .

• Some German reflexives, on the other hand, may be rendered in two or more ways.

Nun *drängt sich* ein weiteres Problem *auf.*	Now a further problem *forces itself* upon us. Now a further problem *is forced* upon us. Now a further problem *arises.*
Diese Ansicht *setzte sich* nicht *durch.*	This view *did* not *gain general acceptance.* This view *was* not *generally accepted.*

c / Impersonal use of the reflexive

A somewhat special case is the use of the reflexive construction to state solely that in a given circumstance an action is going on or may go on in a certain manner. The subject of the German impersonal reflexive is *es;* the subject of the English translation may be the action itself but is often some element of the sentence with which the action is associated.[1]

Es *tanzt* sich hier gut.	The dancing is good here.
	This is a good place to dance.
Im neuen Wagen *fährt es sich* sehr bequem.	The new car is very comfortable to ride in.
	The new car rides very well.

27 / The verb *lassen*

The very common verb *lassen*, like *haben, sein, werden,* and the modals, often has a dependent verb. Since, like these others, *lassen* has several meanings, the whole clause or sentence—especially the end of the clause or sentence—must be taken into consideration in translating this verb.

a / *lassen*, English *let*
The primary meaning of *lassen* is *to let*. Sometimes the effect of *lassen* used in this sense can best be rendered by English *to make it possible to*.

Man *ließ* ihn ungestört arbeiten.	They *let* him work undisturbed.
Er *ließ* es geschehen.	He *let* it happen.
	He *let* things take their course.
Mendelejeffs System *ließ* die Entdeckung einer Anzahl neuer Elemente vorhersehen.	Mendelejeff's system *made it possible* to foresee the discovery of a number of new elements.

b / *lassen*, English *leave, cease*
Lassen can also mean *to leave, cease, refrain from doing.*

Ich *habe* meine Sachen im Büro *gelassen.*	I *left* my things at the office.
Lassen Sie das!	*Stop* that!
Er mußte es aber *lassen.*	However, he had to *keep* from doing it.
Er kann das Rauchen nicht *lassen.*	He cannot *stop* smoking.

c / *lassen*, English *have* (causative)
Another frequent meaning of *lassen* with a dependent infinitive is *to have, cause, effect, get (done)*. The German dependent infinitive in such cases is rendered with a passive participle in English.

Er *läßt sich* einen neuen Anzug *machen.*	He *is having* a new suit *made.*
	He *is getting* a new suit *made.*
Sie *haben* einen Arzt *rufen lassen.*[2]	They *had* a doctor *called.*

[1]*Cf.* Unit Four, §12, c.

[2]Note double infinitive construction. See §24 *Note*.

Note   *Lassen* in its meaning *to cause, have, get* may have a direct object which is the agent (not the object) of the action expressed by the dependent infinitive. In such sentences the German infinitive is translated with an active English infinitive.

Man *ließ ihn* in den Wartesaal *gehen.*	They *had him go* into the waiting room.
Er *läßt den Maurer* einen Herd *machen.*	He *is having the mason make* a fireplace.

d / *lassen* with a reflexive

Very important is the use of *lassen* with *sich* plus a dependent infinitive to express what *may* or *can* (not) *be done.* The infinitive is then often best rendered by a passive in English.

Das *läßt sich* leicht *tun.*	That *may be done* easily.
Diese Reform *wird sich* nur langsam *durchführen lassen.*	This reform *can be carried out* only slowly. It *will be possible to carry out* this reform only slowly. We *will be able to accomplish* this reform only slowly.
Die Lösung *hat sich* noch nicht *finden lassen.*[1]	The solution *has* not yet *been found.* It *has* as yet *not been possible to find* the solution.

Exercises

I   Enter on the answer sheet translations of the reflexive constructions and their subjects in the following sentences.

1 Voltaire beschäftigte sich mit der mannigfaltigen Entwicklung der europäischen Kultur.
2 In Rousseaus Werk kreuzen sich eine leidenschaftliche Aufrichtigkeit und ein heroischer Drang nach Selbsterkenntnis.
3 Martin Luther war ein ausgesprochener Übergangsmensch, in dem sich Altes und Neues in höchst seltsamer Weise mischten.
4 Gegen die einseitige Verstandeskultur erhob sich um die Mitte des 18. Jahrhunderts in ganz Europa eine Gegenbewegung des Gefühls.
5 In William Blake verkörperte sich die Würde des seherischen Dichters.
6 Der Darwinismus gründet sich auf die zwei Prinzipien der Vererbung und der Anpassung.
7 Goethe begeisterte sich für das Straßburger Münster.
8 Um das Wesen der Macht dreht sich nun in der Tat aller politische Kampf.

---

[1]Note double infinitive construction. See §24 *Note.*

9 Nach Rathenaus Tod verschärfte sich in Deutschland die politische Lage.
10 Die Dramen Dürrenmatts bewegen sich zwischen den Polen einer gesellschaftskritischen Satire und einer rührsamen Melancholie.
11 In 1942 befand sich England in einer Krise von außerordentlicher Tiefe.
12 Erst nach dem Ende des II. Weltkrieges zeigte sich organisierter Widerstand gegen Stalin.
13 Jedes Zeitalter hat ein anderes Ideal, und mit dem Ideal ändert sich auch der Blick in die verschiedenen Abschnitte der Vergangenheit.
14 Die Existenzphilosophie entfaltete sich im Rahmen einer europäischen Kulturkrise.
15 Die Stimmen der Zeit vereinigen sich zum Lärm und nicht zur Musik, denn sie wissen nichts voneinander.

II   On the answer sheet enter the letter identifying the most appropriate translation of the verb *lassen.*
1 Ein krankhafter Tätigkeitsdrang ließ Michelangelo mehr Anträge ansammeln, als er ausführen konnte.
   (a) caused   (b) left   (c) let   (d) had
2 Voltaire hatte die pedantischen deutschen Gelehrten hinter sich gelassen.
   (a) had had   (b) had left   (c) had allowed   (d) had caused
3 Den weiteren Briefwechsel mit Chamberlain ließ Roosevelt durch seinen Staatssekretär führen.
   (a) permitted   (b) refrained   (c) had   (d) left
4 Daß Hindenburg seinen Außenminister nur mit großem Bedauern hatte gehen lassen, wußte alle Welt.
   (a) had left   (b) permitted   (c) had let   (d) had stopped
5 Am Ende des 19. Jahrhunderts gab es eine zunehmende Industrialisierung, die eine wirtschaftlich starke Herrenschicht entstehen ließ.
   (a) let   (b) caused   (c) refrained   (d) left
6 Die Mathematik läßt nur das zur Geltung kommen, was durch die Gleichungen beweisbar ist.
   (a) permits   (b) brings about   (c) ceases   (d) causes
7 Das Problem der Blutbewegung ließ Harvey nicht zur Ruhe kommen.
   (a) did (not) have   (b) did (not) cause   (c) refrained   (d) did (not) let
8 Faraday hat seine optischen Untersuchungen ruhen lassen, um auf den Elektromagnetismus weiter einzugehen.
   (a) let   (b) has left   (c) had   (d) dismissed
9 Die Entfaltung der europäischen Idee der Freiheit hat aus einigen der kolonialen Länder selbständige Staaten hervorgehen lassen.
   (a) has left   (b) had allowed   (c) has stopped   (d) caused
10 Volta erfuhr, daß man ein Gemisch aus Gas und Luft explodieren lassen kann, wenn man es mit einem elektrischen Funken zündet.
   (a) permit   (b) cause   (c) stop   (d) leave

III You are given partial translations of the following sentences. On the answer sheet write a verb phrase which would make the translation complete.

1 Adenauer hat eine feurige Rede gehalten, aber das deutsche Volk war nicht bereit, sich überzeugen zu lassen.

Adenauer gave an impassioned speech, but the German people were not ready _____ .

2 Immer wieder hat sich beobachten lassen, wie rücksichtslos Stalin seine Opposition zerstörte.

Again and again _____ how ruthlessly Stalin destroyed his opposition.

3 Weder die Existenz noch die Nicht-Existenz Gottes läßt sich mit Menschenverstand beweisen.

Neither the existence nor the non-existence of God _____ by means of human reason.

4 In 1961 sagte Willy Brandt: „Die Deutschen lassen sich heute in ihrer Friedensliebe von keinem anderen Volk übertreffen."

In 1961 Willy Brandt said: "In their love for peace the Germans at this point _____ by no other people."

5 Der Versuch muß gemacht werden, ein Gebäude des Friedens zu errichten, das Bestand haben kann und das sich ausbauen lassen wird.

The attempt must be made to erect a structure of peace which can have permanence and which _____ .

IV Translate into idiomatic English.
1 Bei diesem Sturm fliegt es sich schlecht!
2 In einer entlegenen Berghütte ruht es sich gut aus.
3 Auf dem Lande lebt es sich gut.
4 Es lohnt sich immer, vorsichtig zu handeln.
5 Meine Freude läßt sich nicht beschreiben.

Working Vocabulary

der *Abschnitt, -e* segment, period
das *Alte* the old, old values (for declension see Appendix §73)
sich *ändern* change, be changed
die *Anpassung, -en* adaptation
  an·sammeln collect, accumulate, gather
der *Antrag, ⸚e* commission, assignment, proposition
die *Aufrichtigkeit* sincerity, honesty, integrity
  aus·bauen expand, build on or out, develop (further)
  aus·führen carry out, execute
  ausgesprochen pronounced, definite
sich *aus·ruhen* relax, rest

der *Außenminister, –* minister of foreign affairs, secretary of state
  außerordentlich exceptional
das *Bedauern* regret
sich *befinden, a, u* be, feel; *sich befinden in* find oneself in, experience
sich *begeistern* be enthusiastic, be interested
  beobachten observe
die *Berghütte, -n* mountain cabin
  beschäftigen occupy, engage, keep busy; *sich beschäftigen mit* be active in, involve oneself in, be concerned with
  beschreiben, ie, ie describe
sich *bewegen* move, shift, swing (back and forth)

beweisbar   provable, demonstrable
beweisen, ie, ie   prove
die *Blutbewegung*   movement, circulation
   of the blood
der *Briefwechsel, —*   correspondence
der *Drang*   drive, yearning
   drehen   turn; *sich drehen um*   hinge
   on, revolve around
   ein·gehen, ·ging, ·gegangen   go in(to),
   go into detail, investigate
   einseitig   one-sided, narrow-minded
   einzeln   individual
sich *entfalten*   develop, unfold
die *Entfaltung, -en*   development, unfold-
   ing, spread
   entlegen   remote, distant
   entstehen, entstand, entstanden   come
   into being, arise, begin
die *Entwicklung, -en*   development
   erfahren (ä), u, a   learn, experience, discover
sich *erheben, o, o*   arise
   erst   only, not . . . until (see Unit Sixteen, §54)
die *Existenzphilosophie*   existential philosophy, Existentialism
die *Freude, -n*   joy
   führen   lead, conduct, carry out
der *Funke (-n), -n*   spark
die *Gegenbewegung, -en*   counter-
   movement, reaction
der *Gelehrte*   scholar (for declension see
   Appendix §73)
die *Geltung, -en*   worth, value, importance;
   zur Geltung kommen   be accepted, be
   regarded as valid
das *Gemisch, -e*   mixture
   gesellschaftskritisch   critical of society
die *Gleichung, -en*   equation
sich *gründen*   be based, base itself
   handeln   act
die *Herrenschicht, -en*   aristocracy, upper
   class
   hervor·gehen, ·ging, ·gegangen   come
   forth, arise, result; *hervorgehen aus*
   develop from or out of
der *Kampf, ⁔e*   struggle, battle, fight
   krankhaft   pathological, abnormal,
   feverish
sich *kreuzen*   intersect, meet, come together; make the sign of the cross
die *Lage, -n*   situation
der *Lärm*   noise, uproar
   leidenschaftlich   passionate
sich *lohnen*   pay, be worthwhile
die *Macht, ⁔e*   power, might

mannigfaltig   varied, diverse
sich *mischen*   be combined, mix, mingle
die *Mitte, -n*   middle
das *Münster, —*   cathedral
das *Neue*   the new, new ideas (for declension see Appendix §73)
der *Pol, -e*   pole (magnetic, geographic, etc.)
der *Rahmen, —*   framework, surroundings,
   context
die *Ruhe*   rest, calm, peace; *zur Ruhe kommen*   come to rest, gain peace of mind
   ruhen   rest, lie idle, come to a standstill
   rührsam   very emotional, sentimental
   schlecht   bad, poor, wretched; plain,
   simple
   seherisch   prophetic
die *Selbsterkenntnis*   knowledge of oneself
   selbständig   independent
   seltsam   peculiar, unusual
der *Staatssekretär, -e*   secretary of state
die *Stimme, -n*   voice
die *Tat, -en*   act, deed, fact; *in der Tat*   in
   fact, indeed
der *Tätigkeitsdrang*   active disposition, ap-
   petite for work
die *Tiefe, -n*   profundity, depth
der *Übergangsmensch(-en), -en*   transi-
   tional figure
   übertreffen (i), -traf, o   surpass, exceed
   überzeugen   convince
die *Untersuchung, -en*   investigation, research
sich *vereinigen*   unite, join, combine, agree,
   coalesce
die *Vererbung, -en*   heredity
die *Vergangenheit*   the past
sich *verkörpern*   be embodied
sich *verschärfen*   become intensified, become more acute, be aggravated
   verschieden   different, various
die *Verstandeskultur*   culture stressing intellect and reason, rationalism
   vorsichtig   careful
die *Weise, -n*   manner, way
das *Wesen, —*   being, reality, essence, condition
der *Widerstand, ⁔e*   resistance
   wirtschaftlich   economic
die *Würde*   dignity, worth
sich *zeigen*   become manifest, show itself,
   develop
die *Zeit, -en*   epoch, age, time
das *Zeitalter, —*   age, period, era
   zünden   ignite, light
   zu·nehmen (·nimmt), ·genommen
   grow, increase

TEN

Pronouns and Adjectives which Refer to Nouns

28 / Pronouns, possessive adjectives and their antecedents

In both German and English, pronouns and possessive adjectives agree with their antecedents in number. But within the singular, the choice of pronouns or possessive adjectives in German is governed by the grammatical gender of the antecedent. In English our choice is determined by whether the antecedent is a male, female, or thing. How we translate words like *er, der, sein* depends, therefore, on their antecedents. Compare,

> *Der Mann, der* an der Ecke steht, wartet auf *seine* Frau. *Er* ist sehr zornig.

> *The man who* is standing at the corner is waiting for *his* wife. *He* is very angry.

> *Der Stuhl, der* dort drüben steht, hat *seine* ursprüngliche Farbe verloren. *Er* war gelb.

> *The chair that* stands over there has lost *its* original color. *It* was yellow.

In the same way *sie* may be the equivalent of *she, it,* or *they* and so on.

Never read or translate a pronoun or possessive adjective without establishing to which noun it refers. Many seeming difficulties and obscurities vanish when the proper relationships of this kind are found.

29 / Possessive adjectives and pronouns which refer to nouns

a / Possessive adjectives

German has only two possessive adjectives which have noun antecedents.

- *Sein* (his, its[1]) may have as its antecedent either a masculine or neuter noun.

der Künstler und *sein* Freund	the artist and *his* friend.
der Staat, *seine* Verfassung	the state, *its* government
das Tier in *seiner* Höhle	the animal in *its* lair

- *Ihr* (her, its, their) may have as its antecedent either a feminine or a plural noun.

die Königin und *ihr* Söhnchen	the queen and *her* little son
die Tatsache, *ihre* Bedeutung	the fact, *its* significance
die Leute in *ihren* Wohnungen	the people in *their* dwellings

---

[1]Sometimes also *her: Das Mädchen* und *seine* Mutter (*The girl* and *her* mother.)

b / Pronouns

The number and gender of pronouns is determined by their antecedents. Their case, however, is determined by their use in the sentence or clause. The tables below give a summary of the forms of the various pronouns with the case of each and with the possible gender and number of its antecedent.

- Personal pronouns[1]

FREQUENT FORMS	CASE AND NO. OF PRONOUN	GENDER AND NO. OF ANTECEDENT			
		MASC.	NEUT.	FEM.	PLURAL
er (he, it)	Nom. sing.	Masc.			
es (it)[2]	Nom. or Acc. sing.		Neut.		
ihm (him, it)[2]	Dat. sing.	Masc.	Neut.		
ihn (him, it)	Acc. sing.	Masc.			
ihnen (them)	Dat. pl.				Plural. . . .
ihr (her, it)	Dat. sing.			Fem.	
sie (she, her, it)	Nom. or Acc. sing.			Fem.	
(they, them)	Nom. or Acc. pl.				Plural. . . .

- Pronouns formed from *dieser-* and *ein*-words[3]

TYPICAL FORMS	CASE AND NO. OF PRONOUN	GENDER AND NO. OF ANTECEDENT			
		MASC.	NEUT.	FEM.	PLURAL
die*se*, kein*e*[3]	Nom. or Acc. sing.			Fem.	
	Nom. or Acc. pl.				Plural. . . .
die*sem*, kein*em*	Dat. sing.	Masc.	Neut.		
die*sen*, kein*en*	Acc. sing.	Masc.			
	Dat. pl.				Plural. . . .
die*ser*, kein*er*	Nom. sing.	Masc.			
	Dat. or Gen. sing.			Fem.	
	Gen. pl.				Plural. . . .
die*ses*, kein*es*	Nom. or Acc. sing.		Neut.		
	Gen. sing.	Masc.	Neut.		

- The pronoun *der, das, die; die*[4]

FORMS	CASE AND NO. OF PRONOUN	GENDER AND NUMBER OF ANTECEDENT			
		MASC.	NEUT.	FEM.	PLURAL
das[5]	Nom. or Acc. sing.		Neut.		
dem	Dat. sing.	Masc.	Neut.		
den	Acc. sing.	Masc.			
denen	Dat. pl.				Plural. . . .
der	Nom. sing.	Masc.			
	Dat. sing.			Fem.	
deren	Gen. sing.			Fem.	
	Gen. pl.				Plural. . . .
dessen	Gen. sing.	Masc.	Neut.		
die	Nom. or Acc. sing.			Fem.	
	Nom. or Acc. pl.				Plural. . . .

[1]For complete tables of personal pronouns, see Appendix §62.

[2]*Es, ihm* are also the equivalent of *she* and *her* when the antecedent is *das Mädchen* or *das Fräulein*.

[3]For translations, formation and declension of the *dieser*-words as pronouns see Appendix §65, for the *ein*-words see Appendix §66.

[4]See §30 below and Appendix §63.   [5]For translations, see §30 below.

30 / Functions of the pronoun *der, das, die; die*

The pronoun *der, das, die; die* has two functions:

a / Demonstrative pronoun
It is, on the one hand, a demonstrative pronoun. It is used instead of *er, es, sie; sie* when a demonstrative or emphatic effect is desired. As such it is translated: *he, she, it, they; that, those, these, etc.*

> Die Weltansicht des 18. Jahrhunderts war überwiegend optimistisch, *die* des 20. wäre wohl als pessimistisch zu bezeichnen.

> The 18th century's way of looking at the world was predominantly optimistic, *that* of the 20th century must probably be described as pessimistic.

b / Relative pronoun
Der, das, die; die is, on the other hand, a relative pronoun corresponding to English *who, which, that.*

> Die Bilder, *die* Talbot erhielt, waren Negative, aus *denen* sich beliebig viele Positive gewinnen ließen.

> The pictures *which* Talbot obtained were negatives from *which* it was possible to obtain any desired number of positives.

c / *der, das, die; die* and the verb
The key to distinguishing between *der, das, die; die* in its two functions is the position of the verb. As a demonstrative this pronoun has no special effect on the position of the verb. As a relative pronoun *der, das, die; die* introduces a subordinate clause, and the verb comes at the end of the clause. Compare the uses of this pronoun in the following example.

> Was wir darüber wissen, sind eigentlich nur Vermutungen. *Die* stützen sich zwar auf Untersuchungen, *die* man vor kurzem unternommen hat.

> What we know about it are really only conjectures. *They (These)* are, to be sure, based on investigations *which* have recently been undertaken.

31 / *wer* and *was*[1]

Wer and *was* also have two functions. They are question words, and they are relative pronouns.

a / *wer* and *was* as question words
As question words *wer* and *was* may introduce a direct question or an indirect question. In either case they are respectively the equivalents of English *who?* and *what?*

> *Wer (Was)* ist das?
> Man weiß nicht, *wer* es getan hat.

> Who *(What)* is that?
> It is not known *who* did it.

[1]For the declension of *wer* and *was*, see Appensix §64.

b / *wer* as a relative pronoun

Wer as a relative pronoun never has an antecedent. It corresponds in use to English *whoever, the person who* and *he who.*

Wer Künstler sein *will,* muß Geduld haben.	*Whoever* wants to be an artist must have patience.
	The person (anyone) who wants to be an artist must have patience.

c / *was* as a relative pronoun

Was as a relative pronoun has three uses.

● *Was* may be used without an antecedent; then *was* corresponds to English *whatever, that which, what.*

Was wir über das Erdinnere *wissen,* sind nur Vermutungen.	*What (Whatever)* we know about the earth's interior are only conjectures.

● *Was* may refer back to an indefinite antecedent such as *alles, nichts, etwas, das Beste;* it will then be translated with English *that.*

Alles, was er durch lange Arbeit gesammelt *hatte,* ging in Flammen auf.	*Everything that* he had collected through work over a long period of time went up in flames.

● *Was* may refer back to a condition or fact stated in the preceding clause; in such cases its English equivalent is *which* or *which is (was) something that.*

Sie ließ ihn eine ganze Stunde allein, was ihn wütend *machte.*	She left him alone for a whole hour, *which* (was something that) threw him into a rage.

32 / Pronoun substitutes with prepositions

When the antecedent is not a human being, certain prefixes replace pronouns as objects of most prepositions which govern the dative or accusative.

a / *da(r)-*

The prefix *da-* or *dar-,* English *it (that)* or *them,* may refer to a noun of any gender if the object or objects named are not human.

Sein Haus ist dort drüben.	*His house* is over there.
Dahinter steht ein schöner Apfelbaum.	*Behind it* is a beautiful apple tree.
Die Bänke sind neu.	*The benches* are new.
Mein Eltern sitzen gern *darauf.*	My parents like to sit *on them.*

Note   Occasionally the prefix *da(r)-* may refer to human beings.

Es waren viele *Künstler* da, *dar*unter der berühmte Franz Marc.	There were many *artists* there, among *them* the famous Franz Marc.

b / *hier-*

The prefix *hier-* may refer to a noun of any gender or number, or to an action, state, circumstance, etc. This prefix has demonstrative force and is translated by *this, that, here,* and expressions with similar emphatic effect.

Er kletterte noch höher. *Hierdurch* gewann er einen Überblick über das ganze Tal.	He climbed even higher. *By so doing (Thereby)* he got a bird's eye view of the whole valley.

c / *wo(r)-*

The prefix *wo-* or *wor-* has two functions.

● In direct and indirect questions, *wo(r)-* is the equivalent of English *what.*

Woran arbeitet man jetzt am eifrigsten?	On *what* are they working most intensely now?

● *Wo(r)-* may serve as the substitute for a relative pronoun if the antecedent is not human. In this use *wo(r)-* is the equivalent of English *which.*

Der Bau, *woran (an dem, an welchem)* man arbeitet, ist eine Fabrik.	The building on *which* they are working is a factory.

Exercises

I   On the answer sheet enter the letter identifying the antecedent of each pronoun. Then indicate the case and number of the pronoun in each instance; if more than one case is possible, give both. Use the usual abbreviations.

☆   QUESTION

Possible antecedents   *Pronoun*
(a) der Mann   (b) das Recht   (c) die Leute   die

ANSWER   (c) *Nom. pl., Acc. pl.*

Possible Antecedents   *Pronoun*

1 (a) der Entdecker (b) die Forderung (c) die Mächte		dem
2 (a) unsere Kenntnis (b) sein Ziel (c) der Begründer		das
3 (a) viele Siegel (b) alle Vorgänge (c) zwei Möglichkeiten		eins
4 (a) einiger Maler (b) der Sphäre (c) dieser Held		dessen
5 (a) mit dem Frieden (b) des Spätmittelalters (c) in kritischen Zeiten		welche
6 (a) solche Vorgänge (b) der Staatsmann (c) dem Vertrauen		deren
7 (a) jeder Maler (b) eines Gesichts (c) die Sonne		die
8 (a) der Rechtfertigung (b) diese Strömungen (c) sein Ziel		jenen
9 (a) des Siegels (b) diese Möglichkeiten (c) der Vergangenheit		denen
10 (a) der Weltgeschichte (b) der Held (c) des Zieles		sie

II   Enter on the answer sheet the word which is the antecedent of each pronoun in italics. Then give the case of the pronoun and an appropriate translation for it.

☆   QUESTION Mit unserer Kenntnis können wir das wirkliche Dasein nie erfassen: was wir durch (1) *sie* ergreifen, ist niemals der Gegenstand selbst, sondern nur unsere Vorstellung von (2) *ihm.*

ANSWER (1) *Kenntnis, Acc., it*   (2) *Gegenstand, Dat., it*

A Faraday ist der Entdecker der Naturvorgänge, (1) *die* der heutigen Starkstromtechnik ihre besonderen Möglichkeiten geben.

B Der Begründer der Silhouettekunst behauptete, den Charakter jedes Menschen aus (2) *dessen* Gesicht ablesen zu können.

C Der Liberalismus war ein Kind der Aufklärung, (3) *die* erst durch (4) *ihn* politisch wurde.

D Das Kernproblem, von dem die ganze reformatorische Bewegung ausging und um (5) *das* (6) *sie* sich drehte, war die Frage nach der Rechtfertigung.

E Deutsche Politik nach 1945 war eine Funktion der Politik der Mächte, (7) *die* Deutschland besiegt und besetzt hatten.

F In Bismarcks Charakter ist etwas, (8) *was* uns davon zurückhält, (9) *ihm* jene unbedingte Verehrung zu schenken, (10) *die* wir anderen Helden so gern entgegenbringen.

III   Enter on the answer sheet translations of the words and phrases in italics in the following sentences.

A Ampère entscheidet zum ersten Male zwischen Erscheinungen der elektrischen Spannung und (1) *denen des elektrischen Stroms.*

B Nietzsche fand sein politisches Ideal nicht in Deutschland, weder (2) *in dem der Gegenwart* noch in dem der Vergangenheit.

C Kopernikus lehrte eine fixe und endliche Welt, (3) *in deren Mittelpunkt* unbeweglich die Sonne steht und (4) *deren äußerste Grenze* von der achten Sphäre gebildet wird eine feste Kugel, (5) *hinter der* nichts mehr ist.

D Die Strömungen, (6) *aus denen* die Reformation entstand, sind weitaus älter als Luther.

E Der bedeutendste Maler des Spätmittelalters war Mathias Grünewald, (7) *dessen* starker Realismus unseren modernen Malern so nahe steht.

F (8) *Wer* jemals die Weltgeschichte betrachtet hat, muß ja wissen, daß jede vergangene Zeit und Kultur für uns mit hundert Siegeln verschlossen ist.

G Es kommt sehr auf den Ton an, (9) *mit dem* politische Forderungen vorgebracht werden.

H In Florenz begann Galilei die Probleme der Bewegungslehre zu studieren, (10) *durch deren Lösung* er später so Großes vollbrachte.

I Die Geschichte Preußens hat zwei Eigenschaften, (11) *welche* (12) *sie* von (13) *der* anderer deutscher Staaten unterscheidet.

J (14) *Wer* diesen Tag der Kriegserklärung miterlebt hat, der kann (15) *ihn* nicht vergessen.

IV   Enter on the answer sheet translations of the phrases in italics in the following
sentences.
(1) Die Welt hat *einen Mann* verloren, *zu dem die Menschen Vertrauen hatten.*
(2) John F. Kennedy war *ein Mann, der es ernst meinte* mit dem Frieden der Welt . . .
(3) Ich erinnere mich an *die Begegnungen* in kritischen Zeiten, *in denen dieser Mann
bewies,* . . . wie sehr er mit uns verbunden war. (4) *Die Ziele, die dieser Mann* der
Menschheit *gesetzt hat,* können nicht niedergeschossen werden. (5) Die Menschheit
hat *einen großen Staatsmann* verloren, *der* mit Phantasie und Nüchternheit, mit Wirklichkeitssinn und Idealismus *neuen Grenzen zustrebte.*

(Willy Brandt, on the occasion of
John F. Kennedy's death.)

Working Vocabulary

ab·lesen (ie), a, e   read off, interpret,
tell (character)
an·kommen, ·kam, o   depend on,
arrive; *ankommen auf*   depend on
die *Aufklärung, -en*   explanation, enlightenment, the (period of) Enlightenment
aus·gehen, ·ging, ·gegangen   emanate,
proceed (from)
äußerst   most remote, most distant,
uttermost
bedeutend   important, meaningful
die *Begegnung, -en*   meeting, encounter
der *Begründer, –*   originator, founder
behaupten   state, contend, assert
besetzen   occupy
besiegen   defeat, conquer
betrachten   view, regard, study
die *Bewegung, -en*   movement
die *Bewegungslehre, -n*   theory of motion,
dynamics
beweisen, ie, ie   prove
bilden   build, form
das *Dasein*   presence, existence
sich *drehen*   turn, revolve
die *Eigenschaft, -en*   characteristic, peculi-
arity, quality
der *Entdecker, –*   discoverer
entgegen·bringen, ·brachte, ·gebracht
extend to, offer
entscheiden, ie, ie   distinguish, decide
entstehen, entstand, entstanden   arise,
originate
erfassen   grasp, comprehend
ergreifen, ergriff, ergriffen   apprehend,
grasp, take hold of

sich *erinnern*   remember, recall
ernst   serious; *es ernst meinen mit*   to
be serious (in concern, in intent) about
die *Erscheinung, -en*   phenomenon, mani-
festation
erst   only, first, not until (see Unit Sixteen, §54)
fix   fixed, firmly established
die *Forderung, -en*   demand
der *Gegenstand, ̈e*   object, thing
die *Gegenwart*   the present
das *Gesicht, -er*   face
die *Grenze, -n*   boundary, edge, horizon
groß   large, important; *Großes*   great,
important things or matters (for declension see Appendix §73)
der *Held (-en), -en*   hero
heutig   contemporary, of today
jemals   ever
die *Kenntnis, -se*   knowledge
das *Kernproblem, -e*   fundamental problem
die *Kriegserklärung, -en*   declaration of war
die *Kugel, -n*   sphere, ball, bullet
lehren   teach, set forth, present
die *Lösung, -en*   solution
die *Macht, ̈e*   power, force
der *Maler, –*   painter, artist
meinen   say, think, express an opinion
(see *ernst*)
die *Menschheit*   mankind
mit·erleben   experience with others,
share experience
der *Mittelpunkt, -e*   middle, center, focus
die *Möglichkeit, -en*   possibility, poten-
tiality

  nahe near; *nahe·stehen, ·stand,*
  ·gestanden be closely connected
  with, be compatible with
der Naturvorgang, ⁔e natural process
  nieder·schießen, o, o shoot down
die Nüchternheit quality of dispassionate
  appraisal
die Phantasie, -n imagination
das Recht, -e right, privilege
die Rechtfertigung, -en exculpation, justification, vindication
  schenken give, grant
das Siegel, – seal
die Silhouettekunst art of drawing silhou-
  ettes
die Sonne, -n sun
die Spannung, -en tension
das Spätmittelalter late middle ages
die Sphäre, -n sphere, orbit
der Staatsmann, ⁔er statesman
die Starkstromtechnik power engineering,
  high-voltage technique
der Strom, ⁔e (electric) current, electricity
die Strömung, -en trend, tendency

der Ton, ⁔e tone, manner, fashion
  unbedingt unconditional, complete
  unbeweglich motionless, immovable
  unterscheiden, ie, ie distinguish, differ-
  entiate, separate
  verbinden, a, u connect, be allied
die Verehrung, -en admiration, esteem
die Vergangenheit the past
  verschließen, o, o lock (up), close
das Vertrauen trust
  vollbringen, vollbrachte, vollbracht
  achieve, complete
  vor·bringen, ·brachte, ·gebracht propose, bring forward
der Vorgang, ⁔e process
die Vorstellung, -en idea, notion
  weder ... noch neither ... nor
  weitaus by far, much
der Wirklichkeitssinn sense for reality,
  realism
das Ziel, -e goal, objective
  zurück·halten (ä), ie, a hold back, re-
  strain, prohibit
  zu·streben strive for, toward (with
  dative)

The Subjunctive: the Conjecture, Wish and Condition Contrary-to-Fact

Perhaps the most frequent reason for error in interpreting a German subjunctive form is that the reader does not see it. The subjunctive mood is infrequent in English, and the English speaking reader is not accustomed to being on the alert for it. Also, English speaking readers often do not know the German verb forms well enough to recognize a subjunctive form easily.

33 / Frequent forms of the subjunctive

There are two sets of the subjunctive mcod in German. One is derived from the simple past; it is here called the *general* subjunctive because it is used more frequently than the other. The second subjunctive set is derived from the infinitive; it is called the *special* subjunctive here because only some of its forms find frequent use and because it has certain special functions.

The endings of both subjunctive sets are: (ich) -e, (du) -est, (er, etc.) -e, (wir) -en, (ihr) -et, (sie, Sie, etc.) -en. For illustrations of the complete conjugation of the subjunctive, see the Appendix §91-95. Here are listed only the third person singular and plural of a few typical verbs and of some especially important forms which occasion frequent errors. To make comparison easier the indicative is also given.

a / General subjunctive (forms derived from the simple past)

In regular weak verbs, i.e. those with a regular past, the general subjunctive mood and the simple past of the indicative are identical. Compare the following forms of these regular weak verbs:

INFINITIVE	PAST INDICATIVE	GENERAL SUBJUNCTIVE
leben	lebte, -n	*lebte, -n*
sagen	sagte, -n	*sagte, -n*

The general subjunctive of weak verbs with an irregular past is the past indicative plus umlaut where possible. Compare:

INFINITIVE	PAST INDICATIVE	GENERAL SUBJUNCTIVE
bringen	brachte, -n	*brächte, -n*
nennen	nannte, -n	*nennte, -n*

The general subjunctive of strong verbs is formed from the past indicative with umlaut where possible and the subjunctive endings. The following forms are typical:

INFINITIVE	PAST INDICATIVE	GENERAL SUBJUNCTIVE
bieten	bot, -en	*böte, -n*
finden	fand, -en	*fände, -n*
gehen	ging, -en	*ginge, -n*
lassen	ließ, -en	*ließe, -n*
sehen	sah, -en	*sähe, -n*

Among irregular verbs the following are very frequent and should have special attention:

INFINITIVE	PAST INDICATIVE	GENERAL SUBJUNCTIVE
haben	hatte, -n	*hätte, -n*
sein	war, -en	*wäre, -n*
werden	wurde, -n	*würde, -n*
dürfen	durfte, -n	*dürfte, -n*
können	konnte, -n	*könnte, -n*
mögen	mochte, -n	*möchte, -n*
müssen	mußte, -n	*müßte, -n*
sollen	sollte, -n	*sollte, -n*
wollen	wollte, -n	*wollte, -n*
tun	tat, -en	*täte, -n*
wissen	wußte, -n	*wüßte, -n*

b / Special subjunctive (forms derived from the infinitive stem)
    With the exception of the verb *sein,* we may say for practical purposes that the sub-
junctive formed from the infinitive stem is used only in the third person singular. The
distinguishing mark of the special subjunctive in the third person singular is the ending
-*e.* Illustrative of regular and irregular verbs are the following:

INFINITIVE	PRESENT INDICATIVE	SPECIAL SUBJUNCTIVE
leben	er lebt	er *lebe*
sagen	er sagt	er *sage*
gehen	er geht	er *gehe*
lassen	er läßt	er *lasse*
sehen	er sieht	er *sehe*
haben	er hat	er *habe*
dürfen	er darf	er *dürfe*
mögen	er mag	er *möge*
sollen	er soll	er *solle*

The verb *sein* is exceptional in that the third person singular form is *sei* (indicative
ist) and in that the distinctive plural form *seien* (indicative *sind*) is frequently used.

34 / Uses of the subjunctive

Once a verb form has been recognized as a subjunctive, the problem of interpretation is usually a rather simple matter. The two main uses of the subjunctive are: (1) to indicate that a statement is a supposition, a conjecture, a contrary-to-fact condition, or a wish or desire which is contrary to fact; and (2) to indicate that a statement is quoted indirectly.

Only the general subjunctive is used in the kinds of statements listed under (1). In the indirect quotation either the general or the special subjunctive may occur.

The special subjunctive is also used to express requests, wishes which may be fulfilled, propositions, concessions, and purpose. Some uses of this subjunctive form that cause difficulty were discussed in Unit Seven, §20, under the heading "The Imperative and Suggestion."

35 / The conjecture, supposition, contrary-to-fact statement and wish

The use of the subjunctive in the conjecture, supposition, and contrary-to-fact statement or wish is easily recognized and translated. For German and English are similar in such usage.

a / English idiomatic use of tense, German subjunctive

- To indicate that a statement referring to present time is contrary-to-fact or expresses a mere supposition, English uses the past tense of the verb (e.g., If we only knew . . . , then we would . . .). In such sentences German makes use of the simple general subjunctive and the general subjunctive of *werden* plus an infinitive.

Wenn das der Fall *wäre, würde* unsere Lage schon günstiger *sein.*	If that *was (were)* the case, our situation *would* indeed *be* more favorable.
Wenn man das nur *wüßte!*	If we only *knew* that!
Das *würde* aber zu weit *führen.*	However, that *would take* us too far.
Täte er es nicht, so *würde* er für seine Mühe nichts *bekommen.*	If he *did* not *do* it, he *would get* nothing for his trouble.

- To indicate that statements referring to the past are contrary-to-fact, hypothetical, etc., English uses the pluperfect form of the verb (e.g., If that *had been* true . . .). German in like sentences uses compound verb forms with the auxiliary in the general subjunctive.

Hätte man das nur *gewußt!*	If they *had* only *known* that!
Würde er es wirklich *getan haben?*	*Would* he really *have done* it?
Wenn die Beobachtungen genauer *gewesen wären, würde* er diesen Fehler nicht *begangen haben.*	If the observations *had been* more exact, he *would* not *have made* this mistake.

b / Alternate verb forms in the result clause or conclusion

In the result clause or conclusion of German conditional sentences, or in a supposition, a choice of verb forms is possible. The German writer may use the general subjunctive form *würde, -n* with a following infinitive or perfect infinitive; or he may use simply the general subjunctive of the main verb, or of *haben* and *sein* when used as auxiliaries.

Wäre das der Fall, dann *würde* unsere Lage schon günstiger *sein*.	If that were the case, our position *would* indeed *be* more favorable.
Wäre das der Fall, dann *wäre* unsere Lage schon günstiger.	
Wenn er das nicht täte, *würde* er für seine Mühe nichts *bekommen*.	If he did not do that, he *would* not *get* anything for his trouble.
Wenn er das nicht täte, *bekäme* er für seine Mühe nichts.	
Wenn dem so wäre, so *würde* er diesen Fehler nicht *begangen haben*.	If that were the case, he *would* not *have made* this mistake.
Wenn dem so wäre, so *hätte* er diesen Fehler nicht *begangen*.	
Es *würde* sich schon machen *lassen*.	It *could be* done (It *would be possible* to do it) to be sure.
Es *ließe* sich schon machen.	

Note   The meanings of the modal auxiliaries in the subjunctive and in the indicative call for special attention. You will find it helpful to study the following forms and their English equivalents.

INDICATIVE	SUBJUNCTIVE
Wir durften tanzen gehen.	Wir dürften vielleicht tanzen gehen.
We were allowed to go dancing.	Perhaps we might be allowed to go dancing.
	Es dürfte ein Leichtes sein.
	It could (will probably) be an easy matter.
Sie konnte es tun.	Sie könnte es tun.
She could (was able) to do it.	She could (would be able) to do it.
	Sie könnte es getan haben.
	She could (might) have done it.
	It is possible that she did it.
Sie hatte es tun können.	Sie hätte es tun können.
She had been able to do it.	She could have done it.
	She would have been able to do it.
Ich mochte es ihm nicht sagen.	Ich möchte es ihm nicht sagen.
I did not like to say it to him.	I would not like to say it to him.

Sie hatten arbeiten müssen.
   They had had to work.

Sie hätten arbeiten müssen.
   They would have had to work.

Er sollte kommen.
   He was supposed to come.

Er sollte kommen.
   He should (ought to) come.

Er hatte kommen sollen.
   He had been supposed to come.

Er hätte kommen sollen.
   He should (ought to) have come.

Ich hatte mitgehen wollen.
   I had wanted to go along.

Ich hätte mitgehen wollen.
   I would have wanted to go along.

Exercises

I   Enter in the answer spaces the letters identifying all of the subjunctive (general or special) forms in each group. Include also forms which may be either indicative or subjunctive depending on use.[1]

1 (a) lebte	(b) lebst	(c) lebt	(d) lebe
2 (a) muß	(b) müsse	(c) mußte	(d) müßtet
3 (a) dachte	(b) denkt	(c) dächte	(d) dachten
4 (a) dürfe	(b) darf	(c) durfte	(d) darfst
5 (a) bin	(b) war	(c) wäre	(d) sind
6 (a) haben	(b) hätten	(c) hatte	(d) habe
7 (a) sähe	(b) sieht	(c) sehe	(d) seht
8 (a) werde	(b) würden	(c) würde	(d) wird
9 (a) kannst	(b) könnten	(c) konnten	(d) kann
10 (a) tue	(b) tat	(c) taten	(d) täte

II   Enter in the answer spaces the letter identifying those forms in each group which are (or may be) forms of the general subjunctive.

1 (a) blieben	(b) bleibe	(c) bleiben	(d) bliebe
2 (a) komme	(b) kam	(c) kamen	(d) kämen
3 (a) soll	(b) sollte	(c) sollten	(d) sollst
4 (a) kaufe	(b) kauft	(c) kaufte	(d) kaufen
5 (a) ließen	(b) lasse	(c) ließ	(d) ließe
6 (a) lesen	(b) läsen	(c) lese	(d) las
7 (a) wollte	(b) will	(c) wollen	(d) willst
8 (a) wissen	(b) wüßten	(c) weiß	(d) wußte
9 (a) mögen	(b) magst	(c) mochte	(d) möchte
10 (a) brachte	(b) brächte	(c) bringe	(d) brachten

---

[1]For complete listings of principal parts and typical forms of the tense auxiliaries, modal auxiliaries, and irregular weak verbs, see Appendix §98-100.

III   Enter on the answer sheet the letter identifying the correct English translation of the words in italics.

Note   The first four passages (questions 1-12) are excerpts from the letters of Thomas Mann. All were written in the years immediately following World War II.

A Mit der Veränderung, daß [Turgenevs] **Väter und Söhne** zu den sechs Werken (1) *gehören würden,* die ich zur Lektüre auf eine einsame Insel (2) *mitnehmen würde,* sollte natürlich nur allgemein meine hohe Schätzung für dieses Meisterwerk ausgedrückt sein. Hinzu (3) *käme* gewiß etwas von Dostojewski, **Die Brüder Karamasov** oder auch **Die Dämonen.**
   1 (a) had belonged   (b) belonged   (c) would belong   (d) belongs
   2 (a) would take along   (b) would have taken along   (c) got taken along
      (d) was taken along
   3 (a) came   (b) comes   (c) is to come   (d) would come

B (4→) *Käme der* allgemeine (←4) *Krieg,* den General MacArthur in Asien anzuzünden (5) *sucht,* so (6→) *würde es* uns allen wohl (←6) *schlecht ergehen.*
   4 (a) The war came   (b) Let the war come   (c) If the war has come
      (d) If the war were to come
   5 (a) would try   (b) is trying   (c) tried   (d) were to try
   6 (a) it would be bad   (b) it was bad   (c) it would have been bad
      (d) it is bad

C Wirklich, es (7→) *wäre* in diesem Europa (←7) *nicht mehr zu leben,* wenn (8→) *nicht* eine individuelle und geistige Sympathie (←8) *erhalten bliebe.*
   7 (a) had no longer been possible to live   (b) is no longer possible to live
      (c) was no longer possible to live   (d) would no longer be possible to live
   8 (a) had not been preserved   (b) would not have been preserved
      (c) has not been preserved   (d) were not preserved

D Es (9) *wäre* gut, wenn aus all unseren Qualen ein neues humanistisches Ethos (10) *sich herausbildete* und ins allgemeine Bewußtsein (11) *eininge.* Das (12) *könnte* heilsam das seelische Klima beeinflussen.
   9 (a) had   (b) was   (c) would   (d) is
   10 (a) evolves   (b) would evolve   (c) will evolve   (d) had evolved
   11 (a) enters   (b) will enter   (c) did enter   (d) would enter
   12 (a) could   (b) was able to   (c) can   (d) could have

E Wir (13) *kämen an kein Ende,* wenn wir die Motive moderner Existenzphilosophie aufzählen (14) *wollten,* die bei Rousseau zum ersten Male vorkommen.
   13 (a) never got finished   (b) never get finished   (c) would never get
      finished   (d) had never got finished
   14 (a) will try to   (b) try to   (c) tried to   (d) had tried to

F Ohne die Katastrophe zweier Weltkriege (15) *wäre* der Existenzialismus nicht so stark zum Ausdruck gekommen.
   15 (a) would (not) have   (b) were (not)   (c) was (not)   (d) would (not) be
      (not) be

G Im Idealfall (16) *wäre* der Kritiker ein Mittler zwischen dem Künstler und dem Publikum.
   16 (a) would have   (b) will be   (c) was   (d) would be

H Es (17→) *hätte* keinen geeigneteren Lehrmeister der Wissenschaft für Faraday (←17) *geben können*, als gerade Davy.
   17 (a) had to be able (not) to be   (b) could (not) have been   (c) would (not) be   (d) would have been able (not) to be

I Selbst wenn die Verhandlungen zwischen Hindenburg und Lloyd George anders (18) *ausgegangen wären*, (19) *muß bezweifelt werden*, daß England einen Frieden (20) *angenommen hätte*.
   18 (a) were to end   (b) ended   (c) had ended   (d) did end
   19 (a) it must be doubted   (b) it would be doubted   (c) it had been doubted   (d) it would have been doubted
   20 (a) accepted   (b) did accept   (c) would accept   (d) would have accepted

IV   Translate the words in italics in the following sentences.
A (1) *Wüßte ich* seine Adresse, dann (2→) *müßten wir nicht* bei der Auskunft (←2) *nachfragen*.
B So ein Fehler (3→) *wäre nicht* wieder (←3) *gutzumachen*.
C (4) *Hätten Sie nur früher geschrieben!*
D Der Polizist (5→) *hätte* die jungen Männer (←5) *nicht anklagen sollen*, ehe ihre Teilnahme (6) *bestätigt wurde*.
E Er (7) *wäre* zufrieden, wenn wir ihm eine neue Wohnung (8) *fänden*.
F Wir (9→) *hätten* länger in Italien (←9) *bleiben können*, aber dann (10→) *wären* wir zu spät in Griechenland (←10) *angekommen*.

Working Vocabulary

allgemein   (in) general, universal
anders   differently, otherwise
an·klagen   accuse
an·nehmen, (·nimmt), ·nahm, ·genommen   accept
an·zünden   ignite, set fire to
auf·zählen   count (up), tabulate
der Ausdruck, ∸e   expression; *zum Ausdruck kommen*   be expressed, become manifest
aus·drücken   express
aus·gehen, ·ging, ·gegangen   end, go out, come out
die Auskunft, ∸e   information, information desk
beeinflussen   influence
bestätigen   confirm, verify

das Bewußtsein   consciousness
bezweifeln   doubt, call into question
bleiben, ie, ie   remain, stay
bringen, brachte, gebracht   bring
denken, dachte, gedacht   think, opine, intend
dürfen (darf), durfte, gedurft   may, be allowed to, dare
ein·gehen, ·ging, ·gegangen   enter, go into
einsam   solitary, lonely
das Ende, -n   end; *an ein Ende kommen*   get finished, get done
ergehen, erging, ergangen   turn out, happen; *einem gut (schlecht) ergehen*   go well (badly) for someone
erhalten (ä), ie, a   keep, preserve

erhalten bleiben be preserved, remain in existence

das *Ethos* ethic, ethos

die *Existenzphilosophie, -n* existentialism, existential philosophy

der *Fehler, –* mistake, error

geeignet suitable, appropriate

gehören belong

geistig spiritual

gerade just, exactly

das *Griechenland* Greece

gut·machen set right, make amends for, make up for

heilsam beneficial, salutary

sich *heraus·bilden* evolve, be formed

hinzu in addition, further

der *Idealfall, ⁻ˈe* ideal case, ideal situation

die *Insel, -n* island

das *Klima* climate

kommen, kam, gekommen come

können, (kann), konnte, gekonnt can, be able to, know

lassen (ä), ie, a let, leave, have or cause

leben live

der *Lehrmeister, –* teacher, mentor

die *Lektüre, -n* reading; *zur Lektüre* as reading matter

lesen (ie), a, e read

das *Mal, -e* time, occasion; *zum ersten Male* for the first time, first

das *Meisterwerk, -e* masterpiece

mit · nehmen (· nimmt), · nahm, · genommen take along

der *Mittler, –* intermediary, mediator

mögen (mag), mochte, gemocht may, like

das *Motiv, -e* theme, motif

müssen (muß), mußte, gemußt have to

nach·fragen inquire

der *Polizist (-en), -en* policeman

das *Publikum* public, audience

die *Qual, -en* torment, anguish

die *Schätzung, -en* estimation, opinion

seelisch spiritual, psychic

sehen (ie), a, e see

selbst self, even

sollen (soll), sollte, gesollt (indicative) be supposed to, be said to; (subjunctive) should, ought to

stark strong, intense

suchen try, seek

die *Teilnahme* participation, sympathy

tun (tut), tat, getan do, make

die *Veränderung, -en* change

die *Verhandlung, -en* negotiation

vor·kommen, ·kam, ·gekommen appear be found, occur

wirklich real

wissen, wußte, gewußt know

die *Wissenschaft, -en* science

die *Wohnung, -en* apartment, house, residence

wollen (will), wollte, gewollt will, intend to, claim to

zufrieden happy, satisfied, content

TWELVE

The Subjunctive: Indirect Discourse
als wenn, als ob

36 / Purpose of the subjunctive in indirect discourse

When a German author uses the subjunctive in quoting ideas or statements indirectly, he may have one or both of two purposes in mind. He may use the subjunctive to indicate that he is quoting statements which he does not necessarily regard as true. Or, he may simply use the subjunctive as a device to indicate that he is restating things he himself or someone else said.

The latter is frequently the only purpose. Using the subjunctive is a very convenient way to indicate that a speaker or writer is relating something stated previously. When an English author summarizes a longer statement by another person, he must keep on reminding the reader that the ideas belong to someone else. This he does with phrases such as: *Z continues, states further, goes on to say, adds,* etc. These reminders are not necessary in German. Having given the origin of his quotation, the German author simply goes on using "quotational" (subjunctive) verb forms and the reader knows he is continuing to restate the thoughts of someone else.

37 / Translation of the subjunctive in "quotational" use

a / The two subjunctives and time

Both the general subjunctive (*wäre, hätte, würde,* etc.) and the special subjunctive (*sei, habe, werde,* etc.) may be used as "quotational" verb forms.

Both subjunctives usually indicate the same time and have the same meaning when they are used in indirect discourse.

Man glaubte damals, daß die Erde flach *sei.*	It was believed at that time that the earth *was* flat.
Man glaubte damals, daß die Erde flach *wäre.*	
Man klagte schon vor 1900, daß der materialistische Geist sich stark *verbreite.*	Even before 1900 the complaint was often made that the materialistic spirit *was spreading* rapidly.
Man klagte schon vor 1900, daß der materialistische Geist sich stark *verbreitete.*	

b / Tense sequence

Whether *sei* or *wäre* is translated as *is* or *was* (*habe, hätte* as *has or had; nehme, nähme* as *takes* or *took,* etc.) depends on the tense of the introductory verb of saying, thinking, believing, etc. We must, therefore, observe carefully the sequence of tenses, i.e., the tense of the introductory verb as compared with the time of the quotational form.

● *Simple quotational forms.* Any simple quotational form *(sei, wäre; habe, hätte; mache, machte; nehme, nähme)* indicates that the action or state is or was contemporary with the time of the introductory verb of saying, thinking, etc.

If the introductory verb is in the present, a simple quotational form is usually translated with an English present tense.

Es *glauben* noch manche Leute, daß die Erde flach *sei.*	Some people still *believe* that the world *is* flat.

If the introductory verb is in the past, the simple quotational forms are usually translated with some past tense form in English.

Gegen Ende des 19. Jahrhunderts *waren* viele der Meinung, daß man sich am Ende einer Epoche *befinde* *(. . . befände).*	Towards the end of the 19th century many people *were* of the opinion that they *were living* at the end of an epoch.

● *Quotational forms of the perfect.* Any quotational form of the perfect (*sei gewesen, wäre gewesen; habe gehabt, hätte gehabt,* etc.) indicates that the action or state preceded the time of saying or thinking.

If the introductory verb is in the present, the quotational form may be translated with English simple past or present perfect.

Die Ärzte *meinen,* daß er nicht schuld daran *gewesen sei.*	The doctors *think* that he *was* not to blame for it.

If the introductory verb is in the past, the quotational forms of the perfect must be translated by the English pluperfect. Thus, both *sei gewesen* and *wäre gewesen* are the equivalent of *had been,* and *habe gehabt* and *hätte gehabt* are translated *had had,* and *sei* or *wäre geblieben,* are translated *had remained,* etc.

Man *dachte* gar nicht daran, daß er krank *gewesen sei (. . . wäre).*	They *did* not *think* at all of the fact that he *had been* sick.

● *Quotational forms of* werden *plus infinitive.* The quotational forms of *werden* *(werde, würde)* plus an infinitive indicate that the action or state is expected or was expected to follow the time of the introductory verb.

If the introductory verb is in the present, the quotational form of *werden* must be translated with the future tense in English.

Man *kann voraussetzen,* daß das Geld zur Verfügung *stehen werde.*	It *can be assumed* that the money *will be* available.

If the introductory verb is in the past, the quotational form of *werden* must be translated with the past form *would* in English.

Man *setzte voraus,* daß das Geld zur Verfügung *stehen werde (. . . würde).*	It *was assumed* that the money *would be* available.

38 / *sollen* in indirect quotation

The verb *sollen* in the meaning *is to, is supposed to* is frequently used in quoting the statement or theory of some other person.

Nach Boyle *soll* das Experiment die Grundlage der Theorie *sein.*	According to Boyle the experiment *is to be (must be)* the basis of theory.
Den Sozialismus *sollen* nach Steinhausen der Industrialismus und der Kapitalismus *erzeugt haben.*	According to Steinhausen, industrialism and capitalism *begot* socialism.

Sollen is also used to quote a command or request indirectly.

Der Arzt sagte, er *solle* das Bett hüten.	The doctor said he *is to (was to)* stay in bed.
Der Arzt sagte ihm, er *solle (sollte)* das Bett hüten.	The doctor told him to stay in bed.

As is shown in both sets of illustrations above, *sollen* may sometimes be omitted in translating indirect statements or commands.

39 / *als wenn* and *als ob*

The conjunctions *als wenn* (as if) and *als ob* (as if) introduce a comparison which is imaginary rather than real. The verb of the clause introduced by these conjunctions will, therefore, be in the subjunctive mood.

Es scheint heute zuweilen, *als ob* Arbeit und Beruf nur als Mittel zum Leben *gälten, als wenn* das Nichtarbeiten das eigentliche Ideal *wäre (. . . sei).*	It seems today *as if* one's work and occupation *are considered* only a means to make a living, *as if* the real ideal *were* not to work at all.

Quite frequently the German author or speaker omits the *wenn* or the *ob* from these conjunctions. When such omission occurs, the inflected verb must follow immediately upon *als* instead of taking its usual position at the end of the subordinate clause. (Cf. the omission of *wenn* and the position of the inflected verb in such instances discussed in Unit Seven.) Thus *als* when followed by a subjunctive verb form is translated by *as if.*

Es scheint heute zuweilen, *als gälten* Arbeit und Beruf nur als Mittel zum Leben, *als wäre* das Nichtarbeiten das eigentliche Ideal.	It seems today *as if* one's work and occupation *are considered* only a means to make a living, *as if* the real ideal *were* not to work at all.

Exercises

I Enter in the answer spaces the letter identifying those forms in each group which are (or may be) forms of the general or special subjunctive.

1 (a) war (b) wäre (c) ist (d) sei
2 (a) brachten (b) bringe (c) brächtest (d) bringt
3 (a) bestreitet (b) bestritt (c) bestreite (d) bestritten
4 (a) halte (b) hieltest (c) hielt (d) hält
5 (a) geht (b) gegangen (c) ginge (d) gehe
6 (a) irrst (b) irre (c) irrte (d) irrt
7 (a) muß (b) mußte (c) müsse (d) müßte
8 (a) wäre geblieben (b) war geblieben (c) bin geblieben (d) seien geblieben
9 (a) wird gehen (b) wirst gehen (c) werde gehen (d) würde gehen
10 (a) habe gearbeitet (b) hätte gearbeitet (c) hat gearbeitet (d) habt gearbeitet

II Translate the words in italics taking into account the context and the sequence of tenses.

1 Er meint, *die Bevölkerung zeige* die Neigung . . .
2 Malthus behauptete, *der Boden* Englands *könne . . . nicht* produzieren.
3 Man hatte geglaubt, *die Newtonsche Lehre . . . sei . . .*
4 Er ist der Meinung, *es handele sich um die Zukunft der Nation.*
5 Er antwortete, *die Ergebnisse seien* ihm *bekannt.*
6 Er hat gesagt, *das dürfe* den Frieden *nicht stören.*
7 *Deutschland,* betonte Stresemann, *sei* treu *geblieben.*
8 Er sagt, *er habe . . . gelesen.*
9 Er verlangte weiter, daß *die Maßnahmen* sofort zu treffen *seien.*
10 Er schlug vor, *daß die Regierung . . .bleibe.*
11 Man konnte einwenden, daß *die Antwort . . . sei.*
12 Seine Ansicht war, *die Sache stehe anders.*
13 Er meinte, *die Soldaten kämen nicht wieder.*
14 Zuerst hat er geantwortet, daß *er . . . nicht bestreiten werde.*
15 Der Kanzler hatte zugeben müssen, daß *er* die Sicherheit *nicht mehr habe.*
16 *Diese Frage,* sagte er, *bleibe besser unbeantwortet.*
17 Es wurde berichtet, *eine Bewegung sei . . . entstanden.*
18 Er erklärte, daß *die Sache nicht zu ändern sei.*
19 Er gab endlich zu, *er habe sich geirrt.*
20 Er fügte hinzu, *er halte* Deutschland für unüberwindlich.

III   Enter on the answer sheet the letter identifying the most appropriate translation
of the verb phrases in italics.

A Die Künstler des Expressionismus meinten, daß die Einheit des Lebens abhanden
gekommen (1) *sei,* und die Zivilisation zugrunde zu gehen (2) *drohe,* wenn man sie
nicht vom Ursprung her (3) *erneuere.*
   1 (a) be   (b) were   (c) was   (d) had
   2 (a) is in danger   (b) had been in danger   (c) was in danger   (d) will be
      in danger
   3 (a) did (not) renew   (b) had (not) renewed   (c) would (not) have re-
      renewed   (d) may (not) renew

B Francis Bacon sagt von der Philosophie, ein Tropfen aus ihrem Becher (4) *führe
zum* Unglauben; (5) *leere man* aber den Becher auf den Grund, so (6) *werde* man
fromm.
   4 (a) lead to   (b) may be leading to   (c) leads to   (d) has led to
   5 (a) if you empty   (b) if you emptied   (c) if you might empty   (d) if
      you had emptied
   6 (a) had become   (b) may (you) become   (c) must become   (d) be-
      come

C Schon seit der zweiten Julihälfte (1918) begann sich in den Kreisen des deutschen
Generalstabes die Überzeugung durchzusetzen, daß der Krieg verloren (7) *sei.*
Deutschland (8→) *solle* sich zu retten (←8) *versuchen* und England den Verzicht
seiner Flotte (9) *anbieten;* dann (10→) *werde* England zu Konzessionen bereit
(←10) *sein.*
   7 (a) had   (b) was   (c) will be   (d) had been
   8 (a) can try   (b) should try   (c) should have tried   (d) shall try
   9 (a) offers   (b) let ... offer   (c) offer   (d) was offering
   10 (a) may (England) be   (b) may become   (c) would be   (d) would have
      been

D Viele Norddeutsche waren der Meinung, man (11) *lebe* noch anders in Wien, ruhi-
ger und beschaulicher, und aus jeder Stadt in Österreich (12→) *klängen einem* die
Namen Mozart und Schubert (←12) *entegen,* und Literatur und Theater (13) *be-
deuteten* dort noch mehr als ein Boxkampf.
   11 (a) may ... live   (b) lives   (c) lived   (d) would live
   12 (a) may one hear   (b) one heard   (c) one hears   (d) one had heard
   13 (a) meant   (b) mean   (c) might mean   (d) had meant

E In Adenauers Brief hieß es, er (14→) *habe* den Eindruck (←14) *gewonnen,* daß
seine Sache durchaus (15) *gut stehe.* Er (16→) *habe* deshalb keinen Zweifel (←16)
gelassen, daß er zu Kompromißlösungen keineswegs bereit (17) *sei.*
   14 (a) had gained   (b) will have gained   (c) might have gained   (d) is
      gaining
   15 (a) might be favorable   (b) had been favorable   (c) was favorable
      (d) would have been favorable
   16 (a) had left   (b) left   (c) leaves   (d) would leave
   17 (a) is   (b) was   (c) might be   (d) may (it) be

F Die Argumentation von Thomas Malthus ist Folgende: die Nahrungsproduktion (18) *vergrößere sich* in arithmetischer Progression; die Bevölkerung (19) *vermehre sich* aber in geometrischer Progression. Dieses Mißverhältnis (20) *könne* nur durch „Checks" ausgeglichen werden.

18 (a) grows larger (b) grew larger (c) might grow larger (d) may (it) grow larger

19 (a) may (it) increase (b) increased (c) increases (d) would increase

20 (a) can (b) could (c) will have been possible (d) had been possible

Working Vocabulary

abhanden· kommen, kam, o get lost, be misplaced

an· bieten, o, o offer (see *Verzicht*)

ändern change, alter

anders differently, otherwise; *anders stehen* be different

die Ansicht, -en view, opinion

aus· gleichen, i, i (re)balance, equalize

der Becher, – cup, goblet

bedeuten mean, signify

behaupten assert, state, say

bereit ready

berichten report

beschaulich contemplative, thoughtful

bestreiten, bestritt, bestritten challenge, dispute

betonen stress, emphasize

die Bevölkerung, -en population

die Bewegung, -en movement, motion

der Boden, – soil, land

der Boxkampf, "e boxing match

bringen, brachte, gebracht bring

drohen threaten, be in danger (of)

durchaus throughout, completely, quite

sich durch· setzen become accepted, prevail

der Eindruck, "e impression; *den Eindruck gewinnen* gain, get the impression

die Einheit, -en unity, oneness; unit

ein· wenden, · wandte, · gewandt object to, take exception to

entgegen· klingen, a, u ring, resound *einem entegegen· klingen* be heard by someone, someone hears (people hear)

entstehen, entstand, entstanden originate, occur

das Ergebnis, -se result, outcome

erneuern renew

die Flotte, -n fleet

fromm devout, wise

führen lead; *zu etwas führen* lead to (produce) something

der Generalstab, "e general staff

gewinnen, a, o gain, win

der Grund, "e base, ground; *auf den Grund* to the bottom

gut good; *gut stehen* be favorable

halten (ä), ie, a hold, regard

sich handeln concern, involve; *es handelt sich um Frieden* peace is at stake

heißen, ie, ei be stated, be called

hinzu· fügen add, say further

sich irren be mistaken, err, be in error

die Julihälfte the half of (the month of) July

keineswegs in no way

die Kompromißlösung, -en compromise solution

der Kreis, -e circle, group

leeren empty

die Lehre, -n theory, idea

die Maßnahme, -n measure, mode of acting

die Meinung, -en opinion; *der Meinung sein* be of the opinion

das Mißverhältnis, -se disparity, disproportion

die Nahrungsproduktion, -en food production

die Neigung, -en tendency, inclination

der Norddeutsche person from northern Germany (for declension see Appendix §73)

das Österreich Austria

die Progression, -en progression

die Regierung, -en government

sich retten save oneself, be saved

die *Sache, -n*   situation, matter, thing
die *Sicherheit, -en*   security, certainty
    sofort   immediately
der *Soldat (-en), -en*   soldier
    stören   disturb, interfere with
    treffen (i), traf, o   hit, affect, reach,
    take (measures)
    treu   loyal, true
der *Tropfen, –*   drop
die *Überzeugung, -en*   conviction, certainty
    unbeantwortet   unanswered
der *Unglaube (ns)*   lack of faith, incredulity
    unüberwindlich   invincible, impregnable
der *Ursprung, ⁻e*   origin, source; *vom Ur-*
    sprung her   from the point of origin

sich *vergrößern*   grow larger, increase
    verlangen   require, demand
sich *vermehren*   increase, enlarge
der *Verzicht, -e*   renunciation; *den Verzicht*
    anbieten   offer not to use, offer to re-
    nounce (give up) use
    vor·schlagen (ä), u, a   propose, suggest
    wieder·kommen, ·kam, o   come back,
    return
    zeigen   show
    zu·geben (i), a, e   admit, concede
    zugrunde gehen, ging, gegangen   perish,
    be ruined
die *Zukunft*   future
der *Zweifel, –*   doubt

THIRTEEN

The Verb as Adjective
Extended Adjective Constructions

40 / Adjective forms of the verb[1]

a / The participles

In both German and English the participles, present and past, are used as adjectives and adverbs.

Der Beweis ist *schlagend*.	The proof is *convincing*.
Der *leidende* Patient . . .	The *suffering* patient . . .
Er ging *stillschweigend* . . .	*Silently* (i.e., *saying nothing*) he went . . .
Das *siedend* heiße Wasser . . .	The *boiling* hot water . . .
Die Entscheidung ist *getroffen*.	The decision is *made* (. . . has been taken).
Die *getroffene* Entscheidung . . .	The decision *taken* . . .
Es ist *entschieden* besser . . .	It is *decidedly* better . . .

b / A construction to say "what is to be done."

German has, in addition, an adjectival verb form which is a mixture of the infinitive and the present participle. It has the infinitive preposition *zu* followed by the present participle: *zu treffend* . . . , *zu leugnend* . . . , *aufzulösend* . . . .

The construction derives from the passive formation *sein* plus an infinitive with *zu* described in Unit Three, §9 (see there), and it indicates *what is to (may, must) be done*.

Die hier *zu treffenden* Vorsichtsmaß-regeln . . .	The precautionary measures *to be taken* at this point . . .
cf. Hier *sind* Vorsichtsmaßregeln *zu treffen*.	Here precautionary measures *are to (must) be taken*.
Seine nicht *zu leugnende* Bega-bung . . .	His ability, *which cannot be denied* . . .
cf. Seine Begabung *ist* nicht *zu leugnen*.	His ability *cannot be denied*.
Die *aufzulösende* Substanz . . .	The substance *to be dissolved* . . .
cf. Die Substanz, die *aufzulösen ist*, . . .	The substance which *is to be dissolved* . . .

[1]See also Appendix §101.

41 / The extended adjective construction

a / Adverbs modify adjectives

Any adjective may have an adverb modifying it. Such an adverb then precedes the adjective, and we have what we shall call an "extended adjective construction."

Die *sehr hohe* Temperatur . . .	The *very high* temperature . . .
Ein *außerordentlich wichtiges* Gebiet . . .	An *extraordinarily important* field . . .

b / Adverbs with adjectival verb forms

Both English and German use adverbial modifiers with verbs which are used adjectivally. Such modifiers may express not only degree but also place, time, and manner.

Die *obenerwähnte* Tatsache . . .	The *above-mentioned* fact . . .
Die *früher beschriebene* Apparatur . . .	The *previously described* apparatus . . .
Der *falsch angeklagte* Jüngling . . .	The *falsely accused* young fellow . . .

c / Translating the extended adjective construction

German has great flexibility in respect to the kinds of modifiers which may precede a noun. In English certain elements may precede the noun, others must follow it. Compare:

Das *1937 errichtete* Institut . . .	The institute *erected in 1937* . . .
Das *hier darzustellende* System . . .	The system *to be described here* . . .

Observe that in both English and German the prime modifier tends to be close to the noun. This means that the order of the elements in German must be reversed in English when the extended adjective construction follows the noun.

Die *obenerwähnte* Tatsache . . .	The *above-mentioned* fact . . .
	The fact *mentioned above* . . .

Note further that the illustrations used above are essentially alternatives for subordinate clauses. The matter in each could also have been stated as follows:

Die Tatsache, *die oben erwähnt wurde,* . . .	The fact *which was mentioned above* . . .
Die Apparatur, *die ich früher beschrieb,* . . .	The apparatus *which I described earlier* . . .
Der Jüngling, *den man falsch angeklagt hatte,* . . .	The young fellow *who had been falsely accused* . . .
Das Institut, *welches 1937 errichtet wurde,* . . .	The institute *which was erected in 1937* . . .
Das System, *das hier darzustellen ist,* . . .	The system *which is to be described here* . . .

Because German has far more flexibility than English with respect to the kinds of modifiers that can precede a noun, the modifying element of the German must in many cases be translated with a relative clause in English.

Die *freigewordene* Stelle . . .   The position *which had become*
                                              open

Die *verstorbenen* Kranken . . .   The sick *who had died* . . .

Die *von einander nicht zu unter-*   The twins *who could not be told*
scheidenden Zwillinge . . .   *apart* . . .

Furthermore, German can expand the pattern illustrated above to include a greater
number of elements than can English. Compare the following German extended adjective constructions with their word-for-word English translations.

Eine *im Dienst des Staates stehende*   An *in the service of the state standing*
Kunst . . .   art . . .

Die *in weiten Kreisen der Bevöl-*   The *in large segments of the popula-*
kerung noch immer verbreitete   *lation still (wide-)spread* opinion . . .
Meinung . . .

Die *durch die Einflüsse der Umwelt*   The *through the influence of the envi-*
hervorgerufenen, also nicht vererb-   *ronment called forth, therefore not*
baren Eigenschaften . . .   *transmissible,* characteristics . . .

In each of these cases it is clearly necessary to have the modifiers follow the noun in
English. Thus,

an art *(which stands) in the service of the state* . . .
the opinion, *still wide-spread in large segments of the population* . . .
  the opinion, *which is still common in large segments of the population* . . .
the characteristics *which are called forth by the environment and which are,*
therefore, not transmissible . . .

42 / Extended adjective construction and independent adjectives

Quite often you will find before the German noun an extended adjective construction plus one or more independent adjectives. In English the independent adjectives
must precede the noun; the extended adjective constructions may precede or follow
the noun.

Das **obenerwähnte** *schwarze* Pferd . . .   The **above-mentioned** *black* horse . . .
                                                  The *black* horse **mentioned above** . . .

Die **noch immer weit verbreitete** *aber-*   The *superstitious* notion, **which is still**
gläubische Vorstellung . . .   **widely held** . . .

Note   When you come upon sentences which contain complex extended adjective
constructions, it will help to follow these steps:
   ● Find the beginning and the end of the construction. Match the article, *dieser-*
word, *ein-*word, etc. with the noun.
   ● Find the adjective(s) and adjectival verb form(s) which modify the noun directly. Then find the modifiers which belong with the adjective(s) and adjectival verb
form(s).

- Translate:
1 first the article (*dieser*-word, etc.), then any adjectives which must precede the noun, and then the noun;
2 following the noun, the other elements, either in a relative clause or in an extended adjective construction which reverses the order of the parts in the German construction.

With these steps in mind, study the examples below.

Der von der Richtigkeit seiner Lehre unerschütterlich *überzeugte Marx* . . .	*Marx,* unshakably *convinced* of the correctness of his theory . . .
Die an früherer Stelle kurz *erwähnten* und hier eingehender *zu besprechenden* außerordentlich *wichtigen Entdeckungen* . . .	*The* extraordinarily *important discoveries* (which were) *mentioned* briefly previously and (which are) *to be discussed* more exhaustively here . . .

43 / Adjective or adverb? a note of warning

In German one and the same word may serve as both adjective and adverb. You must, therefore, be on your guard to avoid mistakes of interpretation.

a / Predicate adjectives and adverbs
Adjectives in a predicate position in German are indistinguishable from adverbs. Only the context can guide the reader to a correct understanding.

Dieses Metall ist sehr *leicht.*	This metal is very *light.*
Dieser Stoff ist *leicht* zugänglich.	This substance is *easily* accessible.

b / Adjectives and adverbs before nouns
Adjectives preceding nouns have declensional endings; adverbs do not.

Die genau*e* Beobachtung . . .	The exact observation . . .
Eine genau bestimmt*e* Menge . . .	An exact*ly* determined amount . . .
Ein entschieden besser*es* Mittel . . .	A decided*ly* better remedy . . .

c / The -er ending
Even before nouns, however, adjectives and adverbs may look alike. Especially the ending *-er* may be misleading. The ending *-er* is: (1) a strong adjective ending (masculine nominative singular, feminine dative and genitive singular, genitive plural; (2) the ending for the comparative degree of adjective and adverb; and (3) part of the stem of a relatively few adjectives.

In interpreting the ending *-er* you will need to keep all possibilities in mind while looking for grammatical indicators and logical relationships. Among aids to interpretation is the presence or absence of commas which can help you tell whether you are reading adjectives in series (usually separated by commas) or an adjective modified by an adverb (where a comma would not be proper). Study the following illustrations:

ein leicht*er* Stoff . . .	a *light* substance . . .
bei sehr hoh*er* Temperatur	at a very *high* temperature
eine Reihe leicht*er* Stoffe . . .	a series *of light* substances . . .
ein leicht*erer* Stoff . . .	a *lighter* substance
Die Arznei war *bitter*.	The medicine had a *bitter* taste.
Es ist *bitter* kalt.	It is *bitterly* cold.
bitter*er* Haß . . .	*bitter* hatred . . .
ein leicht*er*, zugänglich*er* Stoff . . .	a *light, accessible* substance . . .
ein leicht*er* zugänglich*er* Stoff . . .	*a more easily accessible* substance . . .
der leicht*er* zugänglich*e* Stoff . . .	*the more easily accessible* substance . . .
eine Reihe leicht*er*, zugänglich*er* Stoffe . . .	a series *of light, accessible* substances . . .
eine Reihe leicht*er* zugänglich*er* Stoffe . . .	a series *of more easily accessible* substances . . .

Exercises

I On the answer sheet write translations of the following extended adjective constructions. Omit matter in parentheses.

Note The meanings of words you may not know are given below each such word. But you must decide whether the German word is singular or plural; adjective or adverb; past participle, present participle or future passive, etc.

1 eine immer größer werdende Gruppe . . .
/ larger and larger /   / group /
2 die aus der Erfahrung gewonnenen Lehren . . .
/experience/ /gain/   /lesson/
3 Die vor uns liegenden Verhandlungen . . .
/ ahead of us /   / negotiations /
4 für den zu behandelnden Fall . . .
/ deal with / / case /
5 die uns zu Gebote stehenden Mittel . . .
/ at our disposal /   / means /
6 der auf Frankreich gerichtete Druck . . .
/ France /   / direct / / pressure /
7 die hier versammelten Völker . . .
/ assemble /
8 die von Faraday erschlossenen Gebiete . . .
/ open up /   / area /
9 eine nicht wegzuleugnende Tatsache . . .
/ repudiate /   / fact /

10 (die westliche Kultur und) das mit ihr verbundene Christentum . . .
                                / associate   / Christianity /
11 unter ganz besonderen, schwer zu erfüllenden Bedingungen . . .
              / special /   /difficult /   / fulfill /   / condition /
12 (der Vertreter) einer längst abgelebten Ideenwelt . . .
                          / long ago / die out / world of ideas /
13 eine für unsere Zeit charakteristische Ausdrucksform . . .
                          / era / /characteristic / / form of expression /
14 die durchaus ernst zu nehmende Gefahr . . .
        / by all means /   take seriously / danger /
15 die zwischen unseren Regierungen zu führenden Verhandlungen . . .
                        / government /   conduct   / negotiation /

II In this exercise you are to do two things:
—Write down the first and last words of each extended adjective construction.
—Translate the adjective construction.

☆   QUESTION: Die Wurzel des Kapitalismus ist das dem Menschen eigentümliche
       Streben nach einem über die bloße Bedarfsdeckung hinausgehenden Gewinn,
       nach Profit.

       ANSWER: 1 First word: ___*das*___ Last word: ___*Streben*___
                        the striving (which is) peculiar to the human being
                    2 First word: ___*einem*___ Last word: ___*Gewinn*___
                        a gain which goes beyond what is necessary to cover basic needs

1 Faraday machte um 1820 die teilweise gemeinsam mit Davy ausgeführten Untersuchungen über die Verflüssigung der Gase.
2 Ferner entdeckte Faraday auch um 1820 den später so wichtig gewordenen Kohlenwasserstoff.
3 Die von Descartes bis Kant reichende Periode der Philosophie war längst abge-
   schlossen.
4 Es war jetzt möglich, die chemische Analyse an den viele Lichtjahre von uns ent-
   fernten Gestirnen zu erproben.
5 Die Aufklärung bildete die Grundlage der sich in Europa ausbreitenden Rokokokultur.
6 Es kann nur die Aufgabe des Staatsmanns sein, immer wieder von neuem nach der
   im Augenblick günstigsten Wegstrecke zu suchen.
7 Die deutsche Delegation hat die fünf anderen an der Locarno-Konferenz teilneh-
   menden Nationen zu einer Besprechung eingeladen.
8 In seiner Rede in Ost-Berlin sprach Brandt von „der gemeinsam erlebten und gemeinsam zu verantwortenden Geschichte."
9 Die neulich unabhängig gewordenen Völker Afrikas bedürfen unserer Unterstützung.
10 Man findet die erbärmlichste Armut in den noch zu entwickelnden Teilen der
   Welt.

Working Vocabulary

ab·leben   die, die out
ab·schließen, o, o   complete, conclude; lock up; seclude
die *Armut*   poverty
die *Aufgabe, -n*   task, assignment
die *Aufklärung, -en*   explanation, enlightenment; the Enlightenment (18th century)
der *Augenblick, -e*   moment
sich *aus·breiten*   spread (out), expand
aus·führen   carry out, execute
bedürfen (bedarf), bedurfte, bedurft   need, be in want of
behandeln   treat, deal with, manage
die *Besprechung, -en*   discussion, meeting, conference, consultation
bilden   form, build
bloß   mere, pure, only
ein·laden (·lädt), u, a   invite
entdecken   discover
entfernen   remove; *entfernt*   distant, remote
entwickeln   develop
erbärmlich   pitiable, miserable, wretched
erfüllen   fill up, fulfill, perform, realize
erleben   experience, witness
erproben   test
erschließen, o, o   open up, make accessible, explore for the first time
fern   far; *ferner*   further, in addition, moreover
fuhren   lead, conduct
das *Gas, -e*   gas
gemeinsam   in common with, together with
das *Gestirn, -e*   star, heavenly body
gewinnen, a, o   gain, earn, extract
die *Grundlage, -n*   foundation, base

günstig   favorable, beneficial
der *Kohlenwasserstoff, -e*   hydrocarbon, carbureted hydrogen
längst   long ago
das *Lichtjahr, -e*, light year
liegen, a, e   lie, be
nehmen (nimmt), nahm, genommen   take
neu   new; *von neuem*   anew
neulich   recently
die *Rede, -n*   speech, talk
reichen   reach, extend
richten   direct, turn; set right, arrange
die *Rokokokultur*   culture of the rococo period (18th century)
stehen, stand, gestanden   stand
das *Streben*   striving, effort, aim
der *Teil, -e*   part, segment
teil·nehmen (·nimmt), ·nahm, ·genommen   take part, participate
teilweise   partially, in part
unabhängig   independent
die *Unterstützung, -en*   support, assistance, subsidy
die *Untersuchung, -en*   investigation, research
verantworten   be responsible for, bear responsibility
verbinden, a, u   bind, connect, associate
die *Verflüssigung, -en*   liquification
versammeln   gather, assemble
der *Vertreter, —*   representative
weg·leugnen   deny, disavow, repudiate
die *Wegstrecke, -n*   path, stretch of road
westlich   western
wieder   again; *immer wieder*   again and again
die *Wurzel, -n*   root

FOURTEEN

The Prefix *da(r)-*: Reference and Anticipation

44 / *da(r)-* used to refer to an antecedent

The prefix *da(r)-* in its most frequent occurrence replaces the pronouns *es (sie, er)* and *sie* as the objects of prepositions. This substitution takes place when the reference is to previously mentioned inanimate objects, facts, or situations.

a / *da(r)-* referring to objects

When used to refer to previously mentioned objects, *da(r)-* is usually translated with English *it* or *them*. But if the prefix *da(r)-* has demonstrative effect, English usage calls for a translation with *this, that,* or the prefix *there-*.

Die Ärzte standen um *einen Tisch.*
*Dar*auf lag der Patient.

The doctors stood around *a table.* On *it* lay the patient.

Freud ist der Verfasser *vieler Schriften;*
*dar*unter ist eine über die Geschichte
der Psychoanalyse.

Freud is the author *of many works;* among *them* is one about the history of psychoanalysis.

Denke der Leser nur an *den Frieden*
*von Versailles. Dar*auf werden wir
noch zurückkommen.

Let the reader but think of *the Peace (Treaty) of Versailles. To this (topic)* we shall return later.

b / *da(r)-* referring to facts or ideas

If the prefix *da(r)-* refers to a previously mentioned idea or fact, English usage calls for translating it with *this* or *that*, or for substituting a suitable noun for the German prefix.

Napoleon war auch aller Freigeisterei
*bitter feind. Da*von wird aber erst
später die Rede sein.

Napoleon was also bitterly hostile to all free-thinking. But of *that* (of *this, thereof,* of *this matter*) we will not speak until later.

45 / *da(r)-* used to anticipate

In English as well as in German there are verb phrases consisting of a verb plus a preposition, for example, *to speak of.* If we compare use of such a verb phrase with that of a simple verb like *to report,* we find that in certain instances the verb phrase demands somewhat special treatment. Compare:

They *reported that* someone had dis-   They *spoke of the fact that* someone
   covered a new antiseptic.   had discovered a new antiseptic.

The straightforward verb *report* can lead directly to a subordinate clause, but the preposition in the idiom *to speak of* cannot have a subordinate clause as its object. We must, therefore, insert the general term "fact" in order to satisfy the idiom; the subordinate clause then serves as a completion element which explains or defines the general term.

This same phenomenon in a slightly different form occurs in German. Where English inserts a general term (e.g., fact) to anticipate a completion element, German inserts the prefix *da(r)-* before the preposition. The following completion element then explains and defines *da(r)-*.

Man sprach viel *darüber, daß* nichts   There was much talk *of the fact that*
   Neues hervorgebracht worden sei.   nothing new had been brought forth.

Semmelweiß machte die Ärzte *darauf*   Semmelweiss called the doctors' atten-
   aufmerksam, *daß* sie selber an dem   tion *to the fact that* they themselves
   Tode vieler Kinder schuld waren.   were to blame for the death of
                                             many children.

This anticipatory use of *da(r)-* occurs in German also when the completion element is an infinitive phrase. We solve the same problem in English by using a verbal noun (gerund) instead of the infinitive.

Man konnte damals kaum *daran*   At that time people could hardly *con-*
   denken, solche Unternehmungen in   *sider (think of) starting* such under-
   Angriff *zu nehmen.*   takings.

How we translate an anticipatory *da(r)-* and the following clause or phrase depends on the English verb or construction that introduces the completion element.

a / Omit *da(r)-* . . . , translate with clause or phrase
When the introductory element in English may be followed directly by a clause or an infinitive phrase, *da(r)-* may be omitted in translating. The German completion clause or infinitive may then be translated with similar English formations.

Er *erinnerte* sie *daran, daß* er sie vor   He *reminded* them *that* he had warned
   dieser Gefahr gewarnt hatte.   them of this danger.

Roscoe *ging* jetzt *dazu über,* die che-   Roscoe now *proceeded to investigate*
   mischen Wirkungen *zu untersuchen.*   the chemical effects.

b / German *da(r)-* . . . , *daß,* English *the fact that* or gerund
If the English construction introducing the completion element cannot lead directly into a subordinate clause, we may translate *da(r)-* . . . *daß* . . . with English *the fact (conclusion, circumstance) that* . . .

Deutschland kann *darauf* stolz sein,   Germany can be proud *of the fact that*
   daß es Musiker wie Bach, Beethoven   it has produced musicians like Bach,
   und Brahms hervorgebracht hat.   Beethoven, and Brahms.

Erinnern wir uns ferner *daran, daß*   Let us furthermore be mindful *of the*
    diese Strahlung medizinisch wichtig   *fact that* this radiation is important
    ist.   in medicine.

At times we may omit *da(r)-* ... *daß* and translate the verb of the German clause
with an English gerund.

Der menschliche Körper erhält sich   The human body maintains itself *by*
    dadurch, daß er der Außenwelt Luft   *taking* air and food from the (exter-
    und Nahrung *entnimmt.*   nal) world about it.

c / German *da(r)-* ... *zu (infinitive),* English gerund

When the English introductory construction cannot be followed by an infinitive,
we may translate *da(r)-* ... *zu (infinitive)* with an English gerund. The English translation will then have no specific element equivalent to *da(r)-*.

Man hat deshalb *daran* gedacht, diese   They, therefore, thought *of using* this
    Länge als Maß *zu benutzen.*   length as a unit of measure.

Man hatte ihn *davor* gewarnt, *sich* so   He had been warned *against exposing*
    bloßzustellen.   *himself* to criticism in this way.

Exercises

I The following sentences contain *da(r)-* prefixes referring to antecedents or facts.
On the answer sheet write the English translation of each *da(r)-* construction that
would best fit the incomplete rendering below the German.

1 Die Voraussetzungen des Plans, oder was *davon* übrig war, waren jetzt völlig umge-
worfen.

The presuppositions of the plan, or what was left _____, were now completely overturned.

2 Die Verhandlungen schlossen am 24. November. *Darauf* wurde der gesamte Briefwechsel veröffentlicht.

The negotiations ended on November 24. _____ the entire correspondence
was published.

3 Um Kafkas Finanzen stand es miserabel. Sein Tagebuch spricht auf jeder Seite
davon.

Kafka's finances were in miserable shape. Every page of his diary refers _____.

4 Er stand draußen vor der Tür und wollte wieder hinein. *Dazu* brauchte er Hilfe.

He stood outside at the door and wanted to get back in. _____ he needed
help.

5 Luther war ein großer Reformer, und *darauf* allein beruhte seine Macht.

Luther was a great reformer, and his power was due _____ alone.

II   Below each German sentence you will find one or two partial translations of the sentence. On the answer sheet continue these translations with an appropriate English equivalent for the words in italics.

A Das Buch Hiob endet *damit, daß Hiob* durch Leiden *zu höherer Einsicht gelangt.*

    1   The Book of Job ends _____ .

B Ein Hauptgrund für die außerordentliche Wirkung Bacons liegt *darin, daß er* der größte Schriftsteller seines Zeitalters *war.*

    2   A main reason for Bacon's exceptional influence lies _____ .

    3   A main reason for Bacon's exceptional influence is _____ .

C Herder wies *darauf* hin, *daß die Deutschen fähig waren,* eine eigene große Literatur hervorzubringen.

    4   Herder called attention _____ .

D Es ist doch *daran* zu erinnern, *daß es Völker gibt,* denen eine geschriebene Volkspoesie fehlt.

    5   We must remember _____ .

E Schopenhauer begnügte sich nicht *damit, an der Oberfläche* der Philosophie *zu bleiben.*

    6   Schopenhauer was not content _____ .

F Mit seherischem Blick für die kommenden Dinge warnt Bismarck *davor, von der* nüchternen *Wirklichkeit* der Politik *abzulenken.*

    7   With a prophetic eye for things to come, Bismarck warns _____ .

G Bismarcks Entlassung im Jahre 1890 war ein Zeichen *dafür, daß eine neue Zeit angebrochen war.*

    8   Bismarck's dismissal in 1890 was a sign _____ .

    9   Bismarck's dismissal in 1890 indicated _____ .

H Es ging ja *darum, die* militärische *Widerstandskraft* Rußlands durch die Revolution *zu brechen.*

    10   The task to be accomplished, after all, involved _____ .

    11   The objective, after all, was _____ .

I Einsteins letzter Lebensabschnitt wurde *davon* überschattet, *daß er den Anstoß* zum Bau der ersten Atombombe *gab.*

    12   The final period of Einstein's life was darkened _____ .

J DeGaulle versuchte, seine Opposition *dadurch* zu umgehen, *daß er* seine eigenen Kandidaten *vorschlug.*

    13   DeGaulle tried to circumvent his opposition _____ .

K Die Hoffnung der Jugend hat *dazu* beigetragen, *die Verzweiflung,* die dem ersten Weltkrieg folgte, *zu überwinden.*

    14   The optimism of young people contributed _____ .

    15   The optimism of young people helped _____ .

III   In the following sentences translate the words in italics.

1 *Ein kluger Politiker soll nicht daran denken,* sein Parteiprogramm sogleich *auszuführen.*

2 Die Sozialdemokratie hat leider nicht begriffen, *daß es darauf ankam, Hitler nicht zur Macht gelangen zu lassen.*

3 „Wir müssen uns bemühen, *unsere Gegner davon zu überzeugen, daß die Deutschen* mit allen ihren Nachbarn in Frieden und Freundschaft *leben wollen.*" (Willy Brandt)

4 *Die Erfolgsmöglichkeiten hingen davon ab, daß die* europäisch gesinnten *Kräfte* in Frankreich stark genug *blieben,* Briande im Außenministerium zu halten.

5 *Günter Grass hat sich damit beschäftigt, ein* groteskes, von den Kriegsgreueln verzerrtes *Bild* von der deutschen Geschichte unserer Zeit *zu schaffen.*

IV *Review of extended adjective constructions.* Sentences 4 and 5 of the preceding exercise contain examples of extended adjective constructions. They and associated elements are repeated below. In the spaces of the answer sheet (4a and 5a) enter translations of these constructions.

4a ... die europäisch gesinnten Kräfte in Frankreich ...

5a ... ein groteskes, von den Kriegsgreueln verzerrtes Bild von der deutschen Geschichte unserer Zeit ...

Working Vocabulary

ab·hängen, i, a depend (on)

ab·lenken divert, be diverted, turn away, get away

an·brechen (i), a, o begin, dawn

an·kommen, ·kam, o arrive, depend on; *es kommt darauf an* it depends, that's what the issue (the matter, everything) depends on

der *Anstoß, ⁻(ss)e* impetus, initiative, stimulus

aus·führen carry out, execute

das *Außenministerium, -ien* ministry for foreign affairs, department of state

der *Bau, -e* construction, erection; structure (plural *die Bauten*)

begreifen, begriff, begriffen grasp, understand

sich *bemühen* take trouble, endeavor

sich *beschäftigen* be occupied, occupy oneself; *sich mit etwas beschäftigen* be concerned with, endeavor, put effort into

brechen (i), a, o break

eigen own, personal

die *Einsicht, -en* insight, knowledge

der *Erfolg, -e* success; *die Erfolgsmöglichkeit, -en* possibility of success

fähig able, capable

fehlen be missing, be lacking; *mir fehlt das Buch* I do not have the book

folgen follow

der *Gegner, -* opponent, adversary

gelangen reach, arrive at, attain; *zur Macht gelangen* come to power

gesinnt minded, disposed; *europäisch*

gesinnt oriented toward Europe (as a whole)

hervor·bringen, ·brachte, ·gebracht bring forth, produce

hoch, höher, höchst high

klug clever, smart, wise

die *Kraft, ⁻e* power, force, power center

die *Kriegsgreuel* (plural) atrocities (horrors) of war

das *Leiden, -* suffering, affliction

leider unfortunately

die *Macht, ⁻e* power, strength

der *Nachbar (n), -n* neighbor

nüchtern sober, straightforward, prosaic

die *Oberfläche, -n* surface, superficial level

das *Parteiprogramm, -e* (political) party program, political platform

das *Rußland* Russia

schaffen, schuf, a make, create

der *Schriftsteller, -* writer

sogleich immediately, right away

die *Sozialdemokratie* Social Democracy

überwinden, a, u overcome, surmount

überzeugen convince

verzerren distort, deform

die *Verzweiflung, -en* despair

die *Volkspoesie, -n* popular poetry, folk literature

vor·schlagen (ä), u, a propose, suggest, nominate

die *Widerstandskraft, ⁻e* power of resistance, capacity to resist

die *Wirklichkeit, -en* reality

die *Zeit, -en* time, era

The Word *es*

The word *es* finds many uses, some of which present translation problems. The most frequent uses of *es* are summarized in this unit.

46 / *es* used to refer to antecedents

a / *es* with a noun antecedent

Es is the neuter pronoun used to refer to neuter nouns. As such, *es* is translated with an English pronoun appropriate to the reference.

Dieses Verfahren hat aber seine Nachteile. *Es* ist sehr kostspielig.	*This process* has, however, its disadvantages. *It* is very expensive.
Das Mitglied der Royal Society hat gewisse Privilegien. *Es* hat auch seine Pflichten.	*A member* of the Royal Society has certain privileges. *He (She)* also has his (her) duties.

b / *es* referring to a fact or idea

Es may refer to a fact or idea which has been mentioned or is understood. Sometimes an *es* so used can be translated with English *it*. At other times the translation may use English *so*, provide a logical substitute for *es*, or omit any equivalent for *es*.

Die Lage ist gefährlich. Man weiß *es* schon, aber ...	*The situation is dangerous.* We know *it* to be sure, but ...
Die Lage ist *gefährlich.* Sie ist *es* schon lange ...	The situation is *dangerous.* It has been *so* (i.e., dangerous) for a long time ...
Man ist wirklich bange, und spricht *es* ganz offen aus.	*People are really afraid* and say *so* quite frankly.
	People are really afraid and admit *it* quite frankly.
Er war früher *sehr reich,* ist *es* aber nicht mehr.	He was *very rich* at an earlier time but is not any longer.

A frequent use of *es* with modals in such manner was mentioned in Unit Eight, §24. In this case *es* stands for an understood dependent infinitive and its modifiers. Usually *es* used this way need not be translated. But one may insert the dependent infinitive which is understood in German, or substitute the general English *do it*.

Man will *operieren.* Ja, man muß *es.*	The doctors want to operate. Indeed, they must.
	(or) Indeed, they must *operate.*
	(or) Indeed, they must *do it.*

47 / *es* indefinite and impersonal

a / *es,* a general condition

Es in certain expressions can refer to a general condition of things. In translating this *es* one can sometimes substitute the word *things.* At other times no equivalent is possible; one then omits the word in translation, using an English idiom which is equivalent to the whole German expression.

Es geht nicht.	*It* won't do.
	Things are not working out.
Es geht ihm gut.	*Things* are going well for him.
	He feels fine.
Er meint *es* gut.	He means well.
Er meint *es* gut mit mir.	He is kindly disposed toward me.
Man bringt *es* aber auf diese Weise nicht weit.	One does not, however, get very far with this approach.

b / *es,* impersonal subject[1]

Es is also used as the impersonal real subject of a verb. In such cases there may be reference to a vaguely defined agent. Or there may be no reference to any agent but only to the existence of some action or state.

It and *there* may be used to translate the impersonal *es.*

Es ist kalt und *es* schneit.	*It* is cold and *it* is snowing.
Es war spät und sehr dunkel.	*It* was late and very dark.
Es handelt sich um . . .	*It* is a matter of, a question of . . .
	It has to do with . . .
Es gibt Menschen, die . . .	*There* are people who . . .

For some expressions English must provide a logical subject or make the action itself the subject.

Es klopft.	*Someone is knocking.*
Es läutet.	*The bell is ringing.*
Es geht sich hier sehr gut.	*The walking* is very good here.

---

[1]See also *Impersonal use of the reflexive,* §26, c.

48 / *es* used as a filler

There are sentences in German where *es* may or may not occur, depending on word order.

a / *es* used to anticipate

For reasons of emphasis or style a German author may wish the subject of a sentence to follow the verb. He may then insert *es* as the first element so that the verb is the second one. *Es* serves only to fill in and anticipate the following subject whether it is a noun, pronoun, phrase or clause. We can translate such an *es* with English *it* or *there,* or we may omit *es* entirely and let the subject precede the verb.

Es waren *viele Menschen* da. *cf.* Viele Menschen waren da.	*There* were many people there.
Es ist *das* kein Zufall. *cf.* Das ist kein Zufall.	*That* is no chance happening.

Es ist nicht nötig, *dasselbe noch*
    besonders auszusprechen.
    cf. Dasselbe . . . auszuprechen, ist
    nicht nötig.
	It is not necessary to state this again
	 specifically.

Es macht nicht geringe Schwierig- keiten, *diese Erscheinung zu* *erklären.*	*Explaining this phenomenon* occasions no small difficulty.
Es kann ja gar nicht bezweifelt werden, *daß er Begabung hat.*	*It* cannot be doubted that he has talent. *There* can be no doubt about his having talent.

Note 1   Sometimes emphasis on the subject is attained by letting the subject come first and inserting *es* after the verb.

Das ist *es* ja, was ich immer gesagt habe.	*That* is just what I've been saying all the time.

Note 2   Occasionally *es* occurring as the object of the verb anticipates a following infinitive phrase.

Er hat *es* versucht, *mit dieser Gewohn-* *heit zu brechen.*	He has tried *to break this habit.*

b / Sentences without a subject

Certain constructions in German have no real subject at all. They express the fact that a state or action is going on. They may or may not indicate who or what is concerned. *Es* can only appear as the first word in such statements and drops out when some other word takes the first position.

1 *Es* ist meinem Mann übel. *cf.* Meinem Mann ist übel.	My husband does not feel well.

2 *Es* wundert ihn, daß sie noch nicht
   gekommen ist.
   cf. Ihn wundert, daß sie noch
   nicht gekommen ist.

He is surprised that she has not come
yet.

3 *Es* ist schon nach dem Arzt ge-
   schickt worden.
   cf. Nach dem Arzt ist schon ge-
   schickt worden.[1]

The doctor has already been sent
for.

4 *Es* wird hier gearbeitet.
   cf. Hier wird gearbeitet.[1]

Work is going on here.

5 *Es* wird noch geschlafen.[1]

Some people are still sleeping.

Note that the persons affected by the action or state in the first three examples become the subjects of the English equivalents. In the last two examples where the statement expresses solely that an action is going on, a logical subject is provided in English.

Exercises

I   On the answer sheet write translations of the italicized words in the following sentences. Each translation should be suitable to a rendering of the entire sentence.
1 *Man kann es uns nicht verdenken, wenn* wir unsere eigenen Interessen wahren.
2 *Es lag eine Ruhe in seiner Gestalt,* die mich geradezu reizte.
3 *Nun mußte versucht werden,* die neue Verständigung in Europa einzubauen.
4 *Wir haben es doch fertig gebracht,* unseren alten Gegner *zu überzeugen.*
5 Chamberlain war ein Freund Frankreichs gewesen, *Snowden war es nicht.*
6 *Es geht hier um die Verwirklichung einer großen Idee.*
7 *Dem Schauspieler gefällt es immer,* großen Beifall *zu hören.*
8 *Sie nahm es uns besonders übel, daß* wir sie nicht besuchten.
9 *Dem Reichspräsidenten fiel es nicht leicht,* das Abschiedsgesuch des Außenmini-
   sters *anzunehmen,* (10) *aber es blieb ihm nichts anderes übrig.*
11 *In einem Briefwechsel wurde vereinbart, daß* die Verhandlungen im Sommer statt-
   finden sollten.
12 *Beide Seiten hatten es nicht schwer,* die logischen Widersprüche *nachzuweisen.*
13 *Seiner Partei ging es schlecht,* auch wenn er den Kampf siegreich durchgefochten
   hatte.
14 *Die Konservativen lehnten es ab,* für die liberalen Kandidaten *zu stimmen.*
15 *Es lag eine gewitterschwüle Stimmung in der Luft.*
16 Kafka war uns damals ein großes Rätsel, *und er ist es noch heute.*
17 *Eigensinnige Politiker wird es immer geben!*
18 Bei dem Pariser Gespräch *handelte es sich um die Festigung der Saarland-Grenze.*
19 *Es besteht ein organischer Zusammenhang* zwischen Außen- und Innenpolitik.

[1]See Unit Four, §12, c where the use of the passive in such sentences is discussed.

20 *Es wird noch lange dauern, bis* die Brücke fertig ist.
21 *Es gibt viele Verbindungen zwischen Politik und Geschichte.*
22 Die Jugend sprengt alle Formen der Gesellschaftsordnung *oder glaubt es zu tun;* in Wirklichkeit schafft sie eine neue Form.
23 *Es entstand ein großer Sturm auf dem Meer.*
24 *Es hat keine Einweihung stattgefunden.*
25 *Es herrschte,* wie Goethe sich rückblickend ausdrückte, *„eine Gärung aller Begriffe".*

II *Review of extended adjective construction.* Translate the extended adjective constructions in the following sentences and clauses.
1 Jetzt kommen wir wieder zu dem schon einmal früher erwähnten Problem!
2 Der durch lange Verhandlungen zustande gebrachte Vertrag wurde leider nicht von allen Ländern unterschrieben.
3 Die neulich erschienene Ausgabe von Einsteins Briefen ist äußerst interessant; (4) sie zeigt einige bis jetzt wenig betrachtete Seiten seines Charakters.
5 Kants Schriften bieten viele schwer zu erklärende Begriffe der Metaphysik an.

Working Vocabulary

ab·lehnen   reject, turn down, refuse (to)
das Abschiedsgesuch, -e   (letter of) resignation
an·bieten, o, o   offer, present
an·nehmen (·nimmt), ·nahm, ·genommen   accept, assume
sich aus·drücken   express oneself, say
die Ausgabe, -n   edition
der Außenminister, –   secretary or minister for foreign affairs, secretary of state
die Außenpolitik   foreign policy
der Begriff, -e   concept, idea
der Beifall   applause, approval
besonders   especially, very much
bestehen, bestand, bestanden   exist, be
betrachten   study, examine
der Briefwechsel, –   correspondence, exchange of letters
die Brücke, -n   bridge
dauern   last, take (time), be
durch·fechten (i), o, o   fight (it) out
eigensinnig   obstinate, stubborn, headstrong
ein·bauen   build in, fit in, incorporate; *eine Verständigung einbauen*   obtain acceptance of an agreement

die Einweihung, -en   dedication, opening ceremony, initiation
entstehen, entstand, entstanden   arise, originate
erklären   explain, clarify
erscheinen, ie, ie   appear, be published
erwähnen   mention, refer to
fallen (ä), fiel, a   fall; *einem leicht fallen*   be easy for someone
fertig·bringen, ·brachte, ·gebracht   manage, achieve
die Festigung, -en   securing, establishing, determination
die Form, -en   form, convention
die Gärung, -en   ferment, upheaval
gefallen (ä), gefiel, a   please, delight; *das Buch gefällt mir*   I like the book
der Gegner, –   opponent, adversary
gehen, ging, gegangen   go; *es geht um Geld*   it concerns (the issue here is) money
geradezu   directly, actually, downright
die Gerechtigkeit   justice
die Gesellschaftsordnung, -en   social order
das Gespräch, -e   conference, conversation
die Gestalt, -en   figure, appearance, bearing
gewitterschwül   sultry, oppressive (as with an impending storm)

die Grenze, -n   boundary, border

sich handeln um   concern, be a matter of;
Es handelt sich um sein Leben   his life
is at stake (at issue, in question)

herrschen   reign, prevail, be prevalent

die Innenpolitik   domestic policy, politics

die Metaphysik   metaphysics

nach·weisen, ie, ie   prove, point out,
detect

neulich   recently

das Rätsel, –   riddle, mystery

der Reichspräsident (-en), -en   national
president, president of the "Reich"

reizen   provoke, irritate, excite, charm,
attract

rückblickend   retrospective

die Ruhe   composure, peace, calm

das Saarland   the Saar

schaffen, schuf, a   make, create

der Schauspieler, –   actor

die Schrift, -en   writing, (literary) work

die Seite, -n   side, aspect

siegreich   victorious

sprengen   explode, rupture

statt·finden, a, u   take place, occur

stimmen   vote

die Stimmung, -en   mood, atmosphere, feel

*übel·nehmen (·nimmt), ·nahm, ·ge-
nommen*   resent, take amiss; *Ich nehme
es dir übel*   I hold it against you

überzeugen   convince

übrig·bleiben, ie, ie   be left(over, to do)
remain

unterschreiben, ie, ie   sign, approve (of)

die Verbindung, -en   tie, connection, point
of contact, association

verdenken, verdachte, verdacht   blame,
find fault with

vereinbaren   agree, reach a settlement

die Verhandlung, -en   negotiation

die Verständigung, -en   agreement, understanding

der Vertrag, ¨e   treaty, pact

die Verwirklichung, -en   realization

wahren   look after, safeguard

der Widerspruch, ¨e   contradiction

die Wirklichkeit, -en   reality

der Zusammenhang, ¨e   connection, relationship

zustande bringen, brachte, gebracht
achieve, accomplish

More Sentences Beginning with the Verb
Idiomatic Use of Tenses   *erst*

49 / A fourth type of sentence beginning with the verb

In Unit Seven we discussed three types of sentences and main clauses in which the inflected verb is the first element for reasons other than normal word order. These types were: (1) the question, (2) the conditional sentence where *wenn* is omitted, and (3) the request or suggestion.

There is also a fourth instance when the inflected verb may be the first element of the sentence or follow immediately upon a coordinate conjunction. This type of sentence can generally be recognized through the fact that the word *doch* follows rather closely upon the verb.[1]

The intent of this construction beginning with the verb is generally to make the statement stronger. The effect is often one which can best be rendered through an English clause beginning with *for*. At times such a construction can be translated effectively with a rhetorical question in English.

Weiß man doch, woran man ist.	*For (At least, Then) one knows* what one has to deal with.
Lag es doch nahe, diesen Schluß zu ziehen.	*For (After all)* this conclusion obviously suggested itself.
Es war das ein ungeheurer Fortschritt, *lag doch jetzt der Weg* für die weitere Entwicklung *offen.*	That was a tremendous step forward, *for now the way was open* to further development.
	That was a tremendous step forward. *Was not the way open now* to further development?

50 / Idioms beginning with the verb[2]

The following idioms are related to the sentences or clauses beginning with the verb which have already been studied.

---

[1] Compare the "sign-posts" for the other types of sentences beginning with the verb which are listed in Unit Seven, §21.

[2] Like some other expressions, these idioms do not affect the word order of the following clause. See footnote p. 7.

a / *mögen* or *sein* plus *auch (immer, noch) so*

The modal *mögen* in various forms and the suggestion forms of *sein (sei, seien)* will occur in initial position in statements granting or conceding certain conditions. One of the adverbial modifiers *auch so, immer so, noch so, auch immer so,* or *auch noch so* will usually be associated with the quality or element in question. The English translation of such statements will begin with the words *no matter how* or *however.*

Mag es *(auch) noch so* wenig gewesen sein, ein Anfang war es doch.	*No matter how* little it *may* have been, it was a beginning in any case.
Sie wollen sich miteinander darüber nicht verständigen − *mögen* die Folgen *auch (immer) so* ernsthaft sein.	They (simply) won't reach an agreement about it − *however* serious the consequences *may* be. (cf. − *let* the consequences be *as* serious *as they may.*)
Möchte ich den Weg *noch so* langsam zurücklegen, allzubald würde ich zu Hause sein.	*No matter how* slowly I *might* walk, I would get home all too early.
Seien wir *noch so* vorsichtig, die Fahrt bleibt gefährlich.	*However* careful we *may be,* the journey will be dangerous.
Sei es *auch noch so* wenig, dankbar bin ich.	*No matter how* little it *may be,* I am thankful.

b / *sei . . . sei . . .*

Associated with the use of the special subjunctive forms *sei* und *seien* to concede or postulate is the idiomatic use of these forms in stating pairs of possibilities, usually opposites or contrasts, to which a statement of opinion is related. *Sei* or *seien* in these pairs will be in the initial position and the English equivalent of *sei . . . sei . . .* or *seien . . . seien . . .* in this use is *whether (it) be . . . or . . . .*

Sei es gut, sei es böse − wir leben in einer Zeit des fortschreitenden Kollektivismus.	*Whether it be good or bad* − we are living in a time of advancing collectivism.

51 / The present with future implication

Both German and English often use a verb form of the present to state that an action will take place at some future time. Usually an expression of time, or the context, makes it clear that the speaker is thinking of a future period.

Pres. Er hält eine Rede.	He is making a speech.
Fut. Er hält morgen eine Rede.	He is making a speech tomorrow. i.e., He *will make* a speech tomorrow.

Because the two languages are similar in this respect, the German present with future implication seldom causes the English speaking reader any difficulty.

52 / The idiomatic present and past

a / The present and past implying previous action or state
The present in German can be used to express the fact that an action or state going on in the present was begun at a previous point in time.

Er *ist* schon lange hier.   He *has been* here a long time.

In similar fashion the simple past in German can indicate that an action or state going on at some point in the past had been going on during the preceding period.

Er *war* seit einer Woche da.   He *had been* there for a week.

Such is frequently the idiomatic meaning of the present or past when it occurs in conjunction with either: (1) *schon* followed by an expression of time, or (2) *(schon) seit* with a measure of time. See illustrations above and below.

b / Translation of the idiomatic present
In translating the idiomatic present English must use the (progressive) perfect. English usually introduces the time element with the preposition *for*. But see the last example below.

Man *sucht schon ein Jahr* nach einem   They *have been seeking* a better rem-
besseren Mittel.   edy *for a year*.

Sie *arbeiten schon seit zwei Monaten*   They *have been working* in this divi-
in dieser Abteilung.   sion *for two months*.

Ich *gehe seit einem Jahre* zu diesem   *I have been going* to this dentist *for a*
Zahnarzt.   *year*.

Seit 1945 sucht man ein neues Mittel.   We *have been looking* for a new remedy *since 1945*.

c / Translation of the idiomatic past
In translating the idiomatic past English must use the (progressive) pluperfect. The time element in English is usually introduced with the preposition *for*. But see the last example.

Man *suchte schon drei Jahre* ein bes-   They *had been looking* for a better
seres Mittel.   remedy *for three years*.

Sie *arbeiteten (schon) seit langer*   They *had been working* in a factory
Zeit in einer Fabrik.   *for a long time*.

Seit 1824 wirkte Johannes Müller in   Johannes Müller *had been teaching*
Bonn als Dozent.   *(lecturing)* in Bonn *since 1824*.

Note   *Seit* with the past need not always indicate that one has to do with an idiomatic past. *Seit* can be used with the past tense also to indicate simply that an activity or state began at a certain time. That this is the meaning is usually clear from the context or from the sense of the sentence, as in the following illustration.

Seit dem Jahre 1840 begann man die-   *From 1840 on* scholars *began* to
sen Vorgang genauer zu studieren.   study this process more closely.

53 / Idiomatic use of the future and future perfect

Both the future and future perfect tenses can be used to express probability, sometimes with the aid of the word *wohl* (probably), sometimes without.

a / Future
The future can express present probability.

Da man ihn ins Krankenhaus gebracht hat, *wird* er *(wohl)* sehr krank *sein.*	Since he was brought to the hospital, he *is probably* very sick.

b / Future perfect
The future perfect can express past probability.

Da man ihn ins Krankenhaus gebracht hat, *wird* er sehr krank *gewesen sein.*	Since they took him to the hospital, he *was probably* very sick.

54 / *erst*

The word *erst* serves as an important adverb as well as adjective. The meaning of *erst* as an adverb may be *first, at first,* and *first of all.*

Ich muß *erst* packen.	I have to pack *first.*
Erst wollte man es kaum glauben.	*At first* people could hardly believe it.

However, the adverbial use of *erst* often serves to underscore that something has yet to occur, or to stress the time or condition for an occurrence. *Erst* in such instances may be translated with the positive emphasis of English *yet, just, only.*

Das wird sich *erst* zeigen.	That is *yet* (remains) to be seen.
Sie ist eben *erst* angekommen.	She arrived *just* now. She *just* arrived.
Dieser Stahl schmilzt *erst* bei sehr hoher Temperatur.	This (kind of) steel melts *only* at a very high temperature.
Das Wasser soll man kochen und dann *erst* trinken.	You must boil the water and *only* then *(only after* that) can you drink it.

In such use the force of *erst* may in effect say that something *has not (yet) happened,* or that something *did not, will not, cannot, ought not happen* before a given time or condition. This significance of *erst* is translated with a negative approach to the matter being stated, employing modifiers such as *not until, not till, not for.* The last two examples above can also be translated in this way. Compare the following:

Dieser Stahl schmilzt *erst* bei sehr hoher Temperatur.	This steel does *not* melt *until* a very high temperature is reached.
Das Wasser soll man kochen und dann *erst* trinken.	Do *not* drink the water *until* it has been boiled.
Erst 1888 wurde Wagners **Die Feen** gegeben.	Wagner's **Die Feen** was *not* presented *until* 1888.

Der nächste Zug fährt *erst* nach   The next train will *not* leave *for*
zwei Stunden.   (another) two hours.

Exercises

On the answer sheet write translations fitting the context for the words in italics.

1 Die Verfolgung der Jupitermonde nahm Galilei sehr in Anspruch; *gelang es ihm doch schwer,* ihre Umlaufszeiten *zu bestimmen.*

2 Besonders in Österreich findet man glänzende Leistungen in der Musik; *war es doch die Heimat Mozarts und Haydns* und die geistige Heimat Beethovens.

3 Böll hatte keine Empfangsrede bereit, *kam doch der Nobelpreis als eine ganz überraschende Ehre.*

4 *Brachte doch Picasso die Ausdruckskraft der Malerei* auf ein völlig neues Niveau.

5 Die Erfindung der Flugmaschine brachte höchst wichtige Gewinne, *mochten die ersten Folgen davon auch noch so fragwürdig gewesen sein.*

6 Bevor wir uns die Bilder von Paul Klee ansehen, *sei doch erwähnt,* daß er mit Kandinski lange befreundet war.

7 Rußland muß auf den Vorschlag der NATO-Nationen, *sei es durch eine öffentliche Rede, sei es durch heimliche Verhandlungen,* mit irgendeiner Erwiderung antworten.

8 Besuchen Sie uns in Zürich, *sei es während Ihrer Italienreise, sei es später im Winter.*

9 *Seien wir auch immer so müde,* bei der höchst schwierigen Frage der Kriegsschuld müssen wir noch etwas länger bleiben.

10 *Nächstes Jahr findet die Tagung* der Leibniz-Gesellschaft *in Prag statt.*

11 *Zehn Monate arbeitete Baudelaire* an einem einzelnen Gedicht!

12 *Seit Jahrhunderten träumt man davon,* eine Weltordnung *zu schaffen,* in der es keinen Krieg gäbe.

13 *Seit langer Zeit gilt Arnold Schönberg als ein Komponist,* dessen Musik nicht leicht zugänglich ist.

14 *Spannungen* zwischen dem britischen Mutterland und seinen Kolonien in Nordamerika *bestanden bereits seit längerer Zeit,* als in 1776 die Revolution erklärt wurde.

15 *Seit Jahrhunderten lebten die Franzosen* unter dem System eines politischen Absolutismus, ehe die Monarchie endlich gestürzt wurde.

16 *Seit dem Ende des zweiten Weltkrieges haben sich viele europäische Verhältnisse geändert.*

17 *Das Newtonsche Weltbild ist schon längst* als unzulänglich *abgelehnt worden.*

18 *Man wird uns wohl nicht länger warten lassen;* wir sind doch um halb zwölf verabredet.

19 *Viele Physiker werden die Theorien Einsteins falsch verstanden haben.*

20 *Vor dem Ende des 20. Jahrhunderts werden wir sicher neue Energiequellen entdeckt haben.*

21 *Kommt unser Gast nächste Woche,* so werden wir unsere Pläne fallen lassen müssen.
22 *Wird der liberale Kandidat gewählt,* so ist die alte Koalition völlig zerstört.
23 *Erst im 20. Jahrhundert wurde Kierkegaards Philosophie richtig eingeschätzt.*
24 *Erst nach dem Druck von Schönbergs* **Harmonielehre** (1911) *konnte man* die theoretische Grundlage seiner „atonalen" Musik *verstehen.*
25 *Goethe vollendete* seine Faust-Dichtung *erst einige Monate vor seinem Tod* im Jahre 1832.

Working Vocabulary

ab· lehnen   reject, turn down
sich ändern   change
an· sehen (ie), a, e   look at, view
der Anspruch, ⁻e   claim, demand; *in Anspruch nehmen*   make demands on, occupy time of
die Ausdruckskraft, ⁻e   power of expression, expressiveness
befreundet   friendly, acquainted; *befreundet sein mit*   be friends with
bereit   ready
bereits   already
bestehen, bestand, bestanden   exist, be
bestimmen   determine
die Dichtung, -en   poetry, poem
der Druck, -e   publication, printing, pressure
die Ehre, -n   honor, distinction
ein· schätzen   assess, evaluate
einzeln   single
die Empfangsrede, -n   speech, acceptance speech
die Energiequelle, -n   source of energy
entdecken   discover
die Erfindung, -en   invention
erwähnen   mention, say
die Erwiderung, -en   response, answer
fallen (ä), fiel, a   fall; *fallen lassen*   drop, abandon
die Flugmaschine, -n   airplane
die Folge, -n   result, consequence
fragwürdig   questionable
der Gast, ⁻e   guest
das Gedicht, -e   poem
geistig   spiritual, intellectual
gelingen, a, u   be possible (for), succeed; *es gelingt ihm nicht*   he is not able
gelten (i), a, o   be valid; *als etwas gelten*   be regarded (viewed) as something
die Gesellschaft, -en   society

der Gewinn, -e   gain, benefit, profit
glänzend   splendid, excellent, brilliant
die Grundlage, -n   foundation, basis
die Heimat, -en   homeland
heimlich   secret, private
höchst   most, extremely, high
irgendein   some, any
das Italien   Italy; *die Italienreise*   trip to (through) Italy
die Kriegsschuld, -en   war guilt
längst   long ago
die Leibniz-Gesellschaft, -en   the Leibniz Society
die Leistung, -en   achievement, work
die Malerei   painting
das Mutterland   homeland
die NATO-Nationen   nations belonging to the North Atlantic Treaty Organization
das Niveau, -s   level
öffentlich   public
der Physiker, –   physicist
die Quelle, -n   source
die Rede, -n   speech, statement
schaffen, schuf, a   create, make
schwierig   difficult
die Spannung, -en   tension, discord
statt· finden, a, u   take place
stürzen   overthrow, hurl down
die Tagung, -en   meeting, convention
der Tod, -e   death
träumen   dream
überraschen   surprise
die Umlaufszeit, -en   time (length, duration) of revolution
unzulänglich   insufficient, inadequate
verabreden   make an appointment
die Verfolgung, -en   pursuit, study
das Verhältnis, -se   relation, circumstance(s)
die Verhandlung, -en   negotiation

vollenden complete, perfect
völlig complete, fully
der *Vorschlag, -"e* proposal, suggestion
wählen elect, choose

das *Weltbild* view of the universe (world)
die *Weltordnung* world order, world unity
zerstören destroy
zugänglich accessible, open (to)

I On the answer sheet copy the subject of each sentence.

1 Jedem Bürger stellt der Staat weitgehende Bedingungen.

2 Der Schüler hat der zweiten Vorlesung nicht beigewohnt.

3 Den Heimatlosen hilft die Heilsarmee.

4 Ein neues Sozialbewußtsein sucht die heutige Jugend.

5 Einsteins Relativitätstheorie und die damit verbundene Lehre der Dynamik brachten die ganze Welt der Wissenschaft in Aufruhr.

II a) Copy on the answer sheet the complete verb or verb complex of each sentence. Include auxiliaries. b) Also give the dictionary (infinitive) form of the verb or verb complex.

1 Jules Vernes Phantasie lief den aktuellen Ereignissen weit voraus.

2 Eine Fortsetzung des Romans hätte meine Zeit zu sehr in Anspruch genommen.

3 Der Bibliothekar wollte uns auch die Goethe-Sammlung zur Verfügung stellen.

4 Der Sieg Napoleons in der Dreikaiserschlacht von Austerlitz 1805 löste das Ende des Heiligen Römischen Reichs Deutscher Nation aus.

5 Adenauer hat sein Volk gegen feindliche Angriffe immer in Schutz genommen.

III Enter on the answer sheet the letter identifying the most appropriate translation of the verb form(s) in italics in each sentence.

A Die ungeheuere Wichtigkeit von Pasteurs Entdeckungen *war* nicht sogleich zu sehen.

    1   a) were (not)   (b) was (not) being   (c) had (not)   (d) could (not) be

B Wordsworth and Coleridge *waren* die Begründer der englischen Romantik.

    2   (a) had   (b) were   (c) could be   (d) are

C Viele wichtige Schriften der griechischen Antike *sind* verschwunden.

    3   (a) have   (b) were   (c) could be   (d) are

D (4) Der Bau der Berliner Mauer *hatte* deutlich gemacht, (5) daß Fortschritte in Richtung auf eine Lösung der Deutschen Frage nur durch Verbesserungen der Beziehungen zur Sowjetunion zu erzielen *waren*.

    4   (a) owned   (b) has   (c) had   (d) did have

    5   (a) were being   (b) are   (c) had   (d) could be

E Das eigentliche Gebiet der deutschen Aufklärung *ist* die moralische Verbesserung der Menschheit *geworden*.

    6   (a) became   (b) had been   (c) is being   (d) had grown

F Alle Tendenzen der Renaissance *wurden* von der Volksphantasie sehr wirksam in eins zusammengefaßt in der Figur des Faust.

    7   (a) became   (b) had been   (c) were   (d) are being

G (8) Über die Berliner Krisenjahre 1961 und 1962 *ist* viel geschrieben *worden*
(9) und viel *wird* noch darüber geschrieben werden.
8 (a) were (b) has been (c) became (d) is being
9 (a) will (b) is (c) grows (d) is getting
H Das sehr ernste Problem der steigenden Aufrüstung *wird* lange noch ungelöst bleiben.
10 (a) is (b) will (c) is becoming (d) grows

IV Translate the words in italics.
1 *Die Höflichkeit* des Engländers *fällt den Ausländern auf.*
2 In Amerika *sind Menschen aus vielen verschiedenen Ländern* zu einer Nation *zusammengeschmolzen worden.*
3 *Die Entwicklung* des deutschen Nationalismus *nahm* bei der Wahl Hindenburgs zum Reichspräsidenten *an Geschwindigkeit zu.*
4 *Man hat die Zwanzigerjahre* als das Jahrzehnt der neuen Architektur *bezeichnet.*
5 *Man hatte verschiedene Möglichkeiten vor sich.*

V *Review of strong verbs* Fill in the missing principal parts for the verbs listed on the answer sheet. These verbs follow the patterns illustrated below.

ITEMS	INFINITIVE	PRESENT: 3rd PERSON SING.	PAST: 3rd PERSON SING.	PAST PARTICIPLE
1- 2	beißen *(bite)*	beißt	biß	gebissen
3- 4	pfeifen *(whistle)*	pfeift	pfiff	gepfiffen
5- 7	bleiben *(remain)*	bleibt	blieb	geblieben
8-10	fliegen *(fly)*	fliegt	flog	geflogen

Working Vocabulary

der *Angriff, -e* attack, assault
der *Anspruch, ⸗e* claim; *in Anspruch nehmen* make demands on
die *Antike* antiquity
auf·fallen (ä), ·fiel, a strike, be noticeable, attract attention
die *Aufklärung, -en* explanation, enlightenment; the Enlightenment (18th century)
der *Aufruhr* uproar, disturbance; *in Aufruhr bringen* cause a tumult, stir up an uproar
die *Aufrüstung* armament
der *Ausländer, –* foreigner
aus·lösen cause, induce, bring about
der *Bau, -e* construction, erection; structure (plural *die Bauten*)

die *Bedingung, -en* condition, stipulation; *jemandem Bedingungen stellen* place conditions on someone
der *Begründer, –* founder, originator
bei·wohnen attend (with dative)
bezeichnen label, designate, characterize
die *Beziehung, -en* relation, tie
der *Bibliothekar, -e* librarian
der *Bürger, –* citizen
deutlich clear, evident
die *Deutsche Frage* the problem of the political partitioning of Germany into East and West sectors
die *Dreikaiserschlacht* the "battle of the three emperors," a term used to refer to the battle of Austerlitz (1805)

eigentlich   proper, real, true
die *Entdeckung, -en*   discovery
die *Entwicklung, -en*   development
das *Ereignis, -se*   event, fact
ernst   serious
erzielen   achieve, realize, strive for
feindlich   hostile, unfriendly
der *Fortschritt, -e*   advance, progress
die *Fortsetzung, -en*   continuation
das *Gebiet, -e*   domain, field
die *Geschwindigkeit, -en*   speed, velocity
heilig   holy (see *Reich*)
die *Heilsarmee*   Salvation Army
der *Heimatlose*   the homeless (one) (for
   declension see Appendix §73)
heutig   contemporary, of today
die *Höflichkeit, -en*   politeness, courtesy
die *Jugend*   youth, the young, young
   people
die *Krisenjahre*   the years of crisis
die *Lehre, -n*   theory, teaching(s)
die *Lösung, -en*   solution
die *Mauer, -n*   wall; *die Berliner Mauer*
   the wall dividing Berlin into political
   East and West sectors
die *Menschheit*   humanity, mankind
die *Möglichkeit, -en*   possibility, option
die *Phantasie*   imagination
das *Reich, -e*   empire, kingdom; *das Heilige
   Römische Reich deutscher Nation*   the
   Holy Roman Empire (843-1806)
der *Reichspräsident (en), -en*   national
   president, president of the "Reich"
die *Richtung, -en*   direction; *in Richtung
   (auf)*   toward
der *Roman, -e*   novel
die *Romantik*   romanticism
die *Sammlung, -en*   collection
die *Schlacht, -en*   battle, slaughter (see
   Dreikaiserschlacht)

die *Schrift, -en*   writing, work
der *Schüler, –*   student, pupil
der *Schutz*   shelter, refuge, protection; *in
   Schutz nehmen*   defend, protect against
der *Sieg, -e*   victory, triumph
sogleich   immediately, right away
das *Sozialbewußstein*   social awareness or
   consciousness
der *Staat, -en*   country, government, state
steigen, ie, ie   rise, increase
stellen   place, put (see also *Verfügung*)
ungeheuer   huge, immense
ungelöst   unsolved
die *Verbesserung, -en*   improvement, correction
verbinden, a, u   connect, associate, relate
die *Verfügung, -en*   disposal, use; *jemandem
   etwas zur Verfügung stellen*   place
   something at someone's disposal
verschieden   different, various
verschwinden, a, u   vanish, disappear
das *Volk, ⁻er*   people
die *Volksphantasie*   imagination of the people
voraus· laufen (äu), ie, au   precede, run
   in advance (ahead), go before
die *Vorlesung, -en*   lecture
die *Wahl, -en*   election, choice
weitgehend   extensive, far-reaching
die *Wichtigkeit*   importance
wirksam   effective
die *Wissenschaft, -en*   science
*zu· nehmen (· nimmt), · nahm, · genom-
   men*   increase, grow
zusammen· fassen   unite, embrace, summarize
zusammen· schmelzen (i), o, o   fuse
   (weld) together, melt together

I   Indicate on the answer sheet the case and number of each numbered noun in italics. Use the abbreviations: *Nom.* for nominative, *Acc.* for accusative, *Dat.* for dative, *Gen.* for genitive; *sg.* for singular, *pl.* for plural.

A   „Es war Präsident Kennedy, der (1) die *Vorstellungskraft* (2) der jungen *Menschen* in (3) aller *Welt* gefangennahm und sie angefeuert hat. Er gab (4) der jungen *Generation* (5) die *Hoffnung,* daß es unter (6) den *Nationen,* unter Menschen (7) *Frieden* und Verständnis geben kann. Verbunden mit (8) einem bemerkenswerten *Realismus* sah er (9) neue *Horizonte* und machte sie (10) anderen *Menschen* sichtbar. (11) Sein plözlicher *Tod* machte (12) sehr vielen jungen *Menschen* klar: (13) Das *Werk* wurde begonnen, und es muß vollendet werden." (This tribute to Kennedy was made by Willy Brandt in Coventry, England, on April 24, 1965.)

B   (14) Die *Phantasiebewegung* tat mit Herder (15) den großen *Schritt* zu (16) der *Erfassung* (17) des *Völkischen* als des Nährbodens (18) aller wahren geistigen *Entwicklung.*

C   (19) Dem *Dichter* Heinrich Böll ist es am meisten gelungen, (20) den deutschen *Menschen* (21) seinen östlichen *Nachbarn* verständlich zu machen.

D   (22) Die *Arbeitslosigkeit* machte (23) der Roosevelt *Regierung* (24) die größten *Schwierigkeiten* wegen (25) des schlimmen *Zustandes* der amerikanischen Industrie.

II   Enter on the answer sheet the letter identifying the translation of the words in italics which would fit best into a complete rendering of the sentence.

A   Wie Claude Bernard *hat* auch Pasteur die meisten seiner Forschungen unter primitiven Umständen *ausführen müssen.*
   1   (a) must carry out   (b) would have to carry out   (c) had to carry out
      (d) had had to carry out
B   Die Dichter der Aufklärung *wollten* auf unterhaltsame Weise belehren und erziehen.
   2   (a) will   (b) claim   (c) would wish   (d) wanted
C   (3) Es gehört zu den Härten im Leben eines Politikers, daß er nicht immer alles sagen *darf,* was er denkt; (4) daß er seinen Gefühlen nicht immer freien Lauf lassen *kann.*
   3   (a) is permitted   (b) has to   (c) was allowed to   (d) might
   4   (a) was able to   (b) will be allowed   (c) can   (d) could
D   (5) Nachdem die Berliner Mauer gebaut wurde, *mußte* man die politischen Möglichkeiten neu durchdenken, (6) wenn man für die Menschen etwas erreichen und den Frieden sicherer machen *wollte.*
   5   (a) must   (b) had to   (c) has to   (d) would have to
   6   (a) wanted   (b) intend   (c) alleges   (d) had wanted

E Die Entstehung einer Kultur glaubt Toynbee nicht allein mit Argumenten des Ver-
standes verstehen zu *können.*

    7   (a) know   (b) could   (c) be able to   (d) have been able to

F Hermann Hesse *soll sich* eingehend mit Jungs Psychologie *beschäftigt haben,* gerade
bevor er den Roman **Demian** (1919) schrieb.

    8   (a) ought to have concerned himself   (b) should concern himself
         (c) is supposed to concern himself   (d) is said to have concerned himself

G (9) *Lesen Sie* etwas von Hemingway oder Steinbeck, (10) wenn Sie Joyce nicht
mögen.

    9   (a) If you read   (b) Read   (c) Are you reading   (d) Should you
         read

    10   (a) may   (b) might   (c) wish   (d) like

H *Vergessen wir nicht,* daß T. S. Eliot auch einige Werke für das Theater geschrieben
hat.

    11   (a) Let us not forget   (b) If we do not forget   (c) We do not forget
         (d) Are we not forgetting

I *Können wir* dieses Thema richtig behandeln, ohne die **Cantos** von Erzra Pound in
Betracht zu ziehen?

    12   (a) If we can   (b) May we be able to   (c) We can   (d) Can we

J *Betrachten wir* den Dom genauer, so wird uns seine eigenartige Architektur klar und
verständlich.

    13   (a) Let us study   (b) If we study   (c) Are we studying   (d) We
         are studying

K *Möge diese* wichtige *Musik* Stockhausens ein größeres Publikum *finden!*

    14   (a) Is this music finding   (b) If this music should find   (c) May this
         music find   (d) This music may find

L *Ist die* deduktive *Logik* von Descartes auch bei Bertrand Russell *zu finden?*

    15   (a) The logic is to find   (b) If the logic is found   (c) Is the logic
         finding   (d) Can the logic be found

III   Translate the words in italics.

A (1) *Wenn wir* das Lebenswerk Friedrich Meineckes im Innersten *verstehen wollen,*
so müssen wir vielleicht von der Tatsache ausgehen, (2) *daß er* zu einer Zeit *geboren wurde,* (3) *als es noch kein deutsches Reich gab.*

B Hesse beschäftigte sich mit Jungs Psychologie, (4) *gerade bevor er* den Roman
Demian *schrieb.*

C Können wir dieses Thema richtig behandeln, (5) *ohne* die **Cantos** von Ezra Pound
in Betracht zu ziehen?

IV *Review of strong verbs* Fill in the missing principal parts for the verbs listed on the answer sheet. These verbs follow the patterns illustrated below.

ITEMS	INFINITIVE	PRESENT: 3rd PERSON SING.	PAST: 3rd PERSON SING.	PAST PARTICIPLE
1- 3	singen *(sing)*	singt	sang	gesungen
4- 6	spinnen *(spin)*	spinnt	spann	gesponnen
7-10	werfen *(throw)*	wirft	warf	geworfen
11-13	erschrecken *(be alarmed)*	erschrickt	erschrak	erschrocken
14-15	empfehlen *(recommend)*	empfiehlt	empfahl	empfohlen

Working Vocabulary

an· feuern excite, fire

die Arbeitslosigkeit unemployment

die Aufklärung, -en explanation, enlightenment; the Enlightenment (18th century)

aus· führen carry out, execute

aus· gehen, · ging, · gegangen go out, begin, proceed

bauen build, erect

behandeln treat, handle

belehren instruct, teach

bemerkenswert remarkable, noteworthy

sich beschäftigen be busy, occupy oneself, spend time

der Betracht regard, consideration; *in Betracht ziehen* take into consideration, consider, examine

betrachten regard, examine, view

der Dichter, – poet

der Dom, -e cathedral, church

durch· denken, · dachte, · gedacht think over, consider

eigenartig unique, peculiar

eingehend thorough, exhaustive

die Entstehung, -en origin, rise

die Entwicklung, -en development

die Erfassung, -en understanding, grasp

erreichen attain, reach

erziehen, erzog, erzogen educate, instruct

die Forschung, -en research

der Friede (-ns) peace

gebären, a, o bear; *geboren werden* be born

gefangen nehmen (nimmt), nahm, genommen capture, captivate

das Gefühl, -e feeling, emotion, sentiment

gehören belong

geistig spiritual, intellectual

gelingen, a, u be possible (for), succeed; *es gelingt ihm nicht* he is not able, he is not succeeding

genau exact

die Generation, -en generation

gerade just, right

die Härte, -n hardship, rigor

die Hoffnung, -en hope, aspiration

der Horizont, -e horizon

das Innerste essence, depth (for declension see Appendix §73)

klar clear, distinct

der Lauf, ⁻e movement, flow; *freien Lauf lassen* give full expression (to), give vent (to)

das Lebenswerk, -e life work

die Mauer, -n wall; *die Berliner Mauer* the wall dividing Berlin into political East and West sectors

der Mensch (-en), -en human being, person

die Möglichkeit, -en possibility

der Nachbar (-n), -n neighbor

der Nährboden, – soil, land for producing food

die Nation, -en nation

östlich eastern

die Phantasie imagination, inventiveness; *die Phantasiebewegung* literary movement which championed human imagination (18th century)

plötzlich sudden

das Publikum audience, public

der Realismus realism

die Regierung, -en government

das **Reich, -e** empire, kingdom; "Reich" as
a politically unified Germany
der **Roman, -e** novel
schlimm poor, bad
der **Schritt, -e** step, stride; *den Schritt tun*
take the step
die **Schwierigkeit, -en** difficulty
sichtbar visible, evident
sicher secure, safe
das **Tatsache, -n** fact
das **Thema, Themen** theme, topic, subject
der **Tod, -e** death
der **Umstand, ⁻e** condition, circumstance
unterhaltsam amusing, entertaining
verbinden, a, u tie, connect
vergessen (i), a, e forget
der **Verstand** reason, logic

verständlich intelligible, comprehensible; *verständlich machen* make clear
das **Verständnis, -se** understanding, accord
verstehen, verstand, verstanden understand
vollenden complete, achieve
völkisch national; *das Völkische*
spirit, affairs of the people (for declension see Appendix §73)
die **Vorstellungskraft, ⁻e** (power of)
imagination
die **Weise, -n** manner, way
die **Welt, -en** world
das **Werk, -e** work, job, publication
wichtig important
ziehen, zog, gezogen pull, draw (see
Betracht)
der **Zustand, ⁻e** condition, state

I Write on the answer sheet the letter identifying the most appropriate translation of the words in italics.

A Wir dürfen *uns* nicht durch die Berliner Mauer *auseinanderbringen lassen*.

   1   (a) let ourselves divide   (b) cause division   (c) let ourselves be divided   (d) leave us divided

B Das Eintreten Deutschlands in die Weltwirtschaft *ließ* den Kapitalismus zu einem mächtigen Hebel politischen Strebens *werden*.

   2   (a) lets . . . be   (b) causes . . . to grow   (c) caused . . . to become   (d) ceases to be

C Wegen der plötzlichen Flucht aus Deutschland (1933) *hat* Thomas Mann einige wichtige Manuskripte in München *lassen müssen*.

   3   (a) had to leave   (b) had to let   (c) must leave   (d) was forced to stop

D Die weitere Streuung thermonuklearen Machtpotentials *würde* Rüstungskontrollen schwieriger *werden lassen*.

   4   (a) became cause . . . to be   (b) will let . . . grow   (c) prevented . . . from becoming   (d) would cause . . . to become

E (5) Wir werden in diesem Jahr zum zehnten Mal den 13. August vorbeigehen *lassen müssen*, (6) ohne daß *sich* an der Mauer in Berlin etwas *geändert hat*. (Spoken in 1971 by Willy Brandt)

   5   (a) (have to) cause   (b) (have to) let   (c) (have to) stop   (d) (have to) leave

   6   (a) (without anything) to change   (b) (without) having had to change (anything)   (c) (without) our being changed (by anything)   (d) (without anything) having been changed

F Als *sich* der Industrialismus in England *auszubreiten* begann, kam von vielen Menschen eine starke Gegenreaktion.

   7   (a) to spread themselves out   (b) to have expanded   (c) expands   (d) to expand

G Junge Nationen haben es an sich, *sich* als Träger eines Missionsgedankens *zu empfinden*.

   8   (a) to be perceived   (b) to perceive themselves   (c) perceiving   (d) to have perceived

H Nach William Harvey hat man die Lebenserscheinungen auf Gesetze zurückführen wollen, die *sich* auch in der unbelebten Natur *beobachten lassen*.

   9   (a) let themselves observe   (b) observe themselves   (c) can be observed   (d) cause to be observed

117

I In den Vereinigten Staaten *hat sich* eine klassenlose Gesellschaft auf dem Niveau des Mittelstandes *gebildet.*
10   (a) has developed   (b) has to be formed   (c) had to take form
     (d) has had to develop

II   Translate the words in italics. Your translation should suit the idiomatic context of the whole sentence.

A Die Lehren Galileis wirkten so beunruhigend, daß es Leute gab, (1) *die* sich weigerten, in sein Teleskop zu blicken, um (2) *darin* nicht Wahrnehmungen zu machen, (3) *die* die Lehren der bisherigen Philosophie und (4) *die* der Kirche umstürzen könnten.
B Galilei entdeckte die vier Monde des Jupiter, (5) *die* dem unbewaffneten Auge bis dahin verborgen geblieben waren.
C (6) *Keiner* hat so viele neue Wahrnehmungen erlebt, wie Galilei bei seinen Fernrohr-Entdeckungen und (7) *deren* eingehender Verfolgung.
D „Blut und Eisen" sind die Elemente, (8) *aus denen* Bismarck die deutsche Nation schmiedete.
E „Wir können niemanden als Freund des deutschen Volkes empfinden, (9) *dessen* Haltung und Politik die Wiederherstellung unserer staatlichen Einheit verhindert." (Willy Brandt)
F Wagners Lebenslinie verbindet den Anfang des 19. Jahrhunderts (10) *mit dessen Ende.*
G Die psychoanalytische Forschung hat Entdeckungen gemacht, (11) *ohne die* ein großer Teil der Kunst und Literatur unserer Zeit nicht verständlich wäre.
H Eine Herrschaft der Mehrheit, (12) *die* die Minderheit nicht achtet, ist eine Tyrannie.
I Deutschland steht nicht allein mit dieser Hoffnung; die ganze geistige Welt teilt (13) *sie.*
J Einstein und Max Planck schufen die Formeln und Theorien, (14) *wodurch* die Atomenergie möglich geworden ist.
K (15) *Alles, was* die moderne deutsche Philosophie hervorgebracht hat, geht auf die grundlegenden Leistungen Kants und Hegels zurück.

III   Enter on the answer sheet the letter identifying the most appropriate translation of the words in italics.

A Leonhard Euler meinte (in Bezug auf die Newtonsche Lehre vom Licht), man (1) *müßte* eine Abnahme des Sonnenkörpers bemerken, wenn die Ansicht richtig (2) *wäre,* daß das Licht ein feiner Stoff (3) *sei,* der von der Sonne (4) *ausfließe;* das Licht (5→) *komme* (nach Euler) auf analoge Weise (←5) *zustande* wie der Schall.
1   (a) would have to   (b) has to   (c) has had to   (d) is necessary
2   (a) had been   (b) had   (c) were   (d) could be
3   (a) were   (b) is   (c) has   (d) will be
4   (a) emanates   (b) would emanate   (c) were to emanate   (d) could emanate
5   (a) would come into being   (b) were coming into being   (c) comes into being   (d) had come into being

B Wenn Galilei es (6) *verstanden hätte,* sich die Sympathien der Jesuiten zu erwerben, so (7→) *hätte* er über alles mögliche (←7) *schreiben können,* auch über die Umdrehung der Erde.
   6   (a) understood (how)   (b) has understood (how)   (c) would understand (how)   (d) had understood (how)
   7   (a) had been able to write   (b) could have written   (c) was able to write   (d) could write

C Martin Luther war der Ansicht, daß jede Seele sich ihren eigenen Gott aus dem Innersten neu erschaffen (8) *müsse.* Er verkündete weiter, daß jeder Gläubige, jedes Glied der Kirche ein Priester (9) *sei.*
   8   (a) would have had to   (b) has had to   (c) had to   (d) is having to
   9   (a) has been   (b) were   (c) had   (d) was

D Ricarda Huch hat einmal geschrieben, das Deutsche Reich (10→) *sei* nie etwas Festes (←10) *gewesen,* jeder Kaiser (11→) *habe* es neu (←11) *schaffen müssen,* und das (12) *übersteige* menschliche Kräfte.
   10 (a) is being   (b) had been   (c) is   (d) was
   11 (a) had had to create   (b) had to create   (c) would have to create   (d) has to create
   12 (a) would exceed   (b) may (it) exceed   (c) exceeded   (d) had exceeded

E „Wenn in der Bilanz meiner politischen Wirksamkeit (13) *stehen würde,* ich (14→) *hätte* einem neuen Realtätssinn in Deutschland den Weg öffnen (←14) *helfen,* dann (15→) *hätte* sich eine große Hoffnung meines Lebens (←15) *erfüllt. "* (Willy Brandt)
   13 (a) (it) says   (b) (it) would say   (c) (it) had said   (d) (it) will say
   14 (a) would have helped   (b) did help   (c) would have to help   (d) had helped
   15 (a) would have been fulfilled   (b) were being fulfilled   (c) is to be fulfilled   (d) has been fulfilled

IV *Review of strong verbs* Fill in the missing principal parts for the verbs listed on the answer sheet. These verbs follow the patterns given below.

ITEMS	INFINITIVE	PRESENT: 3rd PERSON SING.	PAST: 3rd PERSON SING.	PAST PARTICIPLE
1- 4	essen *(eat)*	ißt	aß	gegessen
5- 6	lesen *(read)*	liest	las	gelesen
7-10	schlagen *(hit)*	schlägt	schlug	geschlagen
11-15	halten *(hold)*	hält	hielt	gehalten

Working Vocabulary

die **Abnahme, -n** decrease, diminution, shrinkage

achten respect, heed

sich **ändern** change, be altered

die **Ansicht, -en** opinion, view; *der Ansicht sein* be of the opinion

sich **aus· breiten** spread, expand

auseinander· bringen, · brachte, · gebracht divide, bring apart

aus· fließen, o, o emanate, flow out (from)

bemerken observe, notice, perceive

beobachten view, observe

beunruhigen upset, disturb

der **Bezug, ⸚e** reference; *in Bezug auf* with regard to

die **Bilanz, -en** balance, result, final accounting

sich **bilden** be formed, develop, educate oneself, improve one's mind

bisherig up to then (now), previous

dahin to that time (place); *bis dahin* until then

eigen own, individual, characteristic

eingehend probing, thorough, searching

die **Einheit, -en** unity

ein· treten (tritt), a, e enter; *das Eintreten* entry

das **Eisen** iron

empfinden, a, u feel, perceive, regard; *sich empfinden* perceive (feel, view) oneself

die **Entdeckung, -en** discovery

sich **erfüllen** be fulfilled, be realized, come true

erleben experience

erschaffen, erschuf, a create, produce

erwerben (i), a, o gain, obtain

das **Fernrohr, -e** telescope

die **Flucht, -en** flight, escape

die **Formel, -n** formula

die **Forschung, -en** research

die **Gegenreaktion, -en** reaction of opposition, counter-movement

geistig intellectual

der **Gläubige** believer (for declension see Appendix §73)

das **Glied, -er** member

grundlegend fundamental, basic

haben (hat), hatte, gehabt have; *es an sich haben* have as part of one's nature, be one's manner

die **Haltung, -en** behavior, attitude

der **Hebel, –** lever

die **Herrschaft** rule, dominion, mastery

hervor· bringen, · brachte, · gebracht produce, create

die **Hoffnung, -en** hope

das **Innerste** the innermost reaches (of one's mind, soul) (for declension see Appendix §73)

klassenlos classless

die **Lebenserscheinung, -en** phenomenon of life, vital symptom

die **Lebenslinie, -n** life (history), life line (palmistry)

die **Lehre, -n** theory, principle, idea

die **Leistung, -en** achievement, accomplishment

das **Machtpotential, -e** power-potential

die **Mehrheit, -en** majority

die **Minderheit, -en** minority

der **Missionsgedanke (ns), -n** mission purpose, missionary ideology

der **Mittelstand** middle class

möglich possible; *alles mögliche* everything possible, every conceivable thing

das **Niveau, -s** level, plane, standard

der **Realitätssinn** sense of reality, pragmatism

die **Rüstungskontrolle, -n** arms control, supervision of arms agreements

schaffen, schuf, a create, establish

der **Schall, -e** sound, noise

schmieden forge, form

die **Seele, -n** soul, creature

staatlich national, political

stehen, stand, gestanden stand, say, be written

das **Streben** striving, endeavor

die **Streuung, -en** dispersion, spreading

der **Träger, –** bearer

übersteigen, ie ie exceed, surpass

die **Umdrehung, -en** revolution, rotation

um · stürzen overthrow, overturn

unbelebt inanimate, lifeless

unbewaffnet unarmed; *mit unbewaffnetem Auge* with the naked (unaided) eye *verbergen (i), a, o*   conceal, hide

vereinigen   unite; *die Vereinigten Staaten*   the United States

die *Verfolgung, -en*   pursuit, continuation, persecution

verhindern   hinder, prevent, interfere with

verkünden   announce, proclaim

verständlich   understandable, comprehensible

vorbei·gehen, ·ging, ·gegangen   pass, go by

die *Wahrnehmung, -en*   perception, observation; *Wahrnehmungen machen*   observe, perceive

der *Weg, -e*   way; *den Weg öffnen*   pave or clear the way (for)

sich *weigern*   refuse, hesitate (to do something)

die *Weltwirtschaft, -en*   world economy

die *Wiederherstellung, -en*   restitution, reestablishment

wirken   effect

die *Wirksamkeit, -en*   effectiveness, activity, career

zurück·führen   trace back (to), attribute (to)

zurück·gehen, ·ging, ·gegangen   go back, derive (from), originate (with); *das geht auf die Römer zurück*   that has its origin with the Romans

zuatande kommen, kam, o   occur, come to be (exist), be produced

REVIEW EXERCISES UNITS 13-16

On the answer sheet write translations of the words in italics. Each English equivalent should fit perfectly into a rendering of the whole sentence.

1 Die meisten Theologen erklärten Kopernikus' Schriften für eine „Hypothese," offenbar weil Luther und Melanchthon sich *dagegen* ausgeprochen hatten.

2 Das Außerordentliche der Goetheschen Faust-Dichtung *besteht darin, daß sie eine* vollständige *Darstellung* der Kulturgeschichte der Renaissance *ist*.

3 *Man hat sich daran gewöhnt,* selbst die weniger gelungenen Bilder eines „berühmten" Malers zu hohen Preisen *zu kaufen*.

4 *Der Herausgeber hat den Sinn seiner Aufgabe darin gesehen,* Grundlage und Entwicklung der abendländischen Musik *dem Leser nahezubringen*.

5 *Dem Künstler fällt es manchmal schwer,* die „Bedeutung" seiner Werke *zu besprechen*.

6 Man mußte überzeugt sein, *wie Hegel es war,* daß der Lauf der historischen Ereignisse auf einer vernünftigen Basis ruhte.

7 Die jüngere Generation *wird dafür sorgen, daß die* menschlichen *Ideale nicht vergessen werden*.

8 *Es kamen viele Briefe und Glückwünsche* aus aller Welt, als die Verlobung der Prinzessin bekanntgemacht wurde.

9 Das Problem *der immer größer werdenden Bevölkerung* muß irgendwie gelöst werden, (10) *sei es durch friedliche Einschränkungen, sei es durch unerwartete Katastrophen.*

11 *Mag Wittgenstein* dem typischen Leser *auch noch so wenig bekannt sein,* ist doch sein Einfluß unter Fachgelehrten außerordentlich groß.

12 *Die seit Jahren bestehenden Begriffe der Politik* waren mit der Jalta-Konferenz und (13) *dem daraus folgenden „kalten Krieg"* völlig umgestaltet.

14 *Die von Henri Bergson entwickelte Theorie des Humors* (15) *wird Freud wohl gut gekannt haben*.

16 Die Erstaufführung von Strawinskijs **Frühlingsweihe** (1913) erregte großes Aufsehen in Paris, *war doch ihre ausgesprochene Sensualität dem damaligen Geschmack ganz fremd*.

17 *Nächsten Sommer feiert die Heinrich Heine-Gesellschaft* ihr hundertjähriges Jubiläum.

18 *Viele Kritiker werden* den **Doktor Faustus** von Thomas Mann *gelesen haben,* ohne (19) *die darin gelegten autobiographischen Züge* zu erkennen.

20 Präsident Kennedys Tod wurde besonders stark in West Berlin beweint; *war er doch* (21) *dafür verantwortlich, daß diese Stadt* frei und lebendig *geblieben war*.

22 *Schon seit Jahren werden die besten Kamera-Objektive* in Deutschland *hergestellt*.

23 *Das noch zu besprechende Thema* wird uns wieder auf die Frage der Gerechtigkeit bringen.

24 Chamberlain *war schon seit langem der Meinung,* daß die Frage der europäischen Spannungen nicht auf dem Schlachtfeld zu lösen sei.
25 Das vollständigste Wörterbuch der englischen Sprache ist *das von der Oxford-Universität herausgegebene* **Oxford English Dictionary**.

Working Vocabulary

abendländisch western, occidental

die Aufgabe, -n task, assignment

das Aufsehen commotion, sensation

außerordentlich exceptional, extraordinary; *das Außerordentliche* the extraordinary fact, circumstances (for declension see Appendix §73)

ausgesprochen explicit

aus·sprechen (i), a, o express, articulate; *sich gegen etwas aussprechen* speak out against something

die Bedeutung, -en meaning, significance

der Begriff, -e concept, notion

bekannt known; *bekannt machen* announce; *bekannt sein* be (generally) known

berühmt famous, well-known

besprechen (i), a, o discuss

bestehen, bestand, bestanden exist, be; *in etwas bestehen* consist in something, lie in something

die Bevölkerung, -en population

beweinen mourn, lament

damalig of that time

die Darstellung, -en presentation, representation

der Einfluß, ̈(ss)e influence

die Einschränkung, -en restriction, limitation

entwickeln develop

das Ereignis, -se event, occurrence, fact

erkennen, erkannte, erkannt recognize

erklären explain, declare, pronounce; *erklären für* pronounce to be, define as

erregen arouse, excite, cause

die Erstaufführung, -en premiere, first presentation (of a drama, etc.)

der Fachgelehrte expert, specialist, scholar (for declension see Appendix §73)

fallen (ä), fiel, a fall; *es fällt mir schwer* it is difficult for me

feiern celebrate, observe

fremd foreign, strange, new

friedlich peaceful

die Frühlingsweihe "Rite of Spring" (composition by Igor Stravinsky)

gelungen successful, good

die Gerechtigkeit, -en justice, justification

der Geschmack, ̈e taste, flavor

die Gesellschaft, -en society, organization

sich gewöhnen (an) become accustomed (to), get used (to)

der Glückwunsch, ̈e congratulation, felicitation

die Grundlage, -n foundation, basis

heraus·geben (i), a, e publish, edit

der Herausgeber, — editor

her·stellen manufacture, produce

hundertjährig centenary, centennial

irgendwie somehow

das Jubiläum anniversary, celebration

das Kamera-Objektiv, -e camera lens

kennen, kannte, gekannt know, be acquainted with

die Kulturgeschichte, -n cultural history

der Künstler, — artist

der Lauf, ̈e course, flow

lebendig alive

legen put, place, lay

der Leser, — reader

lösen solve, resolve

der Maler, — painter

manchmal sometimes, from time to time, not infrequently

die Meinung, -en opinion; *der Meinung sein* be of the opinion

nahe·bringen, ·brachte, ·gebracht bring close (to); *einem etwas nahebringen* make something accessible to someone

das Objektiv, -e (camera) lens, objective, focus

offenbar apparent, evident, obvious

ruhen rest; *ruhen auf* be based on

das Schlachtfeld, -er battlefield

die Schrift, -en writing(s), work(s)

schwer difficult (see *fallen*)

selbst self, even

der *Sinn, -e* purpose, meaning, sense

sorgen care for, worry about; *für etwas*

sorgen take care of, look after

die *Spannung, -en* tension, conflict

das *Thema, Themen* theme, topic, subject

überzeugen convince

um·gestalten revise, restructure, re-define

unerwartet unexpected

verantwortlich responsible

vergessen (i), a, e forget, neglect

die *Verlobung, -en* betrothal, engagement

vernünftig rational, logical, reasonable

völlig completely

vollständig complete, full

der *Zug, ̈-e* trait, feature, element, train

GRAMMATICAL APPENDIX

The Functions of the Cases

55 / The nominative case

The nominative is the case of the subject, the predicate nominative, and the noun of address.

Der Mensch ist sterblich.	*Man* is mortal.
Pasteur war *ein großer Forscher.*	Pasteur was *a great researcher.*
Lieber Koch, . . .	*Dear Koch,* . . .

56 / The accusative case

The accusative is:

a / the case of the direct object of the verb

Der Kranke hat oft *keinen Appetit.*	A sick person often has *no appetite.*

b / the case of the object of certain prepositions and postpositions
   - always (automatically) after: *bis, durch, für, gegen, ohne, um*;[1]
   - always before the postposition: *entlang*;[1]
   - when the intention is to give information about destination after: *an, auf, hinter, in, neben, über, unter, vor, zwischen.*[1]

c / used idiomatically to express definite time and measure
   - Examples of the accusative used to express definite time:

Jeden Tag gehe ich . . .	*Every day* I go . . .
Nächstes Jahr arbeiten wir . . .	*Next year* we will work . . .
Den vierten Juli feiern wir den Unab-hängigkeitstag.	*On the fourth of July* we celebrate Independence Day.

   - Examples of the accusative used to express measure:

Er arbeitet *den ganzen Tag.*	He works *the whole day.*
Der Kasten war *einen halben Meter* breit.	The box was *half a meter* wide.

57 / The dative case

The dative is:

a / the case of reference. It indicates who or what is affected by an action (indirect object, dative of interest); it tells in respect to whom or what a statement is true or a comparison may be made (dative of reference).

[1]For meanings of prepositions and postpositions, see §85.

The dative may, therefore, be translated in several ways. *Dem Stoff* is rendered variously as: *the substance, to the substance, from* or *for the substance.* In some instances, as in the last example below, the dative in German is the equivalent of a possessive form in English.

Man wollte *ihr* keine geldliche Unter- stützung geben.	They would not give *her* any financial support.
Dieser Stoff ist *jenem* sehr ähnlich.	This substance is very like *that one.*
Wir sind *diesen Forschern* sehr dankbar.	We are very grateful *to these research- ers.*
Die Arbeit ist *ihm* zu schwer.	The work is too hard *for him.*
Man nahm *ihnen* alles.	Everything was taken *from them.*
Er warf *dem Patienten* einen Lichtstrahl in die Augen.	He threw a ray of light into *the patient's* eyes.

b / the case of the objects of certain prepositions and postpositions. It is used:
- always (automatically) after: *aus, außer, bei, gegenüber, mit, nach, samt, seit, von, zu;*[1]
- always before the postpositions: *entgegen, gegenüber, nach;*[1]
- when the intention is to express location, after: *an, auf, hinter, in, neben, über, unter, vor, zwischen.*[1]

c / the case of the objects of certain special verbs
- *antworten* (answer), *befehlen* (command), *begegnen* (meet), *danken* (thank), *dienen* (serve), *drohen* (threaten), *folgen* (follow), *gefallen* (please), *gehören* (belong to), *gehorchen* (obey), *gelingen* (succeed, be possible), *glauben* (believe), *helfen* (help), *nützen* (be of use), *passen* (fit, suit), *raten* (advise), *schaden* (harm), *schmeicheln* (flatter), *trauen* (trust), *trotzen* (defy).

58 / The genitive case

The genitive:

a / denotes possession. But it is also used to express a great many other relationships (source, quality, agent, etc.). It is the equivalent of English possessive *'s* and many uses of the preposition *of.*

Franklin*s* Versuche	Franklin*'s* attempts
der Erreger *der* Seuche	the excitant *of the* disease
der Druck *der* Luftsäule	the pressure *of the* column of air
Dinge *dieser* Art	things *of this* kind

---

[1]For meanings of prepositions and postpositions, see §85.

b / is the case of the objects of certain prepositions and postpositions. It is used
- regularly with: *anstatt, statt, außerhalb, innerhalb, oberhalb, unterhalb, diesseit(s), jenseit(s), infolge, mittels, vermittels, trotz, während, wegen, um . . . willen;*[1]
- regularly before the postpositions: *halben, halber, wegen.*[1]

c / is used with many adjectives

Man war sich *dessen bewußt.* People were *aware of that.*
Er war *seiner Sache gewiß.* He was *sure of his case (of himself).*

d / is used idiomatically in certain adverbial expressions

Eines Tages war er weg. *One day* he was gone.
eines Abends (Morgens, etc.) . . . *One evening (morning,* etc.) . . .
letzten Endes . . . *In the final analysis* . . .

Declension of the Noun and Noun Modifiers

59 / Forms of the noun modifiers[2]

a / The definite article: *der, das, die; die* (the)

	MASCULINE	NEUTER	FEMININE	PLURAL
NOM.	der	das	die	die
ACC.	den	das	die	die
DAT.	dem	dem	der	den
GEN.	des	des	der	der

b / The *dieser*-words: *all-* (all), *dieser* (this, these), *jener* (that, those), *jeder* (each, every), *welcher* (which, what), *mancher* (many a, some), *solcher* (such a, such)

	MASCULINE	NEUTER	FEMININE	PLURAL
NOM.	dieser	dieses	diese	diese
ACC.	diesen	dieses	diese	diese
DAT.	diesem	diesem	dieser	diesen
GEN.	dieses	dieses	dieser	dieser

---

[1]For meanings of prepositions and postpositions, see §85.
[2]See also Unit Five, §13.

c / The *ein*-words: *ein* (a, an), *kein* (no, not any), *mein* (my), *unser* (our), *sein* (his, its), *ihr* (her, its, their), *dein* (your *singular*), *euer* (your *plural*), *Ihr* (your *singular and plural*)

	MASCULINE	NEUTER	FEMININE	PLURAL
NOM.	ein, kein	ein, kein	ein*e*, kein*e*	kein*e*
ACC.	ein*en*, kein*en*	ein, kein	ein*e*, kein*e*	kein*e*
DAT.	ein*em*, kein*em*	ein*em*, kein*em*	ein*er*, kein*er*	kein*en*
GEN.	ein*es*, kein*es*	ein*es*, kein*es*	ein*er*, kein*er*	kein*er*

60 / Forms of the nouns[1]

a / The singular of the feminine noun

- A feminine noun never adds any case ending in the singular.
- Typical illustrations of the feminine declension are:

NOM.	*die* Hand	dies*e* Ehre	kein*e* Kraft
ACC.	*die* Hand	dies*e* Ehre	kein*e* Kraft
DAT.	*der* Hand	dies*er* Ehre	kein*er* Kraft
GEN.	*der* Hand	dies*er* Ehre	kein*er* Kraft

b / The singular of the neuter noun

- The neuter noun regularly adds -*(e)s* in the genitive singular.
- Often the ending -*e* is added in the dative singular of monosyllabic neuter nouns. It also occurs occasionally in the dative of certain polysyllabic nouns.
- Typical illustrations of the neuter declension are:

NOM.	*das* Atom	dies*es* Buch	ein Erlebnis
ACC.	*das* Atom	dies*es* Buch	ein Erlebnis
DAT.	*dem* Atom	dies*em* Buch*e*	ein*em* Erlebnis*(se)*
GEN.	*des* Atoms	dies*es* Buch*es*	ein*es* Erlebnis*ses*

c / The singular of the masculine noun

Masculine nouns must be considered in two groups: those which add -*(e)s* in the genitive singular, and those which add -*(e)n* or -*ns* in the genitive singular.

Masculine nouns with -*(e)s* genitive singular

- Most masculine nouns regularly add -*(e)s* in the genitive singular.
- Monosyllabic masculines of this group often add -*e* in the dative singular.
- Typical illustrations of this group are:

NOM.	*der* Teil	dies*er* Vorgang	ein Körper
ACC.	*den* Teil	dies*en* Vorgang	ein*en* Körper
DAT.	*dem* Teil*e*	dies*em* Vorgang*(e)*	ein*em* Körper
GEN.	*des* Teil*es*	dies*es* Vorgang*(e)s*	ein*es* Körper*s*

[1]For nouns formed from adjectives and verbs, see §73 and §102.

Masculine nouns with -*(e)n* or -*(e)ns* genitive singular

- A few masculine nouns add -*(e)n* or -*ns* in the genitive singular.
- These nouns all add -*(e)n* in the accusative and dative singular (and throughout the plural).
- Typical illustrations of this group are:

NOM.	*der* Affe	*dieser* Mensch	ein Name
ACC.	*den* Affe*n*	*diesen* Mensch*en*	ein*en* Name*n*
DAT.	*dem* Affe*n*	*diesem* Mensch*en*	ein*em* Name*n*
GEN.	*des* Affe*n*	*dieses* Mensch*en*	ein*es* Name*ns*

d / The plural forms of nouns

Formation of the plural form of the noun

There are several ways of forming the plural in German. Using the nominative singular as the base, the most frequent are:

- Add no ending, perhaps ⸚: *der Wagen, die Wagen; der Apfel, die Äpfel; das Messer, die Messer; die Mutter, die Mütter.*
- Add -*e*, perhaps ⸚: *der Hund, die Hunde; der Arm, die Arme; der Arzt, die Ärzte; das Jahr, die Jahre; die Hand, die Hände.*
- Add -*er*, ⸚ if possible: *der Mann, die Männer; das Buch, die Bücher; das Ei, die Eier.*
- Add -*(e)n*, no ⸚: *der Affe, die Affen; der Bär, die Bären; der Doktor, die Doktoren; das Ohr, die Ohren; die Frau, die Frauen; die Säure, die Säuren; die Entdeckung, die Entdeckungen.*
- Drop a final -*um*, -*on*, -*us*, and add -*en*: *das Museum, die Museen; das Individuum, die Individuen; das Stadion, die Stadien; der Globus, die Globen.*
- Add -*ien*: *das Fossil, die Fossilien; das Mineral, die Mineralien.*
- Add -*s*: *das Auto, die Autos; das Restaurant, die Restaurants.*

Declension of the plural

- There is a common plural declension for all genders.
- In the plural the noun adds a case ending only in the dative case. All plural nouns except those ending in -*n* or -*s* add -*n* in the dative case.
- Typical illustrations of the plural declension are:

SING..	NOM.	der Wagen	dieses Messer	keine Hand
PLURAL:	NOM.	*die* Wagen	dies*e* Messer	kein*e* Hände
	ACC.	*die* Wagen	dies*e* Messer	kein*e* Hände
	DAT.	*den* Wagen	dies*en* Messer*n*	kein*en* Hände*n*
	GEN.	*der* Wagen	dies*er* Messer	kein*er* Hände

SING.:	NOM.	die Säure	der Mann	das Auto
PLURAL:	NOM:	*die* Säuren	*die* Männer	*die* Autos
	ACC.	*die* Säuren	*die* Männer	*die* Autos
	DAT.	*den* Säuren	*den* Männer*n*	*den* Autos
	GEN.	*der* Säuren	*der* Männer	*der* Autos

61 / Nouns in the dictionary or vocabulary

There are two conventional ways of listing nouns in dictionaries and vocabularies.

a / The traditional way of listing masculine and neuter nouns in dictionaries and vocabularies is to give the nominative singular and indicate the genitive ending and plural form.

> *der Apfel, -s, "*   der Apfel, des Apfels, die Äpfel
> *der Mensch, -en, -en*   der Mensch, des Menschen, die Menschen
> *das Atom, -s, -e*   das Atom, des Atoms, die Atome
> *das Studium, -s, -ien*   das Studium, des Studiums, die Studien

Entries for feminine nouns will normally give only the nominative singular and indicate the plural form. The editor of the dictionary or vocabulary usually omits any indication of the feminine genitive since the feminine noun never changes in the singular.

> *die Hand, "e*   die Hand, die Hände
> *die Nase, -n*   die Nase, die Nasen

b / Many modern texts and dictionaries list the nominative singular and indicate only the plural for most nouns. The editors of these books assume the reader knows: (1) that the feminine noun adds no case ending in the singular, and (2) that masculine and neuter nouns generally add *-s* or *-es* in the genitive singular. Only when a noun is irregular do these editors indicate the genitive.

> *der Mann, "er*   der Mann (*genitive*: des Mannes), die Männer
> *das Jahr, -e*   das Jahr (*genitive*: des Jahres), die Jahre
> *die Säure, -n*   die Säure (*genitive*: der Säure), die Säuren
> *der Mensch, (-en), -en*   der Mensch (*genitive*: des Menschen[1]), die Menschen
> *der Same, (-ns), -n*   der Same (*genitive*: des Samens[1]), die Samen

Forms of the Pronouns

62 / The personal pronouns

	I, me	*we, us*	*you* (sing.)	*you* (pl.)	*you* (sing. and pl.)
NOM.	ich	wir	du	ihr	Sie
ACC.	mich	uns	dich	euch	Sie
DAT.	mir	uns	dir	euch	Ihnen
GEN.	meiner[2]	unser[2]	deiner[2]	euer[2]	Ihrer[2]

[1]Therefore, the accusative and dative end in *-(e)n!* See §60, c.
[2]Occur seldom.

	he, him; it	*it*	*she, her; it*	*they, them*
NOM.	er	es	sie	sie
ACC.	ihn	es	sie	sie
DAT.	ihm	ihm	ihr	ihnen
GEN.	seiner[1]	seiner[1]	ihrer[1]	ihrer[1]

63 / The demonstrative and relative pronoun *der, das, die; die*

For uses and translations of this pronoun, see Unit Ten , §30.

	MASCULINE	NEUTER	FEMININE	PLURAL
NOM.	der	das	die	die
ACC.	den	das	die	die
DAT.	dem	dem	der	denen
GEN.	dessen	dessen	deren	deren, derer

Note   The genitive plural form *derer* is generally used only when followed by a dependent relative clause.

64 / The interrogative and relative pronouns *wer* and *was*

See Unit Ten, §31 for uses and translations of these pronouns.

NOM.	wer	was
ACC.	wen	was
DAT.	wem	—
GEN.	wessen	wessen

65 / Pronouns formed from *dieser*-words

Typical is:

	MASCULINE	NEUTER	FEMININE	PLURAL
NOM.	dies*er*	dies*es*	dies*e*	dies*e*
ACC.	dies*en*	dies*es*	dies*e*	dies*e*
DAT.	dies*em*	dies*em*	dies*er*	dies*en*
GEN.	dies*es*	dies*es*	dies*er*	dies*er*

[1]Occur seldom.

As pronouns the *dies*-words have the following meanings:

> *dieser* — this one, the latter
> *jeder* — each one, every one
> *solcher* — such a one (person); *plural*: such, such things (people)
> *jener* — that one, the former
> *mancher* — many a one (person); *plural*: some things (people)
> *welcher* — which, which one, what; *plural*: which, which ones

66 / Pronouns formed from *ein*-words

There are three ways of forming pronouns from *ein*-words:

a / by adding the endings of the *dieser*-words. Typical is:

	MASCULINE	NEUTER	FEMININE	PLURAL
NOM.	kein*er*	kein*es* (kein*s*)	kein*e*	kein*e*
ACC.	kein*en*	kein*es* (kein*s*)	kein*e*	kein*e*
DAT.	kein*em*	kein*em*	kein*er*	kein*en*
GEN.	kein*es*	kein*es*	kein*er*	kein*er*

b / by prefixing the definite article and declining the *ein*-word as an adjective. Typical is:

	MASCULINE	NEUTER	FEMININE	PLURAL
NOM.	*der* mein*e*	*das* mein*e*	*die* mein*e*	*die* mein*en*
ACC.	*den* mein*en*	*das* mein*e*	*die* mein*e*	*die* mein*en*
DAT.	*dem* mein*en*	*dem* mein*en*	*der* mein*en*	*den* mein*en*
GEN.	*des* mein*en*	*des* mein*en*	*der* mein*en*	*der* mein*en*

c / by prefixing the definite article and using an adjective form derived from the *ein*-word through adding the suffix *-ig*. Typical is:

	MASCULINE	NEUTER	FEMININE	PLURAL
NOM.	*der* uns*rige*	*das* uns*rige*	*die* uns*rige*	*die* uns*rigen*
ACC.	*den* uns*rigen*	*das* uns*rige*	*die* uns*rige*	*die* uns*rigen*
DAT.	*dem* uns*rigen*	*dem* uns*rigen*	*der* uns*rigen*	*den* uns*rigen*
GEN.	*des* uns*rigen*	*des* uns*rigen*	*der* uns*rigen*	*der* uns*rigen*

The meanings of the pronouns formed from *ein*-words are:

> *einer, der eine* (etc.) — one
> *keiner* (etc.) — none
> *meiner, der meine, der meinige* (etc.) — mine

For the other possessive pronouns corresponding to *meiner* the English equivalents are: *ours, yours, his, hers, its, theirs.*

Declension of Adjectives

67 / Predicate adjectives

Predicate adjectives add no case endings.

68 / Adjectives before nouns: types of endings

Adjectives before nouns have case endings. There are two main types of declensional endings for the adjective: (1) strong, which indicate case, number, and gender of the noun; and (2) weak, which are essentially neutral. These endings are:

a / Strong adjective endings

	MASCULINE	NEUTER	FEMININE	PLURAL
NOM.	-er	-es	-e	-e
ACC.	-en	-es	-e	-e
DAT.	-em	-em	-er	-en
GEN.	-en[1]	-en[1]	-er	-er

b / Weak adjective endings

	MASCULINE	NEUTER	FEMININE	PLURAL
NOM.	-e	-e	-e	-en
ACC.	-en	-e	-e	-en
DAT.	-en	-en	-en	-en
GEN.	-en	-en	-en	-en

69 / Use of the strong adjective endings

The strong adjective endings are used when there is no preceding noun modifier or when the preceding noun modifier lacks a characteristic case ending. The one exception is the genitive of the masculine and neuter singular. Here the noun itself has a characteristic ending *(-s)*; the adjective, therefore, takes a weak ending.

	MASCULINE	NEUTER	FEMININE	PLURAL
NOM.	stark*er* Wein	kalt*es* Wasser	frisch*e* Milch	wenig*e* Leute
ACC.	stark*en* Wein	kalt*es* Wasser	frisch*e* Milch	wenig*e* Leute
DAT.	stark*em* Weine	kalt*em* Wasser	frisch*er* Milch	wenig*en* Leute*n*
GEN.	stark*en* Wein*es*	kalt*en* Wasser*s*	frisch*er* Milch	wenig*er* Leute
NOM.	ein stark*er* Wein	ein klein*es* Teilchen		
ACC.		ein klein*es* Teilchen		

[1]See §69 below.

70 / Use of the weak adjective endings

The weak adjective endings are used when there is a preceding noun modifier with a characteristic case ending (cf. §69 above). The weak adjective ending is, therefore, used always after the definite article and *dieser*-words, but after *ein*-words only when the latter have characteristic case endings.

	MASCULINE	NEUTER	FEMININE
NOM.	der gut*e* Arzt	das leichter *e* Gas	die ganz*e* Reihe
ACC.	den gut*en* Arzt	das leichter *e* Gas	die ganz*e* Reihe
DAT.	dem gut*en* Arzt	dem leichter *en* Gase	der ganz*en* Reihe
GEN.	des gut*en* Arztes	des leichter *en* Gases	der ganz*en* Reihe

	MASCULINE	NEUTER	FEMININE
NOM.	*(See §69 above)*	*(See §69 above)*	seine ganz*e* Reihe
ACC.	einen gut*en* Arzt	*(See §69 above)*	seine ganz*e* Reihe
DAT.	einem gut*en* Arzt	keinem leichter *en* Gase	seiner ganz*en* Reihe
GEN.	eines gut*en* Arztes	keines leichter *en* Gases	seiner ganz*en* Reihe

	PLURAL	PLURAL
NOM.	die best*en* Mittel	ihre best*en* Mittel
ACC.	die best*en* Mittel	ihre best*en* Mittel
DAT.	den best*en* Mitteln	ihren best*en* Mitteln
GEN.	der best*en* Mittel	ihrer best*en* Mittel

71 / Adjectives in a series

Adjectives in a series have identical case endings.

ein besser*es*, leichter*es* Gas   eine glücklicher*e*, besser*e* Zukunft

72 / The ordinals

The ordinals are adjectival numbers indicating order, rank, or succession. Except for *erst-* (first), *dritt-* (third), and *acht-* (eighth), they are formed by adding *-t-* to the cardinal numbers through *neunzehn*, *-st-* from *zwanzig* on. The ordinal for *sieben* may also be formed by adding *-t* to the stem only: *siebt-*.

An ordinal is declined like any other adjective.

der ers*te* Forscher	the first researcher
ein fünf*tes* Beispiel	a fifth example
die neunzehn*te* Aufgabe	the nineteenth lesson
des zwanzig*sten* Versuches	of the twentieth experiment

In written German, ordinals may be abbreviated by using the cardinal number punctuated with a period.

Karl *V.* (. . . *der* Fünft*e*)   Karl the fifth
in dem *19.* Jahrhundert (in *dem* neun-   in the nineteenth century
    zehnt*en* . . .)

73 / Adjectives as nouns

Nouns may be formed from adjectives. Such nouns take an appropriate gender, depending on reference. The adjective is capitalized. But in its declension the adjective-noun follows the same rules that govern the ordinary adjective.

der Krank*e*   the sick man (person), patient
ein Krank*er*   a sick man (person)
wegen *der* Krank*en*   because of the sick woman, because
                                                              of the sick people

Neuter nouns formed from adjectives often have a general or abstract meaning. Sometimes no one English word is the equivalent of such a noun.

das Gute   the good, that which is good, the good
                                                              part (aspect, etc.)
das Neue   that which is new
etwas Schönes   something beautiful
alles Gute   everything (that is) good

Adjectives and Adverbs: Comparison and Idioms

74 / The adjective and adverb

In German the same word may be used as either adjective or adverb.

Er ist ein *guter* Mensch.   He is a *good* person.
Er macht die Arbeit *gut.*   He does the work *well.*

75 / Comparison of adjectives and adverbs

The comparative of an adjective or adverb is formed by adding *-er*, the superlative by adding *-(e)st-*.

neu   gründlich
neu*er*   gründlich*er*
neu*est-*   gründlich*st-*

Some adjectives and adverbs also modify the stem vowel in the comparative and superlative.

j*u*ng   k*a*lt
j*ü*ng*er*   k*ä*lter
j*ü*ng*st-*   k*ä*ltest-

There are two forms of the superlative. One is only adjectival; the other functions both
as adverb and adjective.

● adjective only: der jüngste, die jüngste, das jüngste
● adjective and adverb: *am* gründlichst*en, am* schönst*en*

76 / Irregular adjectives and adverbs

Some adjectives and adverbs have irregular comparison.

good	gut	besser	am besten; der (das, die) beste
high	hoch (hoh-)	höher	am höchsten; der (das, die) höchste
near	nah	näher	am nächsten; der (das, die) nächste
much	viel	mehr	am meisten; der (das, die) meiste
willingly	gern(e)*	lieber*	am liebsten*

Gern, lieber, am liebsten are used to express the degree of pleasure with which one
engages in some activity.

Er arbeitet gern.   He likes to work.

Er liest lieber.   He would rather read.
                                    He prefers to read.

Er liest am liebsten.   He likes best of all to read.
                                    He prefers to read above all else.

77 / Degrees below the positive

To express degrees below the positive German uses *minder* and *weniger, am mindesten*
and *am wenigsten.*

minder erfolgreich   less successful
am wenigsten erfolgreich   least successful

78 / Special uses of the comparative and superlative

The comparative and superlative are used in general just as in English. But both may be
used absolutely, i.e., with implication of only a general instead of a direct comparison.

eine ält*ere* Frau   an elderly lady
ein ält*erer* Herr   an older (rather old) gentleman

eine größ*ere* Summe	a rather large sum
läng*ere* Zeit	quite a long time, for some time
zu günstigs*tem* Preis	at a very favorable price

See also §79, c, i, and j.

79 / Some common idioms with adjectives and adverbs

a / *Etwas* (something) with an adjective or adverb means *somewhat*.

etwas teuer	somewhat expensive
etwas schneller	somewhat faster

b / *Zu* with the positive of the adjective or adverb means *too*.

zu heiß	too hot
zu schnell	too fast, too quickly

c / *Sehr, höchst, äußerst* are used with the positive form of the adjective or adverb to express a high degree of the quality.

sehr groß	very large
höchst interessant	most (very) interesting
äußerst spät	exceedingly late

d / *So . . . auch* is the equivalent of English: *as . . . as, however . . . , no matter how . . .*

So sehr er es *auch* will . . .	*However much* he wants to . . .
So groß der Unterschied *auch* ist . . .	*However (no matter how) great* the difference is . . . *As great as* the difference is . . .

e / *Wie* and *als* (or *denn*) are used respectively for *as* and *than* in making comparisons.

so groß *wie* möglich	*as* large *as* possible
Dieser ist größer *als (denn)* jener.	This one is larger *than* that one.

f / *So* in comparison very often means *as*. See illustrations for *d* and *e*.

g / *Immer* plus a comparative expresses continuing increase in degree.

immer größer	larger and larger, ever larger

h / *Je . . . je; je . . . desto; je . . . um so* are the equivalents of English *the* (larger), *the* (better); *the* (larger), *so much the* (better).

Je größer das Volumen, *je kleiner* der Druck.	*The larger* the volume, *the smaller* the pressure.
Je billiger, desto (um so) besser.	*The cheaper, (so much) the better.*

i / *Aufs (auf das)* with a superlative is used to express a high degree without a specific comparison.

Er schreibt *aufs schönste.*	He writes *as beautifully as is possible.*
	He writes *very beautifully indeed.*

j / *Aller-* as a prefix to a superlative means *of all* or *very.*

das *allerkleinste* Tier . . .	The *smallest* animal *of all* . . .
eine *allerliebste* Blume	a *very pretty* flower *indeed*

Prepositions and Postpositions

80 / Case of prepositional objects

The objects of prepositions are in the accusative, dative, or genitive case, namely:

a / With following accusative object: *bis, durch, für, gegen, ohne, um.*[1]

b / With following dative object: *aus, außer, bei, gegenüber, mit, nach, samt, seit, von, zu.*[1]

c / With following genitive object: *anstatt, statt, außerhalb, innerhalb, oberhalb, unterhalb, diesseit(s), jenseit(s), infolge, mittels, vermittels, trotz, während, wegen, um . . . willen.*[1]

d / With following object in either the accusative or dative cases: *an, auf, hinter, in, neben, über, unter, vor, zwischen.*[1]

When the prepositions in *d* above are followed by an object in the dative case, the intention is to express location. When they are followed by an object in the accusative case, the intention is to express destination.

1	Er wanderte in *der* Stadt umher.	He wandered *about in* the city.
	Er wanderte in *die* Stadt.	He wandered *into* the city.
2	Man gießt das Wasser in *der* Wanne aus.	One pours out the water *which is in* the tub.
	Man gießt das Wasser in *die* Wanne aus.	One pours the water out *into* the tub.

[1]For meanings, see §85.

81 / Postpositions

There are also a few important postpositions, i.e., preposition-like words which follow the noun or prounoun:

- with preceding accusative: *entlang*[1]
- with preceding dative: *entgegen, gegenüber, nach*[1]
- with preceding genitive: *halben, halber, wegen.*[1]

82 / Prefixes with prepositions[2]

Instead of using a pronoun object with a preposition, German often substitutes a prefix for the pronoun. This substitution takes place when the reference is to an inanimate object. The most frequent such prefixes are:

- *da*(r)- meaning *it* or *them; that; there-*.

damit	with it, with them; with that
darin	in it, in them; in that; therein
dadurch	through it, through them; through that; thereby

- *hier-* meaning *this; that; here-*.

hiermit	with this; with that; herewith
hierin	in this; in that; herein

- *wo(r)-* meaning *what; which; where-*.

Womit?	With what?
Ein Stoff, worin . . .	A substance in which . . .

83 / Contractions

There are contractions of some prepositions with certain forms of the definite article:

am	= an dem	*im*	= in dem
ans	= an das	*ins*	= in das
aufs	= auf das	*vom*	= von dem
beim	= bei dem	*zum*	= zu dem
fürs	= für das	*zur*	= zu der

[1]For meanings, see §85.
[2]See also Unit Ten, §32.

84 / Prepositions introducing infinitive phrases

Three prepositions, *(an)statt, ohne,* and *um,* frequently introduce an infinitive phrase. Note in the illustrations below the translation of the German infinitive *(-en)* with an English gerund *(-ing).*

Anstatt diese Ansicht *anzunehmen* . . .	*Instead of accepting* this view . . .
Ohne diese Ansicht verteidigen *zu wollen* . . .	*Without wanting* to defend this view . . .
Um auf diesem Gebiete weitere Fortschritte *zu machen* . . .	*(In order) To make* further progress in this field . . .

85 / Meanings of the prepositions and postpositions

The meanings of the prepositions and postpositions are frequently highly idiomatic. In the following the primary meanings of each preposition are given next to this word. But note in each case the idiomatic meanings illustrated.

For convenience in reference the prepositions are here listed alphabetically.

an (dative, accusative) at, on, to

Er geht an das Fenster.	He goes *to* the window.
Er sitzt an dem Fenster.	He is sitting *at* the window.
Das Bild an der Wand	The picture *on* the wall
Das Ding ist an sich nicht neu.	*In* itself (essentially) the thing is not new.
am Mittwoch	*on* Wednesday
am Tage	*in* the day time
Das Land ist reich an Mineralien.	The country is rich *in* minerals.
Ich denke an ihn.	I am thinking *of* him.
Er starb an der Tuberkulose.	He died *of* tuberculosis.

anstatt (genitive) instead of

auf (dative, accusative) on, upon

Er liegt auf dem Bett.	He is lying *on* the bed.
Er setzte sich auf den Stuhl.	He sat down *on* the chair.
Er ist auf dem Lande.	He is *in* the country.
Er geht auf das Land.	He is going *to* the country.
Er ist taub auf einem Ohr.	He is deaf *in* one ear.
Er ist auf der Schule.	He is *at* school.
Auf diesem Gebiet	*In* this line of study (field, etc.)
Er ist stolz auf seine Arbeit.	He is proud *of* his work.
Er freut sich darauf.	He is looking forward *to* it.
Darauf . . .	There*upon* . . . There*after* . . .
Er prüft das Metall auf seine Härte.	He is testing the metal *as to (to determine)* its hardness.

Er prüft das Erz auf Gold.	He is testing the ore *for (to see whether it contains)* gold.
In Bezug auf das Atom	With respect *to,* as *for* the atom . . .
Er geht auf 14 Tage weg.	He is going away *for* a couple of weeks
Auf diese Weise	*In* this way
Auf jeden Fall	*In* any case

aus (dative) out of

aus der Wanne	*out of (from)* the tub
aus London	*from* London
aus der Erfahrung	*from* experience (source of knowledge)
aus diesem Grunde	*for* this reason (motive)
aus Versehen	*by* mistake (origin)
aus Gold	*(made) of* gold (material)

außer (dative) besides, except

niemand außer Freud	no one *except* Freud
außerdem	*besides, in addition*
außer dieser Entdeckung	*except for* this discovery, *in addition to* this discovery
außer Zweifel	*beyond* doubt
außer dem Hause	*out of* doors

außerhalb (genitive) outside of

bei (dative) generally denotes nearness, neighborhood or accompanying circumstance. See below.

bei dieser Temperatur	*at* this temperature
bei Leipzig	*near* Leipzig
bei dem Verbrennen	*in the process of* combustion, *in* burning
bei diesen Vorgängen	*in, in the case of* these processes
bei chemischen Veränderungen	*in connection with* chemical changes
dabei	*in the process, in so doing*
bei diesem Experiment	*in the course of, while making* this experiment
Er wohnt bei ihnen.	He is living *at* their *house, with* them.
So war es auch bei dieser Entdeckung.	Thus it was *with (in the case of)* this discovery too.
bei seiner Stärke	*in view (because) of* its strength
Bei allem Fleiß fiel er doch durch.	*With (in spite of)* all his diligence he failed.

bis (accusative) till, until, up to, as far as, as much as

Er bleibt bis nächsten Montag.	He will stay *until* next Monday.
Sie fahren bis Berlin.	They are driving *as far as* Berlin.

Bis occurs often in conjunction with other prepositions.

Er folgte ihm bis zum Rathaus.	He followed him *as far as* the town hall.
Man erhält bis zu 5% Zinsen.	One gets *as much as* 5% interest.

diesseit(s) (genitive) on this side of

durch (accusative) through

Er geht durch das Haus.	He walks *through* the house.
Durch Versuche bewies Faraday . . .	*By means of* experiments Faraday proved . . .
Durch Überanstrengung wird man krank.	One gets sick *through (by, as a result of)* over-work.

entgegen (dative) against, contrary to; towards

entgegen meinen Wünschen	*against* my wishes
dem Befehl entgegen	*contrary to* command
Er kam uns entgegen.	He came to meet us. He met us half way.

entlang (accusative) along

Er ging den Fluß entlang.	He walked *along* the river.

für (accusative) for

Er tut es für ihn.	He is doing it *for* him.
Er bezahlt zu viel für das Buch.	He is paying too much *for* the book.
Ich halte ihn für einen großen Wissenschaftler.	I consider him *as (to be)* a great scientist.

gegen (accusative) against

Er schwimmt gegen den Strom.	He is swimming *against* the current.
Gegen Ende August . . .	*Toward* the end of August . . .
Er machte gegen hundert Versuche.	He made *about* a hundred experiments.
Gegen früher	*In comparison with* earlier (times)

gegenüber (dative) opposite; in contrast to; in relation to, as concerns

gegenüber dem Rathaus	*across from (opposite)* the city hall
der Welt der Materie gegenüber	*in contrast to* the world of matter
Mir gegenüber wagt er es nicht, solche Töne anzuschlagen.	He doesn't dare use that tone *(in his relations with) to* me.

halben, halber (genitive) on account of, for the sake of

des Scheines halber	*for the sake of* appearances
meinethalben	*as far as I am concerned, for all I care*

hinter (accusative, dative) behind, in back of

Er sitzt hinter dem Tisch.	He is sitting *behind* the table.
Er geht hinter das Haus.	He walks *in back of* the house.
viermal hintereinander . . .	four times *in succession,* four times *running*

in (accusative, dative) in, within

Er arbeitet in einer Fabrik.	He is working *in* a factory.
In zwei Tagen ist er weg.	*In* two days he will be gone.
Er geht in die Stadt.	He is going *into* the city.

infolge (genitive) as a result of, as a consequence of

infolge dieser Umstände	*as a result of* these circumstances

innerhalb (genitive) inside of

jenseit(s) (genitive) on that (the other) side of, beyond

mit (dative) with. But note idioms.

mit ihm	*with* him
Mit dem Buche will er . . .	*With (the help of)* the book he wants to . . .
mit einem Worte	*in* a word
mit einem Schlage	*with (at)* one blow
mit Absicht	*on* purpose
mit der Eisenbahn	*by* rail

mittels (genitive) by means of

nach (dative) to; after; according to

nach Berlin	*to* Berlin
Das Fenster geht nach der Straße.	The window faces *toward* the street.
nach zehn Tagen	*after* ten days
Er geht nach dem Arzt.	He is going *for* the doctor.
Er sucht nach der Ursache.	He is looking *for* the cause.
nach dieser Theorie	*according to* this theory
dieser Ansicht nach	*according to* this view
demnach	*accordingly, therefore*
dem Erfolg nach	*judging by* the success
Es riecht nach Rosen.	It smells *of* roses.

neben (accusative, dative) beside, next to

oberhalb (genitive) above, over

ohne (accusative) without (showing lack)

samt (dative) with, together with, along with

seit (dative) since (but see Unit Sixteen, §52)

seit seiner Krankheit	*since* his illness
Er ist seit drei Wochen krank.	He has been sick *for* three weeks.

statt (genitive) instead of

trotz (genitive, occasionally dative) in spite of, despite

über (accusative, dative) over, above; about (concerning)

das Bild über dem Tisch	the picture *above (over)* the table
Das geht über meine Kräfte.	That goes (is) *beyond* my abilities.

Er ging über das Feld.   He went *across* the field.

Er reiste über Stockholm nach Berlin.   He went to Berlin *via (by way of, passing through)* Stockholm.

heute über acht Tage   a week *from* today

Er blieb über acht Tage.   He stayed *more than* eight days.

überdies . . .   moreover . . .

Darüber weiß er nichts.   He knows nothing *about* that.

um (accusative) around, about

Die Planeten bewegen sich um die Sonne.   The planets move *around* the sun.

Er kam um drei Uhr.   He came *at* three o'clock.

Es handelt sich nicht um Geld.   It is not a matter *of* money.

Ich bitte Sie darum.   I am asking you *for* it.

Er ist um acht Mark ärmer.   He is poorer *by* eight marks.

Er ist um so weiser.   He is *that much (so much the)* wiser.

Je weniger, um so besser.   *The* less, *the* better.

darum   therefore

um . . .willen (genitive) for the sake of

um ihres Kindes willen   for the sake of her child

unter (accusative, dative) under, below; among

unter den Tisch   *under* the table

unter ihm   *below (subordinate to)* him

unter dem Einfluß   *under* the influence

unter den Leuten   *among* the people

Er starb unter großen Schmerzen.   He died *in* great pain.

Unter dieser Bezeichnung verstehen wir . . .   *By* this term we mean . . .

unter Verlust von Wärme   *accompanied by (with)* loss of heat

Unter lautem Gelächter verließ er das Zimmer.   He left the room *amidst* loud laughter.

unterhalb (genitive) under, below

vermittels (genitive) by means of

von (dative) from, of, about (concerning)

von Berlin   *from* Berlin

von Tag zu Tag   *from* day to day

von nun an   *from* now on

von oben bis unten   *from* top to bottom (downward)

Dies Buch handelt von großen Forschern.   This book is *about* great research scientists.

Das kommt von der Gicht her.   That is *because of* the gout.

Dieser Vorgang ist von keiner chemischen Veränderung begleitet.   This process is accompanied *by* no chemical change.

vor (accusative, dative) before; ago

vor Gott und der Welt	*before (in the sight of)* God and the world
Er ging vor den Tisch.	He went *in front of* the table.
vor allem	*above* all
vor zehn Jahren	ten years *ago*
vor acht Uhr	*before* eight o'clock
Er hat Angst vor dem Tode.	He has a fear *of* death.
Er kann vor Schmerz nicht schlafen.	He cannot sleep *because of* pain.

während (genitive) during

wegen (genitive, occasionally dative) because of, on account of

wegen des Gewitters	*because of* the storm
der Krankheit wegen	*on account of* sickness
meinetwegen	*as far as I am concerned, for all I care*

zu (dative) to

Er geht zum Arzt.	He is going *to* the doctor.
Was sagt man zu diesem Vorschlag?	What are they saying *to* this proposal?
Der Druck verhält sich zu der Temperatur wie . . .	The pressure has the same relation *to* the temperature as . . .
zu diesem Zweck	*for* this purpose
Es ist zu nichts nütze.	It is useful *for* nothing.
Wozu?	*To* what purpose? *For* what purpose?
Das ist zum Verzweifeln.	That is *enough to (cause one to)* give up all hope.
der Dom zu Köln	the cathedral *at* Cologne
Er geht zu Fuß.	He is going *on* foot.
Er reist zu Schiff.	He is travelling *by* ship.
zu dieser Zeit	*at* this time
zum letzten Male	*for* the last time

zwischen (accusative, dative) between, among

The Indicative of Verbs

German has two main types of verbs:

a / the weak verb, which forms its past by adding *-(e)te* and whose past participle ends in *-(e)t;*

b / the strong verb, which forms its past by changing its stem vowel and whose past participle ends in *-en.*

86 / The present

a / Both strong and weak verbs form the present from the stem of the infinitive. To this stem are added the endings: *-e, -(e)st, -(e)t, -en, -(e)t, -en.*

b / Most strong verbs with the stem-vowels *-e-, -a-, au-, -o-,* modify this vowel in the second and third person singular of the present. The vowel *-e-* becomes *-ie-* or *-i-; -a-* becomes *-ä-; -au-* becomes *-äu-; -o-* becomes *-ö-.*

c / Typical forms of the present are:

	WEAK		STRONG			
INFINITIVE	such*en*	red*en*	sing*en*	fall*en*	seh*en*	nehm*en*
ich	such*e*	red*e*	sing*e*	fall*e*	seh*e*	nehm*e*
du	such*st*	red*est*	sing*st*	fäll*st*	sieh*st*	nimm*st*
er, sie, es	such*t*	red*et*	sing*t*	fäll*t*	sieh*t*	nimm*t*
wir	such*en*	red*en*	sing*en*	fall*en*	seh*en*	nehm*en*
ihr	such*t*	red*et*	sing*t*	fall*t*	seh*t*	nehm*t*
sie (Sie)	such*en*	red*en*	sing*en*	fall*en*	seh*en*	nehm*en*

d / The present in German corresponds to three English verb forms.

Er *sucht.*   He *looks* for.

He *is looking* for.

He *does look* for.

See also Unit Sixteen, §51 and §52.

87 / The past

a / Weak verbs form the past by adding the tense ending *-(e)te* to the infinitive stem. The personal endings are: –, *-st,* –, *-n, -t, -n.*

b / Strong verbs add no tense ending; instead there is a vowel change in the stem. The personal endings are: –, *-(e)st,* –, *-en, -(e)t, -en.*

c / Typical forms of the past are:

	WEAK		STRONG			
INFINITIVE	suchen	reden	singen	fallen	sehen	nehmen
ich	such*te*	red*ete*	*sang*	*fiel*	*sah*	*nahm*
du	such*test*	red*etest*	*sang*st	*fiel*st	*sah*st	*nahm*st
er, sie, es	such*te*	red*ete*	*sang*	*fiel*	*sah*	*nahm*
wir	such*ten*	red*eten*	*sang*en	*fiel*en	*sah*en	*nahm*en
ihr	such*tet*	red*etet*	*sang* t	*fiel* t	*sah* t	*nahm* t
sie (Sie)	such*ten*	red*eten*	*sang*en	*fiel*en	*sah*en	*nahm*en

d / The past in German corresponds to three forms in English:

Er *sang*.   He *sang*.
              He *was singing*.
              He *did sing*.

See also Unit Sixteen, §52.

88 / The present perfect and pluperfect tenses

The perfect and pluperfect tenses in German are formed with the present or past of *sein* or *haben* plus the past participle of the main verb.

a / Formation of the past participle

- The past participle of the weak verb is formed from the stem of the infinitive with the addition of the prefix *ge-* and ending *-(e)t*.

INFINITIVE	suchen	reden	reisen
PAST PARTICIPLE	*gesucht*	*geredet*	*gereist*

- The past participle of the strong verb may have the vowel of the infinitive or of the past. It may also have a vowel different from those of the infinitive and past. The past participle of the strong verb adds the prefix *ge-;* but it adds the ending *-en*.

INFINITIVE	fahren	schließen	singen
PAST	fuhr	schloß	sang
PAST PARTICIPLE	*gefahren*	*geschlossen*	*gesungen*

- If the first syllable of the verb is not stressed, the past participle of both strong and weak verbs omits the *ge-* prefix.

  This condition obtains always when the verb begins with the prefix *be-*, *emp-*, *ent-*, *er-*, *ge-*, *ver-*, or *zer-;* when the following are used as inseparable (unstressed) prefixes: *durch-*, *hinter-*, *über-*, *um-*, *unter-*, *voll-;* and when the verb infinitive ends in *-ieren*.

WEAK:	INFINITIVE	besuchen	studieren	übersetzen
	PAST	besuchte	studierte	übersetzte
	PAST PART.	*besucht*	*studiert*	*übersetzt*
STRONG:	INFINITIVE	verschließen	ertragen	unterbrechen
	PAST	verschloß	ertrug	unterbrach
	PAST PART.	*verschlossen*	*ertragen*	*unterbrochen*

b / The present perfect and pluperfect tenses

- The perfect auxiliary is *sein* with intransitive verbs which indicate a change of place or condition. *Sein* is also the perfect auxiliary with the participles *geblieben* (remained) and *gewesen* (been).[1]

  All other verbs have the perfect auxiliary *haben.*[1]

- The present perfect tense is formed from the present of *sein* or *haben* plus the past participle. The German perfect tense corresponds sometimes to the English perfect, sometimes to the simple past in English.

Er *ist* (sie *sind*) *gewesen.*	He *has* (they *have*) *been.* He *was* (they *were*).
Er *hat* (sie *haben*) *gehabt.*	He *has* (they *have*) *had.* He (they) *had.*
Er *ist* (sie *sind*) *geworden.*	He *has* (they *have*) *become.* He (they) *became.*

- The pluperfect tense is formed from the past of *sein* or *haben* plus the past participle.

Er *war* (sie *waren*) *gewesen.*	He *had* (they *had*) *been.*
Er *hatte* (sie *hatten*) *gehabt.*	He *had* (they *had*) *had.*
Er *war* (sie *waren*) *geworden.*	He *had* (they *had*) *become.*

- See also Unit Three.

89 / The future and future perfect

a / The future

The future is formed from the present of *werden* plus the infinitive of the main verb.

Er *wird* (sie *werden*) *sein.*	He (they) *will be, is (are) going to be.*
Sie *werden haben.*	They *will have, are going to have.*
Er *wird werden.*	He *will become.* He *is going to get.*

b / The future perfect

The future perfect is formed from the present of *werden* plus the uninflected form of the perfect (the perfect infinitive) of the main verb.

Examples of the perfect infinitive are: to have eaten—*gegessen haben;* to have sought—*gesucht haben;* to have travelled—*gereist sein.*

Wir *werden* viel *gelernt haben.*	We *will have learned* a great deal.
Er *wird* größer *geworden sein.*	He *will have grown* taller.
Sie *wird* müde *gewesen sein.*	She *was probably* tired.

See also Unit Four, §11 and Unit Sixteen, §53.

[1]See Unit Three, §8

90 / The passive

The passive in German is formed from the various tenses of *werden* plus the past participle of the verb of action.

> PRESENT:
> Der Versuch *wird* heute *unternommen.*   The experiment *is being made* today.
>
> PAST:
> Die Pläne *wurden* gestern *besprochen.*   The plans *were discussed* yesterday.
>
> FUTURE:
> Er *wird gesucht werden.*   He *will be sought.*

Note   In the perfect tenses of the passive, the past participle *geworden* drops its *ge-* prefix.

> PERFECT:
> Der Versuch *ist* gestern *unternommen*   The experiment *was undertaken* yes-
>   *worden.*   terday.
>
> PLUPERFECT:
> Die Pläne *waren* schon *besprochen*   The plans *had* already *been discussed.*
>   *worden.*
>
> FUTURE PERFECT:
> Der Versuch *wird* öfters *unternommen*   The experiment *will have been under-*
>   *worden sein.*   *taken* frequently.

See also Unit Four, §12.

Forms of the Subjunctive and the Imperative

91 / The subjunctive endings

The subjunctive[1] has the same endings for both weak and strong verbs, and for both the general and special subjunctives (see Unit Eleven).
    These endings are: *-e, -est, -e, -en, -et, -en.*

92 / The general subjunctive

The general subjunctive forms are derived from the past of the indicative. Weak verbs with a regular past have a general subjunctive which is identical with the past. Weak verbs with an irregular past and strong verbs form the general subjunctive from the past by adding umlaut (if possible) and endings (in the case of strong verbs).

[1]For uses and translations of subjunctives, see Units Eleven and Twelve.

	WEAK		IRREGULAR WEAK		STRONG	
INFINITIVE	sagen	reden	können	wissen	tragen	scheinen
PAST	sagte	redete	konnte	wußte	trug	schien

GENERAL SUBJUNCTIVE

	sagte	redete	könnte	wüßte	trüge	schiene
ich	sagte	redete	könnte	wüßte	trüge	schiene
du	sagtest	redetest	könntest	wüßtest	trügest	schienest
er, sie, es	sagte	redete	könnte	wüßte	trüge	schiene
wir	sagten	redeten	könnten	wüßten	trügen	schienen
ihr	sagtet	redetet	könntet	wüßtet	trüget	schienet
sie (Sie)	sagten	redeten	könnten	wüßten	trügen	schienen

93 / The special subjunctive

The special subjunctive is formed by adding the subjunctive endings to the stem of the infinitive.

The first and third person singular of *sein* are the only irregulars in this set of forms. These two forms lack the ending -e: *ich sei, er sei.*

	WEAK		STRONG		IRREGULAR	
INFINITIVE	sagen	reden	finden	schließen	tragen	sein

SPECIAL SUBJUNCTIVE

	sage	rede	finde	schließe	trage	sei*
ich	sage	rede	finde	schließe	trage	sei*
du	sagest	redest	findest	schließest	tragest	seiest*
er, sie, es	sage*	rede*	finde*	schließe*	trage*	sei*
wir	sagen	reden	finden	schließen	tragen	seien*
ihr	saget	redet	findet	schließet	traget	seiet*
sie (Sie)	sagen	reden	finden	schließen	tragen	seien*

*Only these forms of the special subjunctive are in general use. The others are avoided because of their similarity to the forms of the indicative.

94 / Compound forms of the subjunctive

The compound forms of the subjunctive use the general or special subjunctive of the auxiliary plus the present infinitive, perfect infinitive, or past participle of the main verb.

Wenn er das nur *getan hätte!*	If he *had* only *done* that!
Er sagte, daß er da *gewesen sei (wäre).*	He said that he *had been* there.
Das *würde* aber zu weit *führen.*	That *would,* however, *take* us too far afield.

95 / Request and suggestion forms

a / *The imperative.* There are three forms of the imperative. They are almost all formed from the stem of the infinitive (see Note below). The endings are: *-en* followed by the pronoun *Sie, -e, -(e)t.*

Red*en Sie!*	Speak!	Lauf*en Sie!*	Run!	(Polite request, sing. and pl.)
Red*e!*	Speak!	Lauf*e!*	Run!	(Pronoun *du* understood)
Red*et!*	Speak!	Lauf*t!*	Run!	(Pronoun *ihr* understood)

Note   Strong verbs which change *e* to *i* or *ie* in the present (see §86, b) use this *i* or *ie* in the singular familiar *(du-)* form of the imperative. These forms are irregular also in having no ending.

Sehen Sie!	See!	Vergessen Sie!	Forget!
Sieh!	See!	Verg*iß!*	Forget!
Seht!	See!	Vergeßt!	Forget!

b / For other request forms see Unit Seven, §20.

Separable Verb and Reflexive Construction

96 / The separable verb

The separable verb consists of a verb plus a verb modifier. This verb modifier functions as a partially separate element of the compound.

The modifier of the separable verb, like the past participle and the infinitive, tends toward the end of the clause or sentence.

Der Körper *nimmt* Vitamine mit der Nahrung *auf.*	The body *absorbs* vitamins with food.
Die Drüsen *sondern* Hormone *ab.*	The glands *secrete* hormones.
Nehmen wir an, daß das so ist.	*Let us assume* that it is so.

When both verb and verb modifier come at the end of a clause they are written together as one word.

| Man weiß, daß der Körper Vitamine mit der Nahrung *aufnimmt.* | It is known that the body *absorbs* vitamins with food. |
| Das darf man aber nicht *annehmen.* | However, we must not *assume* that. |

But the infinitive preposition *zu* and the past participle prefix *ge-* are inserted between modifier and verb.

| Diese Ansicht braucht man nicht *anzunehmen.* | There is no need *to accept* this view. |
| Was Galilei *angefangen* hatte, setzten seine Schüler fort. | What Galileo had *begun,* his disciples carried forward. |

97 / The reflexive construction

The reflexive construction consists of a subject, a verb, and a pronoun object; the subject and object are the same person or thing.

The reflexive pronoun is in the accusative case after most verbs. Some verbs, however, govern the dative.

The forms of the reflexive pronoun are identical with those of the personal pronoun except in the third person singular and plural. The third person form (singular and plural) of the reflexive pronoun is *sich*. This one form serves for both the dative and accusative cases.

REFLEXIVE WITH ACCUSATIVE		REFLEXIVE WITH DATIVE	
INFINITIVE	sich fühlen *(feel)*	sich schmeicheln *(flatter oneself)*	
ich	fühle *mich*	schmeichle *mir*	
du	fühlst *dich*	schmeichelst *dir*	
er, sie, es	fühlt *sich*	schmeichelt *sich*	
wir	fühlen *uns*	schmeicheln *uns*	
ihr	fühlt *euch*	schmeichelt *euch*	
sie (Sie)	fühlen *sich*	schmeicheln *sich*	

See also Unit Nine.

Irregular Verbs

98 / Tense auxiliaries

For meanings and translations of the tense auxiliaries, see Units Three and Four.

a / *haben*	PRESENT	PAST	OTHER TENSES: TYPICAL FORMS	
ich	habe	hatte	*Future:*	er wird haben
du	hast	hattest	*Perfect:*	er hat gehabt
er, etc.	hat	hatte	*Subjunctive:*	
wir	haben	hatten	*General:*	er hätte
ihr	habt	hattet	*Special:*	er habe
sie (Sie)	haben	hatten	*Request:*	haben Sie, habe, habt; haben wir; habe man, man habe

b /*sein* | PRESENT | PAST | OTHER TENSES: TYPICAL FORMS

	PRESENT	PAST	
ich	bin	war	*Future:* er wird sein
du	bist	warst	*Perfect:* er ist gewesen
er, etc.	ist	war	*Subjunctive:*
wir	sind	waren	*General:* er wäre
ihr	seid	wart	*Special:* er sei, sie seien
sie (Sie)	sind	waren	*Request:* seien Sie, sei, seid; seien wir; sei man, man sei

c / *werden*

	PRESENT	PAST	OTHER TENSES: TYPICAL FORMS
ich	werde	wurde[1]	*Future:* er wird werden
du	wirst	wurdest	*Perfect:* er ist geworden
er, etc.	wird	wurde[1]	*Subjunctive:*
wir	werden	wurden	*General:* er würde
ihr	werdet	wurdet	*Special:* er werde
sie (Sie)	werden	wurden	*Request:* werden Sie, werde, werdet; werden wir; werde man, man werde

99 / Modal auxiliaries

For meanings and translations of the modal auxiliaries, see Unit Eight.

a / *dürfen*

	PRESENT	PAST	OTHER TENSES: TYPICAL FORMS
ich	darf	durfte	*Future:* er wird dürfen
du	darfst	durftest	*Perfect:* er hat gedurft[2]
er, etc.	darf	durfte	er hat es tun dürfen[2]
wir	dürfen	durften	*Subjunctive:*
ihr	dürft	durftet	*General:* er dürfte
sie (Sie)	dürfen	durften	*Special:* er dürfe

b / *können*

	PRESENT	PAST	OTHER TENSES: TYPICAL FORMS
ich	kann	konnte	*Future:* er wird können
du	kannst	konntest	*Perfect:* er hat gekonnt[2]
er, etc.	kann	konnte	er hat es tun können[2]
wir	können	konnten	*Subjunctive:*
ihr	könnt	konntet	*General:* er könnte
sie (Sie)	können	konnten	*Special:* er könne

[1] Not infrequent in literary German are the past forms: *ich ward* and *er (sie, es) ward*.
[2] See Unit Eight, §24.

c / *mögen*   PRESENT   PAST   OTHER TENSES: TYPICAL FORMS

ich	mag	mochte	*Future:* er wird mögen
du	magst	mochtest	*Perfect:* er hat gemocht[1]
er, etc.	mag	mochte	er hat es tun mögen[1]
wir	mögen	mochten	*Subjunctive:*
ihr	mögt	mochtet	*General:* er möchte
sie (Sie)	mögen	mochten	*Special:* er möge

d / *müssen*

ich	muß	mußte	*Future:* er wird müssen
du	mußt	mußtest	*Perfect:* er hat gemußt[1]
er, etc.	muß	mußte	er hat es tun müssen[1]
wir	müssen	mußten	*Subjunctive:*
ihr	müßt	mußtet	*General:* er müßte
sie (Sie)	müssen	mußten	*Special:* er müsse

e / *sollen*

ich	soll	sollte	*Future:* er wird sollen
du	sollst	solltest	*Perfect:* er hat gesollt[1]
er, etc.	soll	sollte	er hat es tun sollen[1]
wir	sollen	sollten	*Subjunctive:*
ihr	sollt	solltet	*General:* er sollte
sie (Sie)	sollen	sollten	*Special:* er solle

f / *wollen*

ich	will	wollte	*Future:* er wird wollen
du	willst	wolltest	*Perfect:* er hat gewollt[1]
er, etc.	will	wollte	er hat es tun wollen[1]
wir	wollen	wollten	*Subjunctive:*
ihr	wollt	wolltet	*General:* er wollte
sie (Sie)	wollen	wollten	*Special:* er wolle

100 / Other irregular verbs

a / *tun*   PRESENT   PAST   OTHER TENSES: TYPICAL FORMS

ich	tue	tat	*Future:* er wird tun
du	tust	tat(e)st	*Perfect:* er hat getan
er, etc.	tut	tat	*Subjunctive:*
wir	tun	taten	*General:* er täte
ihr	tut	tatet	*Special:* er tue
sie (Sie)	tun	taten	*Request:* tun Sie, tue, tut; tun wir; tue man, man tue

[1]See Unit Eight, §24.

b /*wissen*   PRESENT   PAST   OTHER TENSES: TYPICAL FORMS

ich	weiß	wußte	*Future:*	er wird wissen
du	weißt	wußtest	*Perfect:*	er hat gewußt
er, etc.	weiß	wußte	*Subjunctive:*	
wir	wissen	wußten	*General:*	er wüßte
ihr	wißt	wußtet	*Special:*	er wisse
sie (Sie)	wissen	wußten	*Request:*	wissen Sie, wisse, wißt; (wissen wir); wisse man, man wisse

c / The so-called irregular weak verbs, listed below, are irregular in two ways:

- The past and past participle have a vowel different from that of the infinitive and present. In some instances there is also a difference in the consonants of the stem.

- The general subjunctive of *bringen* and *denken* follows the pattern of the strong verb.

INFINITIVE		PAST	PAST PARTICIPLE	GENERAL SUBJUNCTIVE
brennen	*burn*	brannte	gebrannt	brennte
kennen	*know*	kannte	gekannt	kennte
nennen	*call, name*	nannte	genannt	nennte
rennen	*run*	rannte	gerannt	rennte
senden	*send*	sandte, sendete	gesandt, gesendet	sendete
wenden	*turn*	wandte, wendete	gewandt, gewendet	wendete
denken	*think*	dachte	gedacht	dächte
bringen	*bring*	brachte	gebracht	brächte

The Verb as Adjective and Noun

101 / Adjectival forms of the verb

The adjectival forms of the verb are:

- *the past participle.* For the formation of this form, see §88, a, and §96.
- *the present participle.* This is formed by adding -*end* to the stem of the infinitive.

     glänz(en)   *glänzend*   lauf(en)   *laufend*   sei(n)   *seiend*

  After verbs with stem-final -*el*-, -*er*-, the -*e* of -*end* is dropped.

     handel(n)   *handelnd*   wander(n)   *wandernd*

- *the future passive adjective.* For the formation of this form, see Unit Thirteen, §40.

For illustrations and translations of these forms, see Unit Thirteen.

102 / The verb as a noun

a / Participles as nouns

Like any other adjective, the verb-adjective can be used as a noun (see §73). Such adjective nouns, too, are capitalized, and they have regular adjective endings. Note the English equivalents of the illustrations below.

Folgendes (folgendes)	the following
der Geliebte	the beloved
der Geheilte	the healed person, the recovered patient, he who has/had been healed
die Leidende	the suffering woman, the woman who is/was sick
das Gesuchte	the sought object, that which is/was being sought

b / The infinitive

The infinitive, too, can appear as a noun. It is then capitalized, is neuter in gender, and is declined like any neuter noun. Note the English equivalents of the illustrations below.

das Lesen	to read, reading
das Lachen	to laugh, laughing, laughter

c / Verbs with modifiers as nouns

These verbal substantives may have adverbial modifiers. Such modifiers are often written with the substantive as one word.

der Erstgeborene	the first born
das Festhalten an diesem Glauben	holding firm in this faith
das Sichtbarmachen des Atoms	the making visible of the atom

Verbs in Dictionaries and Vocabularies
Vowel Patterns of Strong Verbs

103 / Verbs in dictionaries and vocabularies

Conventions for listing verbs in dictionaries and vocabularies vary considerably. The purpose of any listing is, however, to give information about the so-called principal parts or key forms. These are: the infinitive, the third person singular of the past, and the past participle. Any irregularities in the conjugation of the present are usually indicated by giving the third person singular form of the present, this making a fourth principal part for verbs with such irregularities.

a / The weak verb

Weak verbs have for the most part a completely regular conjugation. Most editors, therefore, find it enough to list the infinitive with an indication that the verb is *weak (wk.)* or *regular (r.* or *reg.).* Or they may indicate the regularity of the verb by omitting any information about its principal parts. Thus the listings *malen; malen (wk.); malen (reg.)* all indicate that the principal parts of this verb are *malen, malte, gemalt.*

Irregular weak verbs are usually marked by abbreviations such as *ir.,* or *ir. wk.,* or *wk. ir.* Dictionaries using such designations most often contain a special section listing the various parts of such verbs.

Other word lists, especially vocabularies, give either the stem vowels of the principal parts or the entire forms of the principal parts. The listing for *bringen* may be either *bringen, a, a, (wk. ir.),* or *bringen, brachte, gebracht.* The verb *können,* which has an irregular present, may be listed as *können (a), o, o, (wk. ir.),* or *können, (kann), konnte, gekonnt.*

b / The strong verb

Strong verbs are often considered to be irregular verbs. Some editors, therefore, list the infinitive with the designation *ir.* or a corresponding symbol, thus indicating that the reader should turn to another section of the dictionary or book for the listing of the principal parts.

Other editors give the vowels of the principal parts, mostly of three principal parts, sometimes of four principal parts if there is an irregularity in the present. The vowel of the fourth principal part, the third person singular of the present, may be either the second or the fourth vowel listed. Thus the listings for the verb *sehen, sieht, sah, gesehen* may be:

sehen, ir.

sehen, a, e or *sehen (a, e)*

sehen (ie), a, e or *sehen, a, e, (ie)*

A variation of this kind of entry is sometimes used if the consonantal structure, or the length or shortness of the stem vowel is not uniform in all principal parts. Thus for *gehen* or *treffen* the entries might be:

gehen, i, a or *gehen, ging, gegangen*

treffen (i) a, o or *treffen (trifft), traf, getroffen* or *treffen (i), traf, o*

Note   Before using a vocabulary or dictionary it is a good idea to acquaint yourself with the editorial principles used in setting up the book. Read prefatory matter on the listing of inflected words. Also check the entries for familiar words like *sehen, sprechen* or *lassen.*

104 / Vowel patterns of strong verbs[1]

The changes in the stem vowels of many strong verbs follow certain patterns. Knowing these patterns makes it easier to learn the principal parts of these verbs.

The predominant patterns are presented below, with illustrations. In addition there are listed, below each group, some common verbs which follow less frequent patterns related to the dominant ones.

INFINITIVE	PRESENT:3RD PERSON SING.	PAST: 3RD PERSON SING.	PAST PARTICIPLE	
ei	*ei*	*i, ie*	*i, ie*	
beißen	beißt	biß	gebissen	*bite*
reiten	reitet	ritt	geritten	*ride*
bleiben	bleibt	blieb	geblieben	*remain*
steigen	steigt	stieg	gestiegen	*climb, go up*
ie	*ie*	*o* (short or long)	*o* (short or long)	
fließen	fließt	floß	geflossen	*flow*
sieden	siedet	sott	gesotten	*boil*
riechen	riecht	roch	gerochen	*smell*
biegen	biegt	bog	gebogen	*bend*
frieren	friert	fror	gefroren	*freeze, be cold*

Related verbs:

fechten	ficht	focht	gefochten	*fight, fence*
saufen	säuft	soff	gesoffen	*drink, booze*
heben	hebt	hob	gehoben	*lift*
lügen	lügt	log	gelogen	*lie, tell a lie*
saugen	saugt	sog	gesogen	*suck*
schwören	schwört	schwur (schwor)	geschworen	*swear*

i	*i*	*a*	*u, o*	
binden	bindet	band	gebunden	*bind, tie*
singen	singt	sang	gesungen	*sing*
beginnen	beginnt	begann	begonnen	*begin*
spinnen	spinnt	spann	gesponnen	*spin*

---

[1]These "vowel patterns" are normally listed in series called "gradation classes of strong verbs." This term is avoided here because violence has been done to the usual class divisions in order to get a scheme more useful to the reading student.

INFINITIVE	PRESENT: 3RD PERSON SING.	PAST: 3RD PERSON SING.	PAST PARTICIPLE	
e (short or long)	*i, ie*	*a* (short or long)	*o* (short or long)	
gelten	gilt	galt	gegolten	*be valid, be true*
helfen	hilft	half	geholfen	*help*
werfen	wirft	warf	geworfen	*throw*
brechen	bricht	brach	gebrochen	*break*
nehmen	nimmt	nahm	genommen	*take*
treffen	trifft	traf	getroffen	*hit, meet*
stehlen	stiehlt	stahl	gestohlen	*steal*

Related verbs:

gebären	gebiert	gebar	geboren	*bear, give birth to*
kommen	kommt	kam	gekommen	*come, get*

e (short or long)	*i, ie*	*a*	*e* (short or long)	
essen	ißt	aß	gegessen	*eat*
geben	gibt	gab	gegeben	*give*
lesen	liest	las	gelesen	*read*
geschehen	geschieht	geschah	geschehen	*happen*

Related verbs:

bitten	bittet	bat	gebeten	*ask*
liegen	liegt	lag	gelegen	*lie*
sitzen	sitzt	saß	gesessen	*sit*

a	*ä*	*u*	*a*	
graben	gräbt	grub	gegraben	*dig*
schlagen	schlägt	schlug	geschlagen	*hit*
backen	bäckt	buk, backte	gebacken	*bake*

a	*ä*	*ie*	*a*	
blasen	bläst	blies	geblasen	*blow*
braten	brät	briet	gebraten	*roast, fry*
fallen	fällt	fiel	gefallen	*fall*
halten	hält	hielt	gehalten	*hold*

Related verbs:

fangen	fängt	fing	gefangen	*catch*
hängen	hängt	hing	gehangen	*hang*
hauen	haut	hieb, haute	gehauen	*cut, hew*
heißen	heißt	hieß	geheißen	*call, be called*
laufen	läuft	lief	gelaufen	*run, walk*
rufen	ruft	rief	gerufen	*call*
stoßen	stößt	stieß	gestoßen	*push*

ANSWER SHEETS

Date . . . . Name . . . . Grade . . . .

I 1. *N pl. . A .pl* . . . . .   11. . . . .

2. *A .sg* . . . .   12. . . . .

3. *D .sg* . . . .   13. . . . .

X 4. *A .pl. , N .* . . . . .   14. . . . .

5. *A .pl , N p* . . . . .   15. . . . .

6. *G .pl* . . . .   16. . . . .

7. *D .pl* . . . .   17. . . . .

8. *N .sg., A .sg* . . .   18. . . . .

9. *D .pl* . . . .   19. . . . .

X 10. . . . .   20. . . . .

II 1. . . . .   2. . . . .   3. . . . .   4. . . . .

5. . . . .   6. . . . .   7. . . . .   8. . . . .

9. . . . .   10. . . . .

III 1. . . . .

2. . . . .

3. . . . .

4. . . . .

5. . . . .

6. . . . .

7. . . . .

8. . . . .

9. . . . .

10. . . . .

IV 1. . . . .

2. . . . .

3. . . . .

4. . . . .

5. . . . .

. . . .

V 1. . . . .

2. . . . .

3. . . . .

. . . .

4. . . . .

. . . .

5. . . . .

. . . .

Date . . . . Name . . . . Grade . . . .

I   1. . . . .   9. . . . .

      2. . . . .   10. . . . .

      3. . . . .   11. . . . .

      4. . . . .   12. . . . .

      5. . . . .   13. . . . .

      6. . . . .   14. . . . .

      7. . . . .   15. . . . .

      8. . . . .

II   1. . . . .

       . . . .

       . . . .

      2. . . . .

       . . . .

       . . . .

      3. . . . .

       . . . .

       . . . .

      4. . . . .

       . . . .

       . . . .

      5. . . . .

       . . . .

       . . . .

III   1. . . . .
. . . .
. . . .

2. . . . .
. . . .
. . . .

3. . . . .
. . . .
. . . .

4. . . . .
. . . .
. . . .

5. . . . .
. . . .
. . . .

Date . . . . Name . . . . Grade . . . .

I   1. . . . .   2. . . . .   3. . . . .   4. . . . .

    5. . . . .   6. . . . .   7. . . . .   8. . . . .

    9. . . . .   10. . . . .

II   1. . . . .

    2. . . . .

    3. . . . .

    4. . . . .

    5. . . . .

    6. . . . .

    7. . . . .

    8. . . . .

    9. . . . .

  10. . . . .

III 1. . . . .   2. . . . .   3. . . . .   4. . . . .

    5. . . . .   6. . . . .   7. . . . .   8. . . . .

    9. . . . .   10. . . . .

IV   1. . . . .

    2. . . . .

    3. . . . .

    . . . .

    . . . .

    4. . . . .

    5. . . . .

6. . . . .

7. . . . .

8. . . . .

9. . . . .

10. . . . .

Date . . . . Name . . . . Grade . . . .

I   1. . . . .   2. . . . .   3. . . . .   4. . . . .

     5. . . . .   6. . . . .   7. . . . .   8. . . . .

     9. . . . .   10. . . . .   11. . . . .   12. . . . .

     13. . . . .   14. . . . .   15. . . . .

II   1. . . . .

     2. . . . .

     3. . . . .

     4. . . . .

     5. . . . .
       . . . .

     6. . . . .

     7. . . . .

     8. . . . .

     9. . . . .

     10. . . . .

III   1. . . . .
       . . . .

     2. . . . .
       . . . .

     3. . . . .
       . . . .

     4. . . . .
       . . . .

     5. . . . .
       . . . .

Date . . . . Name . . . . Grade . . . .

I   1. . . . .   16. . . . .

      2. . . . .   17. . . . .

      3. . . . .   18. . . . .

      4. . . . .   19. . . . .

      5. . . . .   20. . . . .

      6. . . . .   21. . . . .

      7. . . . .   22. . . . .

      8. . . . .   23. . . . .

      9. . . . .   24. . . . .

    10. . . . .   25. . . . .

    11. . . . .   26. . . . .

    12. . . . .   27. . . . .

    13. . . . .   28. . . . .

    14. . . . .   29. . . . .

    15. . . . .   30. . . . .

II   1. . . . .   2. . . . .   3. . . . .   4. . . . .

      5. . . . .   6. . . . .   7. . . . .   8. . . . .

      9. . . . .   10. . . . .   11. . . . .   12. . . . .

    13. . . . .   14. . . . .   15. . . . .   16. . . . .

    17. . . . .   18. . . . .   19. . . . .   20. . . . .

    21. . . . .   22. . . . .   23. . . . .   24. . . . .

    25. . . . .   26. . . . .   27. . . . .   28. . . . .

    29. . . . .   30. . . . .

Date . . . . Name . . . . Grade . . . .

I 1. die . . . .   5. Als . . . .

    2. wenn . . . .   da . . . .

    3. als . . . .   daß . . . .

      weil . . . .   6. und . . . .

      daß . . . .   denn . . . .

    4. Aber . . . .   daß . . . .

      als . . . .

      denn . . . .

      daß . . . .

		First Word	*Last Word*			*First Word*	*Last Word*
II	1. MC	. . . .	. . . .	5. IP	. . . .	. . . .
	2. MC	. . . .	. . . .	MC	. . . .	. . . .
	IP	. . . .	. . . .	6. MC	. . . .	. . . .
	IP	. . . .	. . . .	IP	. . . .	. . . .
	MC	. . . .	. . . .	MC	. . . .	. . . .
	3. MC	. . . .	. . . .	MC	. . . .	. . . .
	4. MC	. . . .	. . . .				
	MC	. . . .	. . . .				

III 1. . . . .

      . . . .

    2. . . . .

      . . . .

    3. . . . .

      . . . .

4. . . . .
   . . . .

5. . . . .
   . . . .

6. . . . .
   . . . .

7. . . . .
   . . . .

8. . . . .
   . . . .

9. . . . .
   . . . .

10. . . . .
    . . . .

Date . . . . Name . . . . Grade , , , , , , .

I 1. . . . .   2. . . . .   3. . . . .   4. . . . .

5. . . . .   6. . . . .   7. . . . .   8. . . . .

9. . . . .   10. . . . .   11. . . . .   12. . . . .

13. . . . .   14. . . . .   15. . . . .

II 1. . . . .   2. . . . .   3. . . . .   4. . . . .

5. . . . .   6. . . . .   7. . . . .   8. . . . .

9. . . . .   10. . . . .   11. . . . .   12. . . . .

13. . . . .   14. . . . .   15. . . . .

III 1. . . . .

2. . . . .

3. . . . .

4. . . . .

5. . . . .

6. . . . .

7. . . . .

8. . . . .

. . . .

9. . . . .

10. . . . .

11. . . . .

12. . . . .

. . . .

13. . . . .

14. . . . .

15. . . . .

Date . . . . Name . . . . Grade . . . .

I	INFINITIVE	PRESENT (3rd person sing.)	PAST	PARTICIPLE without dependent infinitive	with dependent infinitive
1.	sollen	. . . .	. . . .	. . . .	. . . .
2.	. . . .	darf	. . . .	. . . .	. . . .
3.	. . . .	. . . .	. . . .	. . . .	müssen
4.	. . . .	. . . .	. . . .	gewollt	. . . .
5.	. . . .	. . . .	mochte	. . . .	. . . .
6.	. . . .	kann	. . . .	. . . .	. . . .

II 1. . . . . 2. . . . . 3. . . . . 4. . . . . 5. . . . .

6. . . . . 7. . . . . 8. . . . . 9. . . . . 10. . . . .

III 1. . . . .

2. . . . .

3. . . . .

. . . .

4. . . . .

5. . . . .

. . . .

6. . . . .

7. . . . .

8. . . . .

9. . . . .

10. . . . .

IV   1. . . . .

      2. . . . .

      3. . . . .

      4. . . . .

      5. . . . .

      6. . . . .

      7. . . . .

      8. . . . .

      9. . . . .

   10. . . . .

Date . . . . Name . . . . Grade . . . .

I   1. . . . .
          . . . .

     2. . . . .
          . . . .

     3. . . . .

     4. . . . .

     5. . . . .
          . . . .

     6. . . . .

     7. . . . .

     8. . . . .

     9. . . . .
          . . . .

    10. . . . .

    11. . . . .

    12. . . . .
          . . . .

    13. . . . .
          . . . .

    14. . . . .

    15. . . . .

II   1. . . . .   2. . . . .   3. . . . .   4. . . . .

     5. . . . .   6. . . . .   7. . . . .   8. . . . .

     9. . . . .   10. . . . .

III   1. . . . .

    2. . . . .

      . . . .

    3. . . . .

    4. . . . .

    5. . . . .

      . . . .

IV   1. . . . .

      . . . .

    2. . . . .

      . . . .

    3. . . . .

      . . . .

    4. . . . .

      . . . .

    5. . . . .

      . . . .

Date . . . . Name . . . . Grade . . . .

I   1. . . . .   6. . . . .

     2. . . . .   7. . . . .

     3. . . . .   8. . . . .

     4. . . . .   9. . . . .

     5. . . . .   10. . . . .

II   1. . . . .

     2. . . . .

     3. . . . .

     4. . . . .

     5. . . . .

     6. . . . .

     7. . . . .

     8. . . . .

     9. . . . .

    10. . . . .

III   1. . . . .

     2. . . . .

     3. . . . .

     4. . . . .

     5. . . . .

     6. . . . .

     7. . . . .

     8. . . . .

     9. . . . .

    10. . . . .

11. . . . .

12. . . . .

13. . . . .

14. . . . .

15. . . . .

IV   1. . . . .

2. . . . .

3. . . . .

. . . .

4. . . . .

5. . . . .

. . . .

Date . . . . Name . . . . Grade . . . .

I 1. . . . . 2. . . . . 3. . . . . 4. . . . .

5. . . . . 6. . . . . 7. . . . . 8. . . . .

9. . . . . 10. . . . .

II 1. . . . . 2. . . . . 3. . . . . 4. . . . .

5. . . . . 6. . . . . 7. . . . . 8. . . . .

9. . . . . 10. . . . .

III 1. . . . . 2. . . . . 3. . . . . 4. . . . .

5. . . . . 6. . . . . 7. . . . . 8. . . . .

9. . . . . 10. . . . . 11. . . . . 12. . . . .

13. . . . . 14. . . . . 15. . . . . 16. . . . .

17. . . . . 18. . . . . 19. . . . . 20. . . . .

IV 1. . . . .

2. . . . .

. . . .

3. . . . .

. . . .

4. . . . .

5. . . . .

6. . . . .

7. . . . .

8. . . . .

9. . . . .

10. . . . .

Date . . . . Name . . . . Grade . . . .

I   1. . . . .   2. . . . .   3. . . . .   4. . . . .

      5. . . . .   6. . . . .   7. . . . .   8. . . . .

      9. . . . .   10. . . . .

II   1. . . . .

      2. . . . .

      3, ...

      4. . . . .

      5. . . . .

      6. . . . .

      7. . . . .

      8. . . . .

      9. . . . .

    10. . . . .

    11. . . . .

    12. . . . .

    13. . . . .

    14. . . . .

    15. . . . .

    16. . . . .

    17. . . . .

    18. . . . .

    19. . . . .

       . . . .

    20. . . . .

III   1. . . . .   2. . . . .   3. . . . .   4. . . . .

       5. . . . .   6. . . . .   7. . . . .   8. . . . .

       9. . . . .   10. . . . .   11. . . . .   12. . . . .

      13. . . . .   14. . . . .   15. . . . .   16. . . . .

      17. . . . .   18. . . . .   19. . . . .   20. . . . .

Date . . . . Name . . . . Grade . . . .

I   1. . . . .

     2. . . . .

     3. . . . .

     4. . . . .

     5. . . . .

     6. . . . .

     7. . . . .

     8. . . . .

     9. . . . .

    10. . . . .

    11. . . . .
        . . . .

    12. . . . .
        . . . .

    13. . . . .
        . . . .

    14. . . . .
        . . . .

    15. . . . .
        . . . .

II   1. a. First word: . . . .   Last word: . . . .

        b. . . . .
           . . . .

     2. a. First word: . . . .   Last word: . . . .

        b. . . . .
           . . . .

3. a. First word: . . . .   Last word: . . . .

   b. . . . .

      . . . .

4. a. First word: . . . .   Last word: . . . .

   b. . . . .

      . . . .

5. a. First word: . . . .   Last word: . . . .

   b. . . . .

      . . . .

6. a. First word: . . . .   Last word: . . . .

   b. . . . .

      . . . .

7. a. First word: . . . .   Last word: . . . .

   b. . . . .

      . . . .

8. a. First word: . . . .   Last word: . . . .

   b. . . . .

      . . . .

      . . . .

9. a. First word: . . . .   Last word: . . . .

   b. . . . .

      . . . .

10. a. First word: . . . .   Last word: . . . .

    b. . . . .

       . . . .

Date . . . . Name . . . . Grade . . . .

I   1. . . . .

2. . . . .

3. . . . .

4. . . . .

5. . . . .

II   1. (ends) . . . .

. . . .

2. (lies) . . . .

3. (is) . . . .

4. (attention) . . . .

. . . .

5. (remember) . . . .

6. (content) . . . .

. . . .

7. (warns) . . . . , , ...

. . . .

8. (a sign) . . . .

. . . .

9. (indicated) . . . .

. . . .

10. (involved) . . . .

. . . .

11. (was) . . . .

. . . .

12. (darkened) . . . .

. . . .

13. (circumvent his opposition) . . . .

. . . .

14. (contributed) . . . .

15. (helped) . . . .

III   1. . . . .

. . . .

2. . . . .

. . . .

3. . . . .

. . . .

4. . . . .

. . . .

5. . . . .

. . . .

IV 4a. . . . .

. . . .

. . . .

5a. . . . .

. . . .

. . . .

. . . .

Date . . . . Name . . . . Grade . . . .

I   1. . . . .

    . . . .

  2. . . . .

    . . . .

  3. . . . .

    . . . .

  4. . . . .

    . . . .

  5. . . . .

  6. . . . .

  7. . . . .

    . . . .

  8. . . . .

  9. . . . .

    . . . .

 10. . . . .

    . . . .

 11. . . . .

 12. . . . .

    . . . .

 13. . . . .

    . . . .

 14. . . . .

 15. . . . .

 16. . . . .

 17. . . . .

    . . . .

18. . . . .
    . . . .

19. . . . .

20. . . . .

21. . . . .
    . . . .

22. . . . .

23. . . . .

24. . . . .
    . . . .

25. . . . .
    . . . .
    . . . .

II   1. . . . .
         . . . .

      2. . . . .
         . . . .

      3. . . . .

      4. . . . .
         . . . .
         . . . .

      5. . . . .
         . . . .

Date . . . . Name . . . . Grade . . . .

1. . . . .
. . . .

2. . . . .

3. . . . .
. . . .

4. . . . .
. . . .

5. . . . .
. . . .

6. . . . .

7. . . . .
. . . .

8. . . . .
. . . .

9. . . . .
. . . .

10. . . . .
. . . .

11. . . . .

12. . . . .
. . . .

13. . . . .
. . . .

14. . . . .
. . . .

15. . . . .

16. . . . .
    . . . .
17. . . . .
    . . . .
18. . . . .
    . . . .
19. . . . .
    . . . .
20. . . . .
    . . . .
21. . . . .
22. . . . .
23. . . . .
    . . . .
    . . . .
24. . . . .
    . . . .
25. . . . .
    . . . .
    . . . .

Date . . . . Name . . . . Grade . . . .

I   1. . . . .   2. . . . .

    3. . . . .   4. . . . .

    5. . . . .

II   1. a. Sentence   . . . .

      b. Infinitive   . . . .

    2. a. Sentence   . . . .

      b. Infinitive   . . . .

    3. a. Sentence   . . . .

      b. Infinitive   . . . .

    4. a. Sentence   . . . .

      b. Infinitive   . . . .

    5. a. Sentence   . . . .

      b. Infinitive   . . . .

III   1. . . . .   2. . . . .   3. . . . .   4. . . . .   5. . . . .

    6. . . . .   7. . . . .   8. . . . .   9. . . . .   10. . . . .

IV   1. . . . .

    . . . .

    2. . . . .

    . . . .

    3. . . . .

    . . . .

    4. . . . .

    . . . .

5. . . . .
   . . . .

V	INFINITIVE	PRESENT: 3rd PERSON SING.	PAST: 3rd PERSON SING.	PAST PARTICIPLE	
1.	reißen	. . . .	. . . .	. . . .	*tear*
2.	. . . .	. . . .	schlich	. . . .	*sneak*
3.	. . . .	. . . .	. . . .	geschritten	*stride*
4.	. . . .	. . . .	griff	. . . .	*grasp*
5.	. . . .	. . . .	. . . .	geschienen	*shine, seem*
6.	. . . .	preist	. . . .	. . . .	*praise*
7.	treiben	. . . .	. . . .	. . . .	*drive*
8.	. . . .	. . . .	. . . .	geflossen	*flow*
9.	. . . .	friert	. . . .	. . . .	*freeze*
10.	. . . .	kriecht	. . . .	. . . .	*crawl*

Date . . . . Name . . . . Grade . . . .

I 1. . . . .   2. . . . .   3. . . . .

   4. . . . .   5. . . . .   6. . . . .

   7. . . . .   8. . . . .   9. . . . .

   10. . . . .   11. . . . .   12. . . . .

   13. . . . .   14. . . . .   15. . . . .

   16. . . . .   17. . . . .   18. . . . .

   19. . . . .   20. . . . .   21. . . . .

   22. . . . .   23. . . . .   24. . . . .

   25. . . . .

II 1. . . . .   2. . . . .   3. . . . .   4. . . . .   5. . . . .

   6. . . . .   7. . . . .   8. . . . .   9. . . . .   10. . . . .

   11. . . . .   12. . . . .   13. . . . .   14. . . . .   15. . . . .

III 1. . . . .

   2. . . . .

   3. . . . .

   . . . .

   4. . . . .

   5. . . . .

IV	INFINITIVE	PRESENT: 3rd PERSON SING.	PAST: 3rd PERSON SING.	PAST PARTICIPLE	
1.	zwingen	. . . .	. . . .	. . . .	*force*
2.	. . . .	. . . .	. . . .	gefunden	*find*
3.	. . . .	gelingt	. . . .	. . . .	*succeed*
4.	. . . .	. . . .	begann	. . . .	*begin*
5.	. . . .	. . . .	. . . .	gewonnen	*gain*
6.	schwimmen	. . . .	. . . .	. . . .	*swim*
7.	. . . .	. . . .	half	. . . .	*help*
8.	. . . .	. . . .	. . . .	gestorben	*die*
9.	gelten	. . . .	. . . .	. . . .	*be worth*
10.	. . . .	verbirgt	. . . .	. . . .	*hide*
11.	. . . .	. . . .	sprach	. . . .	*speak*
12.	treffen	. . . .	. . . .	. . . .	*hit, meet*
13.	. . . .	. . . .	. . . .	genommen	*take*
14.	. . . .	befiehlt	. . . .	. . . .	*command*
15.	. . . .	. . . .	stahl	. . . .	*steal*

Date . . . . Name . . . . Grade . . . .

I   1. . . . . . .   2. . . . .   3. . . . .   4. . . . .   5. . . . .

      6. . . . . . .   7. . . . .   8. . . . .   9. . . . .   10. . . . .

II   1. . . . .   9. . . . .

      2. . . . .   10. . . . .

      3. . . . .   11. . . . .

      4. . . . .   12. . . . .

      5. . . . .   13. . . . .

      6. . . . .   14. . . . .

      7. . . . .   15. . . . .

      8. . . . .

III   1. . . . . . .   2. . . . .   3. . . . .   4. . . . .   5. . . . .

      6. . . . . . .   7. . . . .   8. . . . .   9. . . . .   10. . . . .

      11. . . . . . .   12. . . . .   13. . . . .   14. . . . .   15. . . . .

IV

	INFINITIVE	PRESENT: 3rd PERSON SING.	PAST: 3rd PERSON SING.	PAST PARTICIPLE	
1.	geben	. . . .	. . . .	. . . .	*give*
2.	. . . .	mißt	. . . .	. . . .	*measure*
3.	. . . .	. . . .	trat	. . . .	*step*
4.	. . . .	. . . .	. . . .	vergessen	*forget*
5.	. . . .	sieht	. . . .	. . . .	*see*
6.	. . . .	. . . .	. . . .	geschehen	*happen*
7.	tragen	. . . .	. . . .	. . . .	*carry*
8.	. . . .	. . . .	lud	. . . .	*load*

INFINITIVE	PRESENT: 3rd PERSON SING.	PAST: 3rd PERSON SING.	PAST PARTICIPLE	
9.	gräbt	. . . .	. . . .	*dig*
10.	. . . .	. . . .	gefahren	*go, drive*
11.	. . . .	schlief	. . . .	*sleep*
12. fallen	. . . .	. . . .	. . . .	*fall*
13.	bläst	. . . .	. . . .	*blow*
14.	. . . .	. . . .	geraten	*advise*
15.	läßt	. . . .	. . . .	*let, leave, have*

·Date . . . . Name . . . . Grade . . . .

1. . . . .
2. . . . .
. . . .
3. . . . .
. . . .
4. . . . .
. . . .
5. . . . .
. . . .
6. . . . .
7. . . . .
. . . .
8. . . . .
. . . .
9. . . . .
. . . .
10. . . . .
. . . .
11. . . . .
. . . .
12. . . . .
. . . .
13. . . . .
. . . .
14. . . . .
. . . .

15. . . . .
    . . . .

16. . . . .
    . . . .

17. . . . .
    . . . .

18. . . . .
    . . . .

19. . . . .
    . . . .

20. . . . .

21. . . . .
    . . . .

22. . . . .
    . . . .

23. . . . .
    . . . .

24. . . . .
    . . . .

25. . . . .
    . . . .

GRAMMATICAL INDEX

GRAMMATICAL INDEX

with accented adverb or modifier §5, 96
with dative objects §57c
with *gern, lieber, am liebsten* §76
see   auxiliaries, future, future perfect, *haben,*
    impersonal constructions, infinitive, inflec-
    tion (verb), irregular weak verbs, modal
    auxiliaries, participles (present and
    past), passive, past, pluperfect, present,
    present perfect, reflexive constructions, *sein,*
    separable verb, strong verbs, subjunctive,
    tense, *tun,* verb complex, weak verbs, *werden,*
    wissen, word order
verb complex §6a
verb phrase §5, 96
verbal nouns §102
von with passive §12
vowel patterns of strong verbs §104

was §17c, 31, 64
weak adjective declension §15, 68, 70
weak irregular verbs §100c
weak verb
    definition p. 146
    imperative §95a
    in dictionary or vocabulary §103a
    past §87
    past participle §88a, 96
    present §86
    subjunctive §33, 92-93
welcher §17c, 64
wenn omission §19, 21, 39
wer §17c, 31, 64
werden
    future auxiliary §11, 53, 89
    independent verb §10
    paradigm §98c
    passive auxiliary §12, 90
wie in comparison §79e
wissen paradigm §100b

wollen
    meanings and translations §23f, 35 *Note*
    paradigm §99f
wo-, wor- §17c, 32c, 82
word order
    accented adverb or modifier with verb §5, 96
    adverbs §6
    composite verb forms §4, 8, 11
    conjunctions and verb §17
    double infinitive §24c
    emphasis §12c, 48a
    es inserted or omitted §12c, 48
    imperative §20
    infinitive §4b
    infinitive phrase §18
    inflected verb §1, 4, 19-21, 49, p. 41 foot-
        note 1
    main clause §1, 4, 19-21, 49 p. 41 footnote 1
    nicht §6
    omission *wenn* or *ob* §19, 39
    past participle §4b
    position of verb   normal §1, 4, 24, p. 41 foot-
        note 1
    position of verb "verb first" §19-21, 49
    position of verb and *da* §17c
    position of verb and *der, das, die; die* §30c
    predicate adjectives §6b
    question p. 41, §21
    reflexive pronoun §25b
    sentences without a subject §12c, 48b
    separable verb §5, 96
    statement, §1, 4
    subordinate clause §4
    verb complex §6a
worden §12, 90

zu with adjective and adverb §79h
    with separable verb §5